Research Among

Learners of Chinese

as a Foreign Language

NFLRC Monographs is a refereed series sponsored by the National Foreign Language Resource Center at the University of Hawai'i under the supervision of the series editor, Richard Schmidt. NFLRC Monographs present the findings of recent work in applied linguistics that is of relevance to language teaching and learning, with a focus on the less commonly-taught languages of Asia and the Pacific.

Toward Useful Program Evaluation in College Foreign Language Education
  John M. Norris, John McE. Davis, Castle Sinicrope, Yukiko Watanabe (Editors), 2009
  ISBN 978–0–9800459–3–2

Second language teaching and learning in the Net Generation
  Raquel Oxford & Jeffrey Oxford (Editors), 2009
  ISBN 978–0–9800459–2–5

Case studies in foreign language placement: Practices and possibilities
  Thom Hudson & Martyn Clark (Editors), 2008
  ISBN 978–0–9800459–0–1

Chinese as a heritage language: Fostering rooted world citizenry
  Agnes Weiyun He & Yun Xiao (Editors), 2008
  ISBN 978–0–8248328–6–5

Perspectives on teaching connected speech to second language speakers
  James Dean Brown & Kimi Kondo-Brown (Editors), 2006
  ISBN 978–0–8248313–6–3

ordering information at nflrc.hawaii.edu

Research Among Learners of Chinese as a Foreign Language

Chinese Language Teachers Association Monograph Series, Volume IV

edited by
MICHAEL E. EVERSON
HELEN H. SHEN

NATIONAL FOREIGN LANGUAGE RESOURCE CENTER
University of Hawai'i at Mānoa

ⓒ 2010 Chinese Language Teachers Association
Some rights reserved. See: http://creativecommons.org/licenses/by-nc-nd/2.5/
Manufactured in the United States of America.

The contents of this publication were developed in part under a grant from the U.S. Department of Education (CFDA 84.229, P229A060002). However, the contents do not necessarily represent the policy of the Department of Education, and one should not assume endorsement by the Federal Government.

ISBN: 978–0–9800459–4–9

Library of Congress Control Number: 2009940758

∞ The paper used in this publication meets the minimum requirements of the American National Standard for Information Sciences–Permanence of Paper for Printed Library Materials.
ANSI Z39.48–1984

cover photo taken in 龙兴古镇, Chongqing © 2006 Scott Relyea | book design by Deborah Masterson

distributed by
National Foreign Language Resource Center
University of Hawai'i
1859 East-West Road #106
Honolulu HI 96822–2322
nflrc.hawaii.edu

About the
Chinese Language Teacher Association
Monograph Series

This volume is the fourth in the monograph series sponsored by the Chinese Language Teachers Association. In the preface to the third volume, Professors Feng-sheng Hsueh and Timothy Light wrote, "[the monograph series] grew out of the increasing attention that has been given to theory and practice in Chinese language teaching over the past twenty years." Serving to introduce the field to then such revolutionary concepts as proficiency-based learning, starting a Chinese program in secondary schools, the emerging need for principled teacher development, and the use of computer-aided language learning in Chinese, the monograph series has provided state-of-the-art guidance for teachers, researchers, and administrators in Chinese language education. In selecting the theme of this, the fourth volume of the series, a committee determined that empirical research needed to be showcased to emphasize its importance to the development of our field. This volume, then, presents a collection of studies employing a variety of research designs, theories, topics, and perspectives to inform interested readers about issues that are currently receiving scholarly attention. These studies make for compelling reading and remind us of just how much our field has evolved in the past few decades.

NFLRC Advisory Board

Robert Bickner
University of Wisconsin–Madison

Mary Hammond
East-West Center

Frederick Jackson
independent language education consultant

Madeline Spring
Arizona State University

Elvira Swender
American Council on the Teaching of Foreign Languages

About the
National Foreign Language Resource Center

THE NATIONAL FOREIGN LANGUAGE RESOURCE CENTER, located in the College of Languages, Linguistics, & Literature at the University of Hawai'i at Mānoa, has conducted research, developed materials, and trained language professionals since 1990 under a series of grants from the U.S. Department of Education (Language Resource Centers Program). A national advisory board sets the general direction of the resource center. With the goal of improving foreign language instruction in the United States, the center publishes research reports and teaching materials that focus primarily on the languages of Asia and the Pacific. The center also sponsors summer intensive teacher training institutes and other professional development opportunities. For additional information about center programs, contact us.

Richard Schmidt, Director
National Foreign Language Resource Center
University of Hawai'i at Mānoa
1859 East-West Road #106
Honolulu, HI 96822–2322

email: nflrc@hawaii.edu
website: nflrc.hawaii.edu

Contents

Editors' introduction
 Michael E. Everson & Helen H. Shen 1

1 The Acquisition of the *ba* Construction by Adult English Speakers
 Hang Du 5

2 Language Attrition in Grammar and Receptive Skills in Mandarin Chinese
 Miao-fen Tseng. 35

3 Analysis of Radical Knowledge Development Among Beginning CFL Learners
 Helen H. Shen 45

4 The Effects of Word-Knowledge Depth, Part of Speech, and Proficiency Level on Word Association Among Learners of Chinese as a Second Language
 Chan Lü. 67

5 See How They Read: An Investigation Into the Cognitive and Metacognitive Strategies of Nonnative Readers of Chinese
 Cecilia Chang. 93

6 Free Recall from Japanese Learners of Chinese
 Aiqun Liu. 117

7 Discourse Features and Development in Chinese L2 Writing
 Yun Xiao 133

8 Intermediate Distance Learners of Chinese Look Back: A Survey Study
 Isabel Tasker. 153

About the Contributors 179

Editors' introduction

Michael E. Everson
Helen H. Shen
The University of Iowa

Those of us who have been active in the many efforts to foster Chinese language learning have been very busy during the last few years. Enrollments in Chinese have been increasing, and the demand for programs to educate students and teachers of Chinese, which are supported by both the U.S. and Chinese governments, is on the rise. Yet, as Brecht and Walton (1994) have written, creating a language field involves more than just language programs; a language field needs, among other things, a research tradition that identifies and investigates problems germane to our understanding of language itself.

While Chinese has a long history of being taught to Western learners, empirical research investigating the learning of Chinese is relatively new. This research has been respectably disseminated among Chinese language practitioners through important synthesis articles written in both English (Everson, 1993; Ke & Everson, 1999) and Chinese (Ke & Shen, 2003). Writing by scholars in China (Jiang, 2008) also interested in research has been beneficial in uniting resources across continents and countries, as have the proceedings from major conferences devoted to Chinese language research (Guder, Jiang, & Wan, 2007). A promising direction from this research is that compilations are starting to appear that apply research to the actual teaching of Chinese (Everson & Xiao, 2008; Xing, 2006). The current collection, sponsored by the Chinese Language Teachers Association as their fourth monograph, provides another collection of studies that is cutting-edge in its approach and international in its authorship. It cuts across a variety of themes and perspectives, while the studies are united by the fact that they all draw their data from learners of Chinese as a foreign language (CFL).

Hang Du begins this volume with a mixed-methods study that used both qualitative and quantitative data to investigate learners' acquisition of the *ba* construction. In her study, three groups of Chinese language learners of different proficiency levels (as well as a native-speaker group used to supply baseline data) were asked to judge whether certain sentences using the *ba* construction were correct. The participants also were asked to view videos specifically selected to elicit their spoken production of this construction to investigate whether the learners would use the form correctly in discourse. Her findings are important in showing how this form has been acquired by these learners and how they use it under which circumstances. An excellent review of previous studies is also provided for scholars wishing to know more about the kinds of studies that have been done to investigate this structure.

The second study, by Miao-fen Tseng, asked a question near and dear to the hearts of all Chinese language educators—how much do our learners remember after having taken a summer off from learning Chinese? This study investigated this question among beginning learners of Chinese by collecting data measuring both their proficiency in the language and self-reported measures of their confidence with the language. This study is important not so much for measuring "how much" but for indicating that certain aspects and skills within the language-learning framework may be more influenced by a summer break, at least among these beginning learners. The study is also important for beginning a line of inquiry that recognizes that many learners will have breaks in their language-learning development for a number of reasons, so understanding how the different modalities of language are affected by breaks in learning is very important.

The third study, by Helen H. Shen, adds to an already impressive body of work in CFL literacy development that investigates how learners adapt to a nonalphabetic writing system. Shen's study focused on a small but extremely important element of Chinese characters—the radical. She tested 1st-year students' abilities to recognize the sounds, shapes, and meanings of radicals and analyzed quantitative and qualitative data from a survey in which learners evaluated the difficulties of learning different aspects of radicals and indicated how they used radicals (if at all) to learn characters. In essence, this study investigated learners' first steps in constructing Chinese characters and gets at the importance of this in the overall reading process. Her findings provide a compelling glimpse into some of the strategies learners use and difficulties learners have with the use of radicals, yet indicate convincingly that radicals are viewed by students as an important feature for character learning. Shen's discussion of how her study impacts Chinese pedagogy will make for compelling reading for any Chinese teacher whose students are about to embark upon the learning of characters.

Chan Lü contributed the fourth study, which investigated how Chinese language learners seem to organize their mental lexicons and how this organization changes over time as learners become more proficient. Using a word-association task, she investigated the variables of knowledge depth, part of speech, and proficiency level, thus providing a unique glimpse into the processes learners use when coming to grips with words in Chinese. Her findings about the role of sound and meaning are important for understanding how learners process Chinese words and suggest that different pedagogical strategies be used for vocabulary learning when teaching learners of differing proficiency levels. As the role of phonology in recognizing Chinese characters has provided for controversy and debate in the field of word recognition, Chan Lü's study will be of interest to anyone wishing to know more about the processing of Chinese orthography.

While studies focusing on the character and word level provide an understanding of how Chinese characters are learned by CFL students, Cecilia Chang presents a comprehensive study investigating how learners of different proficiency levels read longer units of text specifically geared for their respective proficiency levels. To give the detail that she felt was necessary to carry out this study, Chang collected data on a variety of measures, such as reading comprehension and reading strategy usage. Her analysis highlights some of the differences between readers of different proficiency levels in terms of text processing and points out some of the strategic choices learners of different proficiency levels seem to make. The study also indicates that trying to correlate strategy use and reading performance is anything but straightforward, thus leaving the door open for more research in this area.

Many argue that if word recognition, reading, and the acquisition of language forms have made up the lion's share of research in CFL, we also need to understand the process of listening comprehension because it may be the first skill that needs to be mastered in a foreign language. Aiqun Liu presents an important study that addresses the processes learners of Chinese use when tasked with recalling the content of a listening passage in Chinese. Liu's study is unique in that the learners of Chinese in this study are Japanese, thus introducing the role of the learner's first language as a variable of interest. Liu's study follows the time-honored tradition that values the role of memory limitations and the schema-theoretic principles important for organizing and recalling information.

One of the areas that has only recently been the topic of empirical investigation in CFL is writing. Perhaps this is because writing Chinese characters from memory is a highly labor-intensive process requiring serious amounts of time and effort, with many of our students never achieving this goal. Yet, many researchers believe that if our learners aim to work in Chinese-speaking environments, they will need to develop their writing skills. Yun Xiao's study provides an important glimpse into the world of heritage and nonheritage learners of Chinese with a longitudinal study using written student diaries as the data source. Xiao's study reveals important trends in the learners' writing development, focusing not only on grammatical forms but also on discourse structures that indicate that writing is very slow to develop to native-like proficiency. Xiao's data also lead her to some interesting pedagogical conclusions that will be enlightening to teachers who are interested in improving their students' writing abilities.

This volume concludes with Isabel Tasker's contribution that deals with Chinese in a distance-learning setting. Most of our students will ultimately be learning Chinese through nontraditional means; that is, not everyone will have a Chinese classroom and traditional Chinese course materials available to them, so understanding nontraditional settings for learning Chinese is of critical importance. Tasker's study used a survey with largely open-ended questions to elicit qualitative data that can be investigated for emerging themes that highlight learners' experiences, attitudes, and feelings about learning Chinese both in general and in the distance-learning setting. Using rich personal stories of learners at different stages in their Chinese language learning careers, Tasker highlights the voices of her participants, who explain their beliefs and attitudes toward how to navigate the distance-learning setting to learn Chinese.

A volume of this scope could not have been accomplished without the efforts of many people. We first would like to thank the authors who contributed their research studies, and who worked so closely and patiently with us during the editing process. The Chinese Language Teachers Association (CLTA) also deserves our thanks. CLTA has provided the leadership necessary to insure that a vibrant and well-prepared organization was in place to respond to the challenges of the "Chinese language boom" that its members knew would eventually materialize. Sponsoring the Chinese monograph series is only one of the many examples of foresight and vision it has demonstrated since its inception in 1962. We would also like to thank the members of the National Foreign Language

Resource Center at the University of Hawai'i for its confidence that our volume would be an important addition to their already impressive list of publications, and for their understanding of the value of research to the field of Chinese language education. Among this group of professionals, we would like to single out the publications specialist, Deborah Masterson, for special recognition. Deborah's hard work and open communication with us in preparing this volume eased our burden immensely, and presented an efficient plan to see this project through to completion.

Michael E. Everson
Helen H. Shen
Iowa City, IA

References

Brecht, R. D., & Walton, A. R. (1994). National strategic planning in the less commonly taught languages. In R. D. Lambert & A.W. Heston (Eds.), *The annals of the American academy of political and social science* (pp. 190–212). Thousand Oaks, CA: Sage Publications.

Everson, M. E. (1993). Research in the less commonly taught languages. In A. O. Hadley (Ed.), *ACTFL Foreign Language Education Series. Research in language learning: Principles, processes, and prospects* (pp. 198–228). Lincolnwood, IL: National Textbook Company.

Everson, M. E., & Xiao, Y. (Eds.). (2008). *Teaching Chinese as a foreign language*. Boston: Cheng & Tsui Company.

Guder, A., Jiang, X., & Wan, Y. (Eds.). (2007). *The cognition, learning, and teaching of Chinese characters*. China: Beijing Language and Culture University Press.

Jiang, X. (2008). 对外汉语字词与阅读学习研究 [*Research on foreign learners' acquisition of Chinese characters, words and reading*]. China: Beijing Language and Culture University Press.

Ke, C., & Everson, M. E. (1999). Recent research in CFL reading and its pedagogical implications. In M. Chu (Ed.), *Mapping the course of the Chinese language field* (pp. 188–203). Kalamazoo, MI: Chinese Language Teachers Association.

Ke, C., & Shen, H. H. (2003). 回顾与展望: 美国汉语教学理论研究述评 [Research and theory building in teaching Chinese in the U.S.: A comprehensive review and critique]. *Yuyan jiaoxue yu yanjiu, 94*(3), 1–17.

Xing, J. Z. (2006). *Teaching and learning Chinese as a foreign language*. Hong Kong University Press.

The Acquisition of the *ba* Construction by Adult English Speakers

Hang Du
Middlebury College, Vermont

Despite the theoretical attention that the ba construction has drawn, little research has investigated its acquisition. This experimental study aims to fill this gap. It involved 65 adult learners of Chinese and two tasks: elicited production and grammaticality judgment prompted by video clips. The data were analyzed both quantitatively and qualitatively. The results show that even though the learners produced fewer ba constructions than native speakers, their judgments of most of the sentences were quite good, indicating that they had internalized some crucial aspects of this construction. Pedagogical implications are discussed.

虽然历年来把字句吸引了理论语言学家的广泛注意，但是在其习得方面的研究极其有限。本研究旨在填补这项空白。参加本实验研究的是65名在加州国防语言学院(DLI)学习中文的、以英文为母语的学生和20名以中文为母语的人组成的对照组。这65名学生处于三个组：低组的学生在DLI学了30个星期，中组的学生在DLI学了45个星期，高组的学生在DLI学了60个星期。他们的两项任务是用中文描述录像中人物的动作及判断一些对这些动作描写的句子的正误。调查的目的是揭示学生是否能够正确使用把字句，特别是能否遵循"把"不能与动词单独使用，而要与结果补语或"了"一起使用的规则。语料经过了统计分析及描述性分析，结果表明在录像描述中，这三组学生用的把字句都没有对照组的那么多，但是他们对多数句子正误的判断却很好，表明他们已经领会了把字句的一些关键因素。在使用把字句时，用错的情况，特别是与动词单独使用的情况不多，表明他们使用把字句时比较谨慎，只有在有把握的时候才用。出现的一些错误跟第一语言研究的结果相符，但有些错误是这些学生独有的，大概是母语的影响。特别值得注意的是，第一语言研究表明以中文为母语的儿童很少将"把"与动词单独使用，但是包括本研究在内的第二语言习得的研究显示第二语言习得者的确犯这个错误。结果亦表明虽然其它研究揭示儿童习得中文时结果补语的掌握落后于"了"，但是参加本实验研究的成人学生对"把"及结果补语相对于"把"及"了"的句子的判断并无区别。本研究使用三组中文水平不同的学生的目的是

Du, H. (2010). The Acquisition of the ***ba*** Construction by Adult English Speakers. In M. E. Everson & H. H. Shen (Eds.), *Research among learners of Chinese as a foreign language* (Chinese Language Teachers Association Monograph Series: Vol. 4). (pp. 5–34). Honolulu: University of Hawai'i, National Foreign Language Resource Center.

揭示把字句的习得过程，但三组学生的表现区别并不明显，可能的原因有三：1。也许中文学习的时间本身并不是中文水平高低的最好标准。2。也许本研究不足以测出15个星期学习时间的差别导致的把字句掌握方面的区别。3。也许和DLI的课程有关。学生学把字句学得比较早，学的时候练习得很多，但学完之后巩固不够。心理语言学和认知科学的研究结果表明，新学的知识只有反复练习巩固才能转化为随时灵活运用的知识。在教学方面，本研究有如下启示：参加本研究的学生对多数句子的正误判断很好，但是他们用的把字句远没有对照组的多，表明他们有很好的被动的知识，但对使用还没有把握。因此如果学生不能马上使用新学的语法，并不表明他们对此一无所知，老师应该创造条件引导他们正确使用。鉴于把字句的难度，老师应该对其使用规则给予清楚的讲解，并给予大量的例句，鼓励学生大胆使用，不要怕犯错。最初的介绍之后，也要定期复习巩固。鉴于DLI的学生都经过严格的筛选，针对其它学生群体的调查能否取得类似的结果还有待进一步研究。另一方面，尽管DLI的学生经过筛选，但他们把字句的使用比对照组还是低得多，进一步证明了这个句式的难度。下一步应该研究水平更高的学生，如已学习中文几年，并在中文环境中生活过的学生，以揭示第二语言习得者是否有可能完全掌握这一句式。

The *ba* construction is one of the best-known constructions in Modern Standard Chinese, also known as Mandarin Chinese. Over the years, researchers have analyzed this construction within various linguistic frameworks. The major frameworks can be categorized as functional, syntactic, and semantic. Classified under the functional approach are the disposal/transitivity approach (Sun, 1995; Thompson, 1973; Wang, 1947) and the topic-comment approach (Chen, 1983; Tsao, 1987). Classified under the syntactic approach are generative syntactic analysis (Goodall, 1990; Huang, 1982, 1989, 1992; A. Y.-H. Li, 1985; Travis, 1984; Zou, 1993), syntactic/semantic analysis (Sybesma, 1999), and verbal analysis (e.g., Bender, 2000; Ross, 1991). Classified under the semantic approach is aspectual analysis (e.g., Liu, 1997; Yong, 1993). In addition, Feng (2001) offered an interesting analysis of the *ba* construction based on prosody, and Yang (2004) offered an analysis of *ba* based on systemic functional linguistics (Halliday, 1994).

In contrast to the rich literature on the theoretical aspects of the *ba* construction, little has been done on the acquisition of it by either children during first-language (L1) acquisition or adult second-language (L2) learners. This research aims at filling this gap.

Literature review

A review of L1 research is important because whether L1 and L2 acquisition are similar is still controversial. The comparison of the results of the current study with existing L1 research can potentially shed light on this issue.

Cheung (1992) examined how the *ba* construction developed in children. His analysis of *ba* was within a syntactic/semantic framework, using the object affectedness linking rule (Gropen, Pinker, Hollander, & Goldberg, 1991), which is illustrated in the alternation between Examples 1a and b below (Pinker, 1984). According to this rule, the affected entity is in the object position. In 1a, the goal, "the truck," is the affected entity, so it is the object of the sentence. In 1b, the theme, "hay," is the affected entity, so it is the object of the sentence.

1a. Load the truck with hay.

1b. Load hay onto the truck.

Cheung (1992) suggested that *ba* marks the affected entity in Chinese. In other words, the *ba* NP is affected. The sentences in Example 2 below indicate such an alternation (Cheung,

p. 3). In 2a, the *ba* noun phrase (NP) *men* (door) is the locative, so Cheung called such sentences "locative *ba*". In such sentences, the locative is affected. In 2b, the *ba* NP *xiao xingxing* (little star) is the theme, so Cheung called such sentences "theme *ba*." In such sentences, the theme is affected.

2a. 老师　　把　　门　　贴　　满　　了　　小　　星星.
    teacher BA   door stick full ASP little star
    The teacher stuck the door full of little stars.

2b. 老师　　把　　小　　星星　　贴　　在　　门　　上.
    teacher BA   little star   stick at   door LOC
    The teacher stuck a little star on the door.

Against this background, Cheung (1992) wanted to find out whether the object affectedness linking rule governs the acquisition of the *ba* construction. Cheung's participants were 32 children in Taiwan in two age groups (4.3–5.4 and 5.5–6.5 years) and 16 adults. Three experiments were conducted: comprehension, production, and imitation. Cheung concluded that the object affectedness linking rule did not apply in the comprehension of the two kinds of *ba* sentences. The results of the imitation experiment were that the children were more accurate at imitating the theme sentences than the locative sentences. The order of accuracy was grammatical theme *ba*>grammatical locative *ba*>ungrammatical theme *ba*>ungrammatical locative *ba*. Results of the production experiment were that overall, participants produced more theme-*ba* than locative-*ba* structures. The 6-year-olds produced more locative *ba* than the 5-year-olds and adults.

Fahn (1993) tested Chinese-speaking children's acquisition of the following five constraints on the *ba* construction. (a) Progressive: The progressive marker *zai* cannot occur in the *ba* construction. (b) Verb selection: Only accomplishment verbs can occur alone in the *ba* construction. (c) Modifier: Stative, action, and achievement verbs need modifiers to occur in the *ba* construction. (d) Compound verb: Only resultative verb compounds can occur in the *ba* construction. (e) Definiteness: The *ba* NP cannot be indefinite.

A group of 100 children from 2.6 to 7.5 years old living in Taiwan participated. They were divided into 10 groups of 10 children each. The method used was grammaticality judgment.

Fahn (1993) found that age 5 was the demarcation point for the progressive, verb selection, and modifier constraints, and age 6 was the demarcation point for the compound verb and the definiteness constraints. She concluded that the progressive, verb selection, and modifier constraints were acquired before the compound verb and definiteness constraints. Note that according to these explanations, resultative verb compounds are acquired later than *le*.

P. Li (1993) studied a group of 99 kindergarten children in Beijing. They were in four age groups: 3-, 4-, 5-, and 6-year-olds. The method used was elicited production. A total of 1007 sentences produced by the children were analyzed. *Ba* was found in 296 of them. There was no significant difference in the production of *ba* across the age groups. Li concluded that children from age 3 on used the *ba* construction correctly in obligatory contexts. Of the 296 sentences with *ba*, 90% contained resultative verb complements (RVCs). Li noted that all but three of the *ba*-sentences had the perfective marker *le*. He therefore concluded that the high correlation between the *ba* construction, the perfective aspect marker *le*, and resultative verb constructions in sentences produced by the children indicated that the children were highly aware of these constraints on the *ba* construction from age 3.

Jin (1992) performed a major L2 study on the acquisition of the *ba* construction by adults. Treating the *ba* construction as a topic-prominent (Tp) feature of Chinese, Jin (1992) asked whether learners whose native language was a subject-prominent (Sp) language (English) could transfer such features to a Tp language (Chinese). The participants were 46 adult learners of Chinese from four proficiency levels. They were all native speakers of English. The study used three tasks: grammaticality judgment, translation, and retelling a story based on a wordless cartoon. The participants' scores from the judgment task formed three clusters, with scores decreasing from Cluster 1 to 3. In Cluster 1, the *ba* NPs were direct objects (patients), and the word order was SOV. The participants in all of the groups performed well on these sentences. In Cluster 2, the *ba* NPs were attributives, and the word order was S + NP + V + O. Higher-level participants performed better than lower-level participants on these sentences. In Cluster 3, the *ba* NPs were adverbials (theme or experiencer), and the word order was S + PP + V + O. No group performed well on these sentences. The results of the translation task were similar to those of the judgment task. In the story-retelling task, the learners produced fewer *ba* constructions than native speakers. Jin attributed this to an avoidance strategy. Five types of errors were identified in both the learners' translation and story-retelling data: "(a) misplacement of negative particles, (b) bare verbs, (c) substitutions, (d) misuse of indefinite NPs after *ba*, and (e) avoidance of *ba* constructions" (p. 41). The study concluded that there was evidence of transfer from English to Chinese. In the story-retelling and judgment tasks, the participants were clearly searching for grammatical clues. The *ba* NPs were mostly the direct objects of the verbs, and the surface word order was SOV. On the other hand, the learners had trouble with the *ba* constructions in the third cluster, where the *ba* NPs were not the direct objects of the verbs, and the use of the *ba* construction was optional, depending on the pragmatic function of the discourse. The learners displayed difficulty judging these sentences because English does not have similar structures.

The researcher concluded that the learners went through three stages of pragmaticization. In the first stage, instead of treating the *ba* NP as the second topic of the sentence, the learners treated it as the preposed object. In the second stage, the *ba* NP could be treated as either an object or a topic. In the third stage, the learners began to analyze the *ba* NP as the second topic of the sentence. The author also presented the difficulties for English speakers acquiring the *ba* construction. This is shown in Table 1, adapted from Jin (1992, p. 47).

Table 1. Learning difficulty hierarchy of *ba* constructions (Jin, 1992)

	cluster 1	cluster 2	cluster 3
	easy <-->difficult		
grammatical	direct object	attributive	place
semantic	patient	theme	theme/experiencer
disposability of verbs	most strong	less strong	least strong
likelihood of using ba	most likely	likely	less likely

Current study

Focus of the study

Despite differing theoretical analyses of the *ba* construction, researchers have reached some consensus about the major constraints on the *ba* NP and on the *ba* VP, although the explanations for these constraints differ widely. The main constraint on the *ba* NP is that it has to be definite, generic, or specific (C. N. Li & Thompson, 1981; Liu, 1997). The main constraint on the *ba* VP is that the verb has to be morphologically complex (Sybesma, 1999). This means the verb in a *ba* sentence must co-occur with some kind of verbal complement or an aspect marker. Liu (1997) summarized nine environments for the *ba* VP: (a) V + RVC; (b) V + *de* (resultative); (c) V + retained object; (d) V + perfective marker *-le*; (e) V + PP (dative or locative); (f) V + quantified phrase; (g) V + *yi* + V; (h) V + durative marker *-zhe* (irrealis); (i) Adv + V. Liu suggested that these nine environments indicate bounded events. Events can be bounded in two ways: by situation aspect or viewpoint aspect. Environments (d) and (h) are bounded by viewpoint aspect because the aspect markers *-le* and *-zhe are* needed. The other seven environments are bounded by situation aspect.

Against this theoretical background, the acquisition of the complexity constraint on the *ba* VP by second-language learners was investigated. Of the nine environments discussed above, RVC and *le* were chosen for the following three reasons. (a) Theoretically, these two each represent one of the two aspects that can bound an event: RVC for situation aspect and *le* for viewpoint aspect. (b) Of the nine environments listed above, RVC and *le* are probably the most common verbal complements for the *ba* construction. P. Li (1993) found that 90% of the *ba* sentences produced by his child participants contained RVCs and that all but three of these sentences contained *le*. (c) L1 research has shown that RVC is acquired later than *le* probably because of RVC's morphological complexity. Whether this is also true with adult L2 learners is worth investigating.

Research questions

1. Have the learners acquired the complexity constraint on the *ba* VP, as realized in RVC and *le*?
2. How do the results of this study compare to the results found in the existing L1 and L2 studies of the acquisition of the *ba* construction?
3. What stages and processes characterize the acquisition of the constraints on the *ba* VP by learners of different proficiencies?

Methods

Participants

The study had 85 participants: 20 native speakers (Gn) and 65 L2 learners in three groups (G1, G2, and G3). The native speakers (NSs) ranged in age from 20 to 47. The age range in the learner groups was 19–38. The NS group was crucial because data from this group can be used as a baseline for comparison.

The three learner groups consisted of students learning Chinese at three different levels in the intensive Chinese program at the Defense Language Institute (DLI) in Monterey, California. The students' levels were defined by the number of weeks that they had studied Chinese in the program at the time of the study. The 21 participants in G1 had studied Chinese for about 30 weeks. The 23 participants in G2 had studied Chinese for about

45 weeks. The 21 participants in G3 had studied Chinese for about 60 weeks. None were heritage speakers of any Chinese dialect. The learner groups are summarized in Table 2.

Table 2. Background information of participants in the learner groups

group	G1	G2	G3
# of participants	21	23	21
male	16	13	17
female	5	10	4
age range	18–38	19–34	19–31
mean age	21	25	23
# of weeks	30	45	60

Design

This study included a production experiment and a grammaticality-judgment experiment to assess complementary aspects of learners' knowledge and as a validity check. The production experiment tested the learners' production of the *ba* construction as they described the actions presented in video scenes. If they failed to use the *ba* construction or used it inappropriately, whether this structure was in their grammar would still not be clear. Therefore, the grammaticality-judgment task was used. The use of tasks requiring both production and grammaticality judgment was supported by data from the pilot study, which showed that some learners produced no *ba* constructions in the production task, while their judgments of all of the target sentences were correct. Such a discrepancy between production and grammaticality-judgment data has been confirmed in the L1 acquisition literature (McDaniel, McKee, & Bernstein, 1998), but this issue has not attracted much attention in L2 acquisition research. A combination of the production and judgment data, therefore, is essential to adequately assess learners' knowledge of any linguistic form.

Fillers were used in the design of both experiments. They were easy items so that the participants would feel confident if they could do them easily. They also helped break patterns that repeated uses of the target items established.

Instrumentation

Production task

The production task was designed to elicit *ba* constructions that included RVCs and *le*. Video scenes showed a woman performing various actions in a home. The actions were presented in pairs of connected actions. For example, in one pair of actions titled "hand washing," the first action was the woman washing her hands under a faucet (Figure 1); the second action was her drying her hands by wiping them with a towel (Figure 2). However, there was no connection across pairs. For example, another pair of actions was her picking up a pair of eyeglasses from a table in the first action and putting them on in the second action, in a different location from where the "hand washing" pair of actions occurred.

The videos contained 19 pairs of actions: 1 was a model pair, 2 were practice pairs, 1 was a pretest pair, 5 were filler pairs, and the remaining 10 were target pairs used to elicit the *ba* construction. Of the 10 target pairs, 5 were designed to elicit *ba* in constructions including RVCs, and the other 5 were designed to elicit *ba* in constructions including *le*. Each part of a pair of actions was designed to elicit one sentence. The pairs of actions and sentence types that they were designed to elicit are summarized in Table 3.

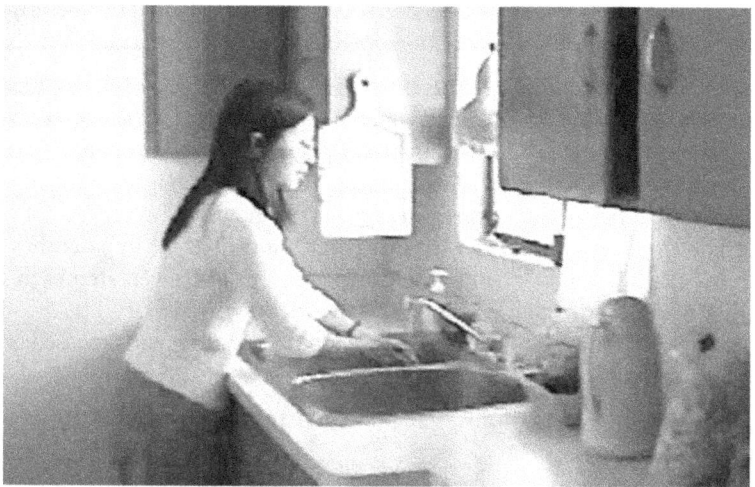

Figure 1. The first action in the hand-washing pair of actions.

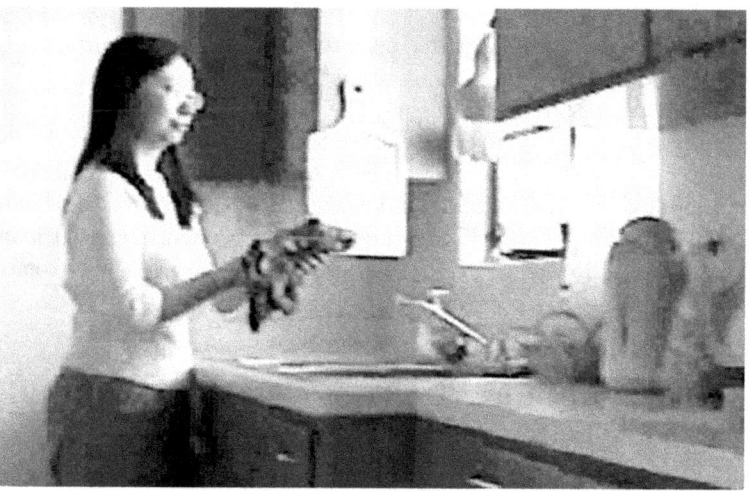

Figure 2. The second action in the hand-washing pair of actions.

Table 3. Type and number of items for the production experiment

		target (10)		filler (5)	model (1), practice (2), pretest (1)
		RVC (5)	le (5)		
action 1	sentence 1	no ba	no ba	no ba	no ba
action 2	sentence 2	ba	ba	no ba	no ba

In the first action of each target pair of actions, an object was introduced as new information. It was therefore assumed to require indefinite reference, and thus, the use of *ba* is ungrammatical in describing the actions. In the second action, the same object was manipulated again, making it old information and thus, definite. In this case, *ba* is required in describing the action. To be consistent with the target pairs, the filler, model, practice, and pretest pairs also depicted two successive actions that elicited two descriptive sentences that should not include *ba*. These actions were easy to describe using SVO sentences.

The experimental materials were presented to the participants as follows. First, video scenes of a pair of actions were played on a computer screen. After that, the screen went black, and words that were supposed to be used in describing the two actions appeared on the screen. The first two words were the verbs for the respective actions, given in the order that the actions appeared. Below the verbs, either one or two nouns appeared. All of the words that appeared on the screen were given in *pinyin* with numbers (1–4) in parentheses after each word to indicate the tones. The English translation was also given after each word to prevent unfamiliar vocabulary from hindering the participants' production. The second reason that the words were given was to help ensure that all of the participants focused on the same actions for their descriptions.

Example 3 shows how these words were presented on the screen after the hand-washing pair of actions was shown.

3. xi (3): to wash

    ca (1): to wipe

    shou (3): hand

A picture of a woman's face was posted on the wall in front of the participants, who were asked to pretend that they were telling this hypothetical person, who could not see the scenes, what had happened in the scenes. The participants were then asked to produce two sentences using these words. They were asked to use these two verbs in the two sentences, respectively, but to use the same noun in both sentences because both actions were about the same object. They were asked to use *ranhou* (then) to connect the two sentences. They were also told that they could add constituents if they wanted. The participants had no time limit to finish the sentences. The response to Example 3 should be something like Example 4:

4. 她 洗 手, 然后 把 手 擦 干净.

    she wash hand then BA hand wipe RVC (clean)

    She washed her hands, (and) then wiped her hands clean.

Grammaticality judgments

This experiment involved a paper-and-pencil task. The video scenes used in the production task were used to facilitate the judgments of sentences. Only the second actions in the items in the production experiment were related to the *ba* construction, so the second actions of 8 of the 10 target pairs of actions in the production experiment (4 for RVCs and 4 for *le*) were used as situations for the grammaticality-judgment experiment. Each scene had one action. For example, the second action of the hand-washing pair of actions (Figure 2) was given to facilitate the judgment of related sentences.

A given action had 6 sentences to judge. Therefore, a total of 60 sentences were used in the grammaticality-judgment experiment. Of the 60 sentences, 48 were based on eight video scenes about the target actions used in the production experiment (four for RVCs and four for *le*). There were 6 sentences based on a filler action in the production experiment as items for modeling. Another 6 sentences based on yet another filler action in the production experiment were items for practice. The presentation of the RVC and *le* scenes in the experiment was randomized.

The 6 sentences for a given action were 1 that had an RVC or *le* with *ba* and 1 that was its *minimal pair* without an RVC or *le*, 1 that had an RVC or *le* without *ba* and 1 that had its RVC or *le*-less minimal pair, and 2 fillers. In other words, 6 sentences were judged for each of the four RVC actions, resulting in 24 sentences. Similarly, 24 sentences were judged based on the four *le* actions. The order of the 4 target sentences and the 2 fillers for each action was randomized in the experiment so that the participants could not find a pattern.

The +*ba*, +RVC and +*ba*, +*le* sentences satisfied the complexity constraint on the *ba* VP; these sentences were grammatical. They tested whether the participants knew that the *ba*-sentences with appropriate verbal complements were grammatical. The +*ba*, −RVC and +*ba*, −*le* sentences were sentences that did not have any verbal complements. They had bare verbs. They were designed to test whether the participants knew that the *ba* sentences without verbal complements were ungrammatical. The other sentences were used to test whether the participants judged the sentences as ungrammatical if they indeed were ungrammatical. In other words, they tested whether the participants overgeneralized the use of the *ba* construction.

The answer grid for the grammaticality-judgment experiment that appeared under each sentence is shown in Table 4. The answer grid had two dimensions: grammaticality and confidence. The horizontal dimension, marked by "Natural/Unnatural," indicates grammaticality. The vertical dimension, marked by "Sure/Unsure," indicates confidence. The rationale of this design is to distinguish between marking an answer with confidence and simply guessing. The answer grid offers four possible answers for each sentence.

Table 4. Sample answer grid for grammaticality judgments

	natural	unnatural
sure		
unsure		

Procedures

Both experiments were conducted with the NS group first to ensure that the items elicited what they were designed to elicit and to establish baseline data. For all of the participants, the production experiment preceded the grammaticality-judgment experiment so that the participants could not guess what the purpose of the study was.

Both experiments with the learners were conducted at the DLI during a 2-week period. The production task was individually given to each participant. A laptop computer was used to show the video scenes, and an audio recorder was used to record the participants' speech. They were administered the grammaticality-judgment task in small groups. Each participant in the NS group was administered both tasks individually during one session.

Data coding and analyses

Production task

The number of *ba* constructions in the second sentences the participants correctly produced for each pair of actions was calculated. Because there were 10 sentences, the highest possible score was 10. Even though RVCs and *le* were the target structures, *ba* sentences with other verbal compounds were also accepted if they were correct. For example, one of the pairs of actions showed the woman opening a book in the first action, then throwing the book to the floor in the second action. This item was designed to elicit *ba* with *le*, as Gn.P13, Participant 13 in the native-speaker group, did in Example 5.

5. 她 拿 了 一 本 书, 看 了 看, 然后 把 它 扔　　 了. (Gn.P13)
   she take ASP one CL book look ASP look then BA it throw ASP
   She took a book, looked at it, and then threw it.

Instead of using *le*, some participants used a PP with *ba*, as shown in Example 6.

6. 她 打开 了 一 本 手册,　　 然后 把 它 扔　 到 一边. (Gn.P18)
   she open ASP one CL handbook then BA it throw to side
   She opened a handbook, and then threw it aside.

Both Examples 5 and 6 are grammatical and appropriate in describing this situation. Therefore, in the coding of the data, as long as the *ba* sentences were produced correctly, the participants were credited for producing them, regardless of what they used with *ba*.

Data from the production task were analyzed by using one-way ANOVAs. Qualitatively, grammatical patterns that the learners used to substitute for the *ba* construction and error patterns were also identified and analyzed.

Grammaticality judgment

Participants got one point for the box that they marked under each sentence. In the analysis of the grammaticality-judgment data, the scores on the confidence dimension were combined.

The statistical analyses of data were approached from three different angles: across the groups, across conditions (+RVC/+*le* vs. −RVC/−*le*), and across items (RVC vs. *le*). The comparison across the groups aimed at capturing possible developmental trends. The comparison across conditions addressed the question of whether the participants accepted *ba* sentences with RVC/*le* and rejected *ba*-sentences without RVC/*le*. The comparison across items addressed the theoretical question of whether RVC was more difficult than *le*. This was addressed in response to claims made by L1 acquisition researchers that children acquired verb compounds later than *le*.

Results

Production

Number of *ba* constructions produced

The numbers of *ba* constructions produced in the second sentences are summarized in Table 5.

Table 5. *Ba* constructions in the second sentences

groups	G1	G2	G3	native
mean (SD)	1.71 (1.76)	2.30 (1.96)	2.24 (2.28)	6.10 (1.71)
range	0–4	0–8	0–7	3–10

A one-way ANOVA used to analyze the data in Table 7 was found to be statistically significant, $F(3, 81)=22.02$, $p<.001$. A posthoc Tukey HSD test indicated that the mean of the NS group (M=6.10) was significantly greater than that of G1 (M=1.71), G2 (M=2.30), and G3 (M=2.24). However, the means of the three learner groups did not significantly differ from each other.

In each of the learner groups, some participants did not produce any *ba* constructions, so they are referred to as *nonproducers*. There were 5 in G1, 9 in G2 and 8 in G3. By contrast, there were no nonproducers in the NS group. In fact, all participants in Gn produced at least three *ba* constructions.

Types of *ba* constructions produced

A breakdown of the *ba* constructions that the participants produced indicates that most of them were with RVCs, *le*, or a combination of the two. This was the case in each group. As Table 6 shows, across the groups, a total of 258 *ba* constructions were produced. Of these, 236 (91%) involved RVCs, *le*, or a combination of them.

Table 6. Types of *ba* constructions in the second sentences

group	RVC	le	RVC + le	other	total
G1	11	16	7	2	36
G2	35	7	6	5	53
G3	25	7	15	0	47
native	57	30	20	15	122
total	128	60	48	22	258

TheThe main structures that the learners used to substitute for the *ba* construction were SVO sentences and object-drop sentences. From their production and error patterns, they seemed uncomfortable finishing *ba* sentences with bare verbs, thereby showing their knowledge of the complexity constraint on the *ba* VP.

Grammaticality judgments

Because there were four scenes to judge for RVC and four for *le*, the highest possible score for each scene was 4. The group scores used in all of the statistical tests were the mean scores.

The main statistical procedure used here was the comparison of the mean scores of each group. When the means of different groups were compared, one-way ANOVAs were used because the independent variable had more than two levels (four when all groups were included and three when the native-speaker group was excluded). In the other two kinds of comparisons, across conditions and across items, paired *t*-tests were used because the values of both condition (+ vs. −) and item (RVC vs. *le*) were binary. Therefore, the independent variable had only two levels, and the dependent variable was within subjects.

Comparisons across groups

These comparisons aimed at capturing possible developmental trends among the groups.

Four one-way ANOVAs were used to compare the scores of the four groups. One ANOVA was for the +*ba*, +RVC sentences, one was for the +*ba*, +*le* sentences, one was for the +*ba*, −RVC sentences, and the last was for the +*ba*, −*le* sentences. The results of these four ANOVAs are presented in Table 7.

Table 7. ANOVAs comparing group means in grammaticality (+ba)

item type		df	F	sig.
+RVC	between groups	3	0.58	.63
	within groups	81		
+le	between groups	3	1.20	.32
	within groups	81		
−RVC	between groups	3	3.58	.02
	within groups	81		
−le	between groups	3	1.51	.22
	within groups	81		

There were statistically significant differences only in the judgments of the +ba, −RVC sentences across the groups (p=.02), as Table 7 shows. Posthoc Tukey HSD tests showed that the difference between G3 and G2 was significant (p=.05) and that the difference between G3 and the NS group was also significant (p=.02). G3's mean score was significantly lower than that of G2 and the NS group. The differences between the other groups were not statistically significant. The results are shown graphically in Figure 3.

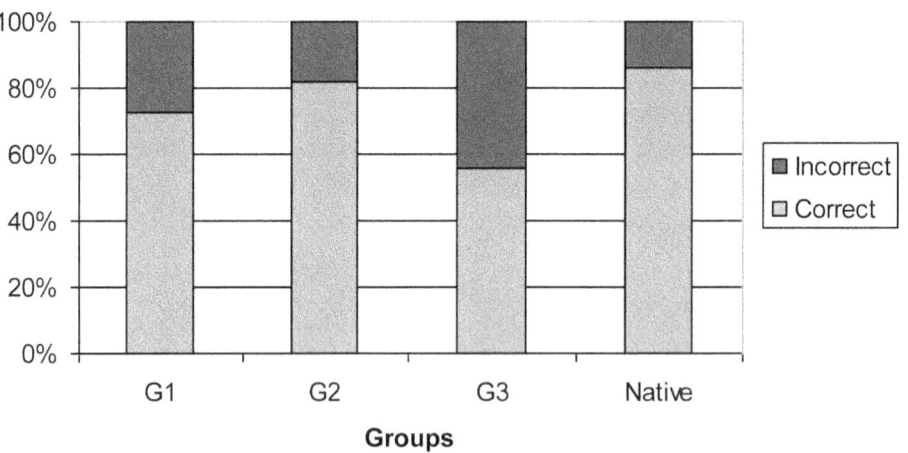

Figure 3. Grammaticality of +ba, −RVC sentences.

Comparisons across conditions (+ba, +RVC/+le vs. +ba, −RVC/−le)

These comparisons focused on the most important aspect in this investigation, namely, whether the learners knew that the *ba* VP has to be morphologically complex. In other words, *ba* cannot appear with bare verbs. It has to appear in a syntactic environment (RVC or *le*).

Paired sample *t*-tests compared the grammaticality scores on the +ba, +RVC and +ba, −RVC, and the +ba, +le and +ba, −le sentences from each group. Thus, eight tests were conducted (four for +RVC vs. −RVC and four for +le vs. −le). The +ba, +RVC/+le sentences are grammatical, so the "natural" scores were used as the correct scores. The +ba, −RVC/−le sentences are ungrammatical, so the "unnatural" scores were used as the correct scores.

+ba, +RVC *versus* +ba, −RVC

The *t*-test results for the +RVC versus −RVC sentences are presented in Table 8.

Table 8. Grammaticality of +RVC versus −RVC within each group (+*ba*)

group	comparison	n	mean	SD	t	sig. (2-tailed)
G1	+*ba*, +RVC vs. +*ba*, −RVC	21	.98 .73	.07 .33	3.42	.00
G2	+*ba*, +RVC vs. +*ba*, −RVC	23	.94 .81	.13 .26	2.15	.04
G3	+*ba*, +RVC vs. +*ba*, −RVC	21	.98 .56	.08 .40	4.71	.00
native	+*ba*, +RVC vs. +*ba*, −RVC	20	.97 .86	.08 .29	1.63	.12

All of the learner groups judged the +RVC sentences more correctly than the −RVC sentences, as Table 8 shows. However, the NSs' judgments of these two types of sentences did not differ significantly (Figure 4).

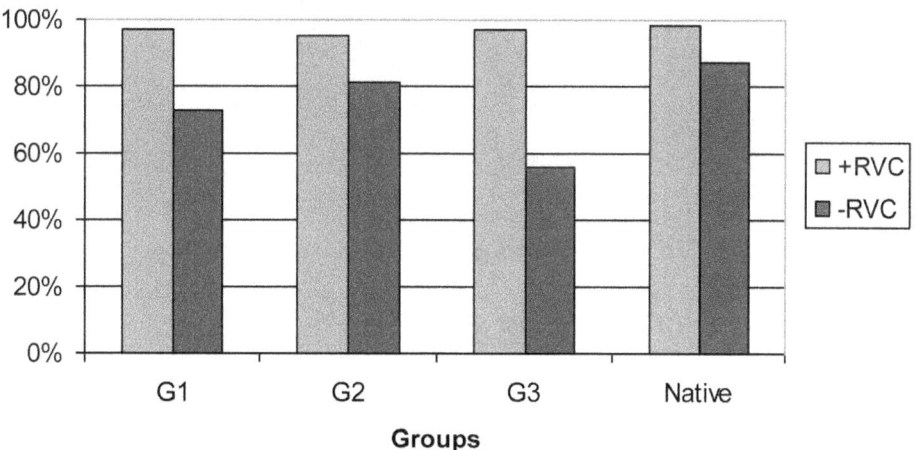

Figure 4. Grammaticality of +*ba*, +RVC versus +*ba*, −RVC sentences.

+ba, +le *versus* +ba, − le

The *t*-test results from the +le versus −le sentences are presented in Table 9.

Table 9. Grammaticality of +*ba*, +*le* versus +*ba*, −*le* within each group (+*ba*)

group	comparison	n	mean	SD	t	sig. (2-tailed)
G1	+*ba*, +*le* vs. +*ba*, − *le*	21	.99 .86	.05 .36	1.6	.12
G2	+*ba*, +*le* vs. +*ba*, − *le*	23	.96 .89	.12 .29	0.98	.35

continued...

Table 9. Grammaticality of +ba, +le versus +ba, −le within each group (+ba) (cont.)

group	comparison	n	mean	SD	t	sig. (2-tailed)
G3	+ba, +le vs. +ba, −le	21	.98 .68	.08 .43	3.34	.00
native	+ba, +le vs. +ba, −le	20	1.00 .84	.00 .33	2.16	.04

The results from G1 and G2 are not significant, as Table 9 shows. This indicates that the correctness of judging +ba, +le versus +ba, −le sentences did not differ within these groups. The results from G3 and the NS group are significant. This indicates that participants in these two groups judged the +le sentences more correctly than the −le sentences. This is shown in Figure 5.

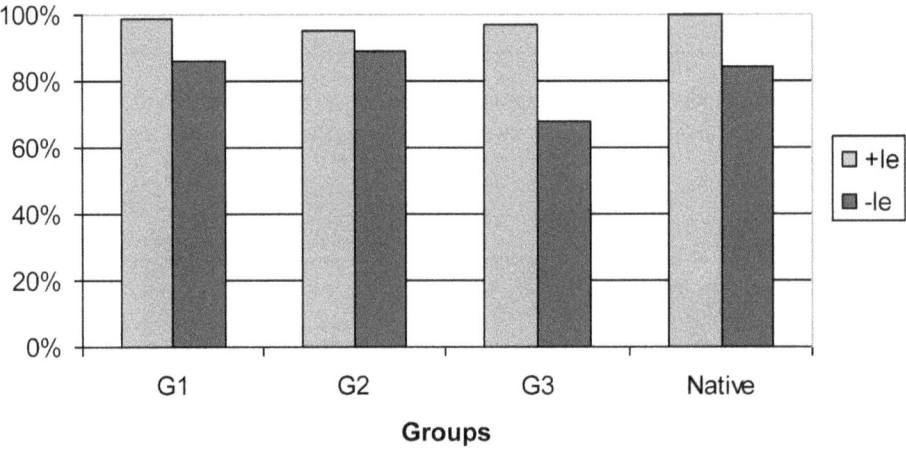

Figure 5. Grammaticality of +ba, +le versus +ba, −le sentences.

Comparison across items (+ba, +RVC versus +ba, +le)
These comparisons addressed the question of whether the adult learners judged the RVC sentences better than the *le* sentences.

Four paired *t*-tests were conducted. Because both types of sentences are grammatical, the "natural" scores were used as the correct scores. The results are shown in Table 10.

Table 10. Grammaticality of +RVC versus +le within each group (+ba)

group	comparison	n	mean	SD	t	sig. (2-tailed)
G1	+ba, +RVC vs. +ba, +le	21	.98 .99	.08 .05	−0.59	.58
G2	+ba, +RVC vs. +ba, +le	23	.95 .96	.13 .12	−0.27	.79
G3	+ba, +RVC vs. +ba, +le	21	.98 .98	.07 .07	−2.91	1.00
native	+ba, +RVC vs. +ba, +le	20	.97 1.00	.08 .00	0.81	.16

As Table 10 shows, the differences between the participants' judgments of +*ba*, +RVC and +*ba*, +*le* sentences are not statistically significant in any group, and all of the scores are near or at the ceiling, as shown in Figure 6.

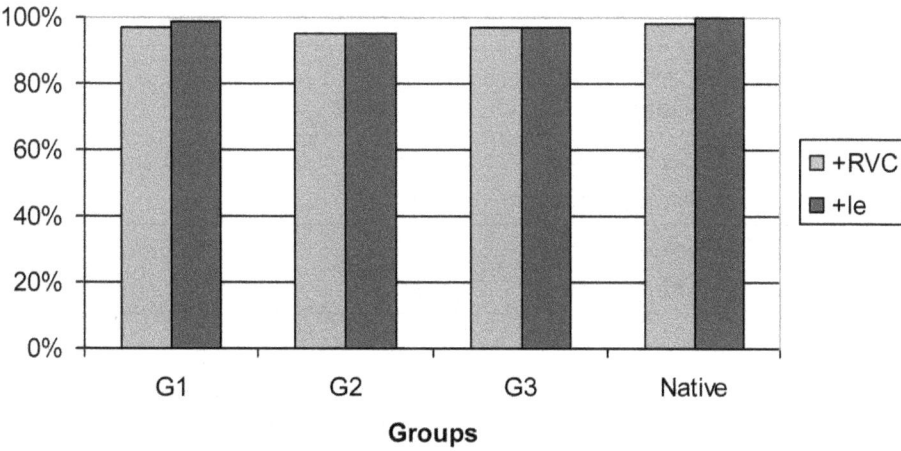

Figure 6. Grammaticality of +*ba*, +RVC versus +*ba*, +*le* sentences.

Analyses of production and judgment data in combination

This part of the analysis focuses on whether groups of learners who had different production patterns also performed differently in the grammaticality-judgment experiment. Recall that the rationale of using both a production experiment and a grammaticality experiment is to cross-check patterns found in one type of data. Therefore, the learners were regrouped according to their production data to create two groups of learners whose production differed to the largest extent. Then the judgment data of these two groups were compared. At the low end was the group of 22 nonproducers from the three learner groups. At the high end was a group of 19 *good producers*, participants who produced at least four correct *ba* constructions (Table 11).

Table 11. Numbers of good producers, nonproducers, and NSs

group	# of participants
good producer	19 (G1: 6; G2: 7; G3: 6)
nonproducer	22 (G1: 9; G2: 5; G3: 8)
NS	18

Four one-way ANOVAs were performed, comparing the mean scores among the three groups on four types of sentences containing *ba*: +*ba*, +RVC; +*ba*, +*le*; +*ba*, −RVC; and +*ba*, −*le*. The results are given in Table 12.

Table 12. Judgments of good producers, nonproducers, and NSs (+ba)

sentence type	comparison	df	F	sig.
+RVC	between groups	2	3.53	.04
	within groups	56		
+le	between groups	2	2.77	.07
	within groups	56		
−RVC	between groups	2	12.56	.00
	within groups	56		
−le	between groups	2	4.11	.02
	within groups	56		

There was no statistically significant difference between the judgments of the sentences containing le (+ba, +le) among the three groups (p=.08), as shown in Table 12. In other words, the nonproducers judged the +ba, +le sentences as well as the good producers and the NSs.

The other three ANOVAs yielded significant results, indicating that there were significant differences in the judgments of the other three kinds of sentences across the three groups. Posthoc Tukey HSD tests showed that the good producers' judgments of the sentences with RVC (+ba, +RVC) were significantly better than those of the nonproducers (p=.03), although the difference between the good producers and the NSs was not significant (p=.66). The good producers' judgment of the sentences without RVCs (+ba, −RVC) was significantly better than that of the nonproducers (p=.002), but the difference between the good producers and the NSs was not statistically significant (p=.50). Additionally, the good producers' judgment of the sentences without le (+ba, −le) was significantly better than that of the nonproducers (p=.04), but the difference between the good producers and the NSs was not statistically significant (p=.999). These results are shown in Figure 7.

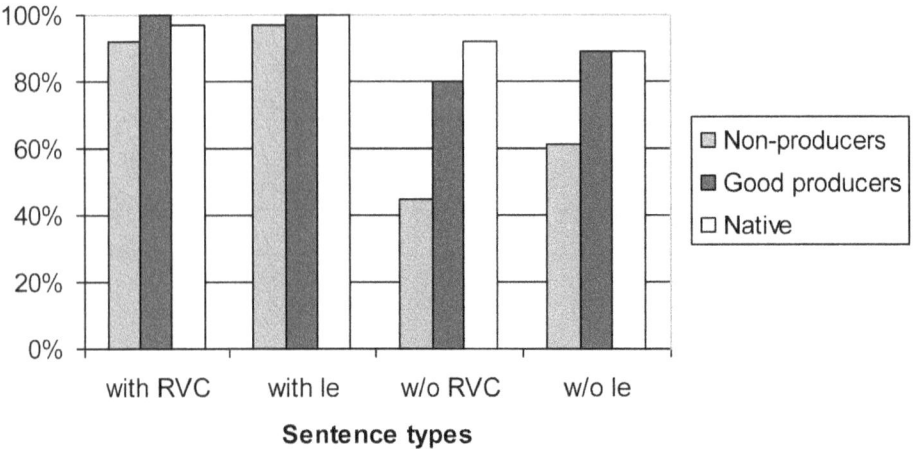

Figure 7. Judgments of four types of sentences across groups (+ba).

One striking finding from these results was that the good producers' judgments of all four types of sentences were not statistically different from those of the NSs. This raised the question of whether their production was significantly different from that of the NSs. A 2-tailed independent groups *t*-test was conducted, comparing the mean production scores from the good-producer and the NS groups. The results indicated that the good-producer group's mean production score was significantly lower than the NS group's ($p=.000$), as shown in Table 13.

Table 13. Production scores of good producers versus NSs

group	n	mean	SD	t	sig. (2-tailed)
good producer	19	4.63	1.16	4.23	.00
NS	18	6.44	1.42		

Thus, even though the good-producer group produced significantly fewer *ba* constructions than the NS group, their grammaticality judgments of all four sentence types with *ba* were the same as those of the NSs. Even the nonproducers' judgment of one of the sentence types, *ba*-sentences with *le* (+*ba*, +*le*), was not significantly different from either the judgment of the good producers or that of the NSs.

Discussion

Research Question 1. Have the learners acquired the complexity constraint on the *ba* VP, as realized in RVC and *le*?

As discussed above, the constraint on the *ba* VP is that it has to be complex. In other words, the verb in the *ba* construction cannot appear alone, but must have some kind of verbal complement within the nine environments discussed by Liu (1997). The two environments investigated in this study involved RVC and *le*, with the production experiment designed to see whether the participants would produce *ba* with some verbal complement and not produce *ba* with bare verbs. Reflected in the grammaticality-judgment experiment, the participants should have accepted *ba* sentences with RVC and *le* (+RVC and +*le*) and should have rejected *ba* sentences without RVC and *le* (–RVC and –*le*).

The overall results of the production experiment demonstrate that the learners' production rate of *ba* constructions was low, which was similar to the findings of other studies (e.g., Jin, 1992). The primary patterns that the learners used to substitute for the *ba* construction were SVO and object-drop sentences. However, when they did produce the *ba* construction, they rarely did so with bare verbs. This suggests that they were conservative producers. They seemed to know that something should come after the verb in the *ba* construction, even though they sometimes seemed to have a hard time finding it, as the following examples illustrate.

Some learners, for example, did not finish the *ba* sentences that they started producing with bare verbs until they finally came up with a verbal complement after a long pause. As Example 7 shows, after a long pause, the participant finally came up with the perfective aspect marker *le*.

7. 她 先…她 先 看 电视, 就 把 电视 关…了. (G1.P10)
   she first…she first watch TV then BA TV turn off…ASP
   She first watched TV, and then turned off the TV.

Some learners started using *ba*, but did not finish the sentences with bare verbs. They seemed to know that something should come after *si* (to tear) but had a hard time finding a complement, so they switched to SVO as Example 8 shows, or object drop, as Example 9 shows.

8. 她 读 那 张 信, 然后⋯信⋯然后⋯把 信 撕⋯然后 撕⋯撕⋯信. (G1.P15)

    she read that CL letter then…letter…then…BA letter tear…then tear…tear…letter

    She read the letter, then…letter…then…tore the letter.

9. 她⋯她 读 信, 然后⋯然后 把 信 撕⋯撕⋯然后 撕⋯撕 了. (G3.P5)

    she…she read letter then…then BA letter tear…tear…then tear…tear ASP

    She read the letter, and then tore (it).

A few learners from G2 and G3 started *ba* sentences but showed clear discomfort leaving a bare verb with *ba*, so they simply said "don't know how to say it" after the verb, as Example 10 shows.

10. *她 先⋯洗 手, 然后 用⋯纸⋯把 手 擦⋯不 知道 怎么 说. (G2.P7)

    she first…wash hand then use…paper…BA hand wipe…not know how say

    She first washed her hand, and then used paper to wipe hand…don't know how to say it.

The results of the grammaticality-judgment task showed that the learners' judgments of the *ba*-sentences with RVC and *le* (+RVC and +*le*) were not significantly different from those of the NSs. This suggests that they knew that it was right when the verbs in *ba* constructions had verbal complements and that as groups, the learners knew that the sentences that satisfied the complexity constraint of the *ba* VP were correct.

As for the judgments of *ba* sentences without RVC or *le* (−RVC and −*le*), there was no difference between the learners and the NSs in the −*le* sentences, but G3 performed significantly worse than G2 and the NSs in the −RVC sentences. This indicates that all of the groups except G3 knew that the sentences were incorrect that did not satisfy the complexity constraint on the *ba* VP.

However, in the comparisons of each group's judgments of the same types of sentences in different conditions (+RVC vs. −RVC and +*le* vs. −*le*), all three learner groups judged the +*ba*, +RVC sentences significantly better than the +*ba*, −RVC sentences. The NS group's judgments of these two types of sentences were not different. As for +*ba*, +*le* versus +*ba*, −*le* sentences, G1 and G2 did not show any difference in their correctness of judgments, while G3 and the NS group more accurately judged the +*le* sentences than the −*le* sentences.

The above discussion of both the production results and judgment results suggests that the learners who participated in this study have acquired a good knowledge of the complexity constraint on the *ba* VP, reflected in their overall correct judgments of *ba*-sentences with RVCs or *le* (+RVC/+*le*) and *ba* sentences without RVCs or *le* (−RVC/−*le*). Their production was still lower than that of the NS group, but when they did produce the *ba* construction, they rarely had bare-verb errors, which, again, suggests that they had some knowledge of the complexity constraint on the *ba* VP.

Research Question 2. How do the results of this study compare to the results found in the existing L1 and L2 acquisition studies of the *ba* construction? In particular, L1 acquisition studies have suggested that RVC is acquired later than *le* because of RVC's morphological complexity (e.g., Fahn, 1993). Is this also true with adult L2 learners?

Comparisons of patterns

Five types of *ba* sentences were found to be produced by the learners in this study, namely, RVC, *le*, RVC+*le*, the tentative aspect, and prepositional phrases (PPs). These are a subset of the types of *ba* sentences that the children in the Cheung (1992) study produced.

Some errors, such as missing post-NP localizers in a PP, were found in both L1 studies and this L2 study. Example 11 was found by Cheung (1992), where the post-NP localizer in a PP, 里 (inside), is missing and is shown in parentheses.

11. *他 把 衣服 吊 在 衣柜 (里).

   he BA clothes hang at closet (LOC)

   He hung clothes into the closet.

Some participants in the present study had similar errors, as shown in Example 12. In this example, the localizer 里 (inside) after the NP 碗儿 (bowl) is missing.

12. *她 煮 水, 然后 把 面条儿 拿 起来 放 在 碗儿__. (G1.P12)

   she boil water then BA noodle take RVC (up) put at bowl__

   She boiled water, and then took the noodles out and put them in the bowl.

Another kind of error, found in the present data but not found in the L1 data, is one reflecting possible transfer, as Example 13 shows. In Example 13, the participant mistakenly used the Chinese durative marker 着 in the same way as the English progressive.

13. *她 先 读 信, 然后 把 信 撕 着. (G2.P20)

   she first read letter then BA letter tear DUR

   Intended?: She first read the letter, and then was tearing the letter.

One striking difference between the L1 results (Cheung, 1992; Erbaugh, 1982; P. Li, 1993) and the L2 results from Jin (1992) and the current study is that the L1 children did not produce bare verbs in their *ba* sentences, but the adults did. This is significant because this concerns the complexity constraint on the *ba* VP, one of the most important aspects of the *ba* construction. Even though the learners in this study did not produce many *ba* constructions with bare verbs, the fact that some did may suggest that they still had problems with this constraint. Their judgment data partially supported this point. Jin also found such errors. The difference between the children's lack of such errors and the presence of such errors in the adult data may suggest that the children acquired this constraint early on. This is especially striking considering that the ages of the children across the different studies ranged from 1 to 6 years. On the other hand, some of Jin's participants had been learning Chinese for several years.

RVCs versus le

As discussed in the literature review, Fahn (1993) found that the children in her study acquired *le* earlier than verbal compounds, which consisted of both verbs and their RVCs. The reason, Fahn argued, was that the literature showed that the aspect system was acquired early by Chinese-speaking children. On the other hand, the verb compound was difficult to acquire because it involved two sets of argument structures.

Fahn's (1993) verbal compound included both the verb and RVC. Even RVC alone is both syntactically and semantically more complex than *le* because it is a verbal element and because it has a thematic role relationship with the object. On the other hand, *le* is simply a grammatical particle belonging to the aspect system and has no relationship to the object. These differences are summarized in Table 14.

Table 14. Comparison of linguistic characteristics of RVC and *le*

	RVC	*le*
syntactic structure	verbal element	particle, perfective aspect marker
semantic structure	has a thematic relation with the object	has no thematic relation with the object
function	indicating results	indicating completion

In the current study, however, there was no difference across the groups in the correctness of their judgments of +*ba*, +RVC and +*ba*, +*le* sentences.

Research Question 3. What stages and processes characterize the acquisition of the constraints on the *ba* VP by learners of different proficiencies?

The cross-sectional design involving participants of three proficiency levels was intended to capture some possible developmental trends. Ideally, the learner groups' performance in both the production and grammaticality-judgment experiments would have been G3>G2>G1. However, no statistically significant trend was found in either the production data or the judgment data. The judgments by G3 of +*ba*, −RVC sentences were even poorer than those by G2. However, some possible developmental trends were identified based on some qualitative and descriptive statistical analyses of the data.

Possible developmental trends
The general tendency was that G1 did not perform as well as the other two groups on the production task. G2 shared errors with both G1 and G3, indicating that it was somewhere in between, but it also had its unique errors. G3 had many individual differences, including a large number of nonproducers. Without the nonproducers, G3's production would have been the best among the three learner groups.

G1's performance was poorer than that of G2 and G3 on the production task
Several indicators have shown that G1 did not perform as well as the other two groups in the production experiment. G1 produced fewer *ba* constructions than the other two groups, even though the differences between the groups were not statistically significant (Table 15).

Table 15. Mean production

group	production (SD)
G1	1.71 (1.76)
G2	2.30 (1.96)
G3	2.24 (2.28)
native	6.10 (1.71)

Examining the highest production score by single participants across the learner groups shows that G1's score is still the lowest. G1's highest production score is 4, but G2's is 8, and G3's is 7.

In all three groups, some participants produced *ba* with bare verbs such as in Example 14.

14. *她 先…洗 手, 然后 把 手 擦. (G1.P10)

    she first…wash hands then BA hand wipe

    She washed her hands first, and then wiped her hands.

However, only in G2 and G3, not in G1, did some participants clearly express discomfort in leaving a bare verb with *ba*, as Example 9 shows, repeated below.

9. 她…她 读 信, 然后…然后 把 信 撕…撕…然后 撕…撕 了. (G3.P5)

   she…she read letter then…then BA letter tear…tear…then tear…tear ASP

   She read the letter, and then tore (it).

G2 shared errors with both G1 and G3 but also had unique errors
G2's production was slightly better than G1's. However, some of G2's grammaticality-judgment scores were significantly better than those of G3.

Error patterns show that G2 was between G1 and G3. For example, some errors from G1 and G2 were not found in G3, suggesting that they are developmental errors. One example is using the wrong NP as the *ba* NP, as in Example 15, where *ba* should have been used with the object *miantiao* (noodles) instead of the instrument *kuaizi* (chopsticks).

15. *她 煮 面条, 然后…把 筷子 拿 上来…拿 下来. (G1.P15)

    she boil noodle then…BA chopsticks take RVC (up)…take RVC (down)

    Intended?: She boiled noodles, and then took them out with chopsticks.

(The English translation reconstructs what the participant probably intended to say.)

On the other hand, some of the errors found in G2 were only shared with G3, such as the use of a single pattern of the *ba* construction to describe different situations. For example, some participants used the tentative aspect with all of their *ba* constructions; others produced all of their *ba* constructions with *haole* (good-*le*). No participant in G1 used such patterns.

The participants in G2 had errors that were not found in the data from the other two groups. For example, the *ba* construction cannot be used with *-zhe* except in its irrealis sense. Such an error can be seen in Example 13, repeated below.

13. *她 先 读 信, 然后 把 信 撕 着. (G2.P20)

    she first read letter then BA letter tear DUR

    Intended?: She first read the letter, and then was tearing the letter.

This sentence was likely produced due to transfer from English because the Chinese durative aspect is being used in the same way as the English progressive.

G3 had more individual variation
G3 and G2 were similar in their production. However, G3's judgments of certain types of sentences were worse than G2's. In the analyses where only grammaticality was considered, G3's score on *ba* sentences without RVC (–RVC) was statistically significantly lower than both G2's and the NS group's. This is contrary to expectations, so individual differences may

explain this finding. Only 5 nonproducers were in G2, but 8 were in G3. The nonproducers in G3 displayed serious problems in their grammaticality-judgment task and error patterns in the production task. Some errors were basic, such as word-order problems or sentences that did not make much sense. Such errors were not common even in G1. Example 16 illustrates this. This sentence has no translation accompanying it because the intended meaning is not clear. The gloss reflects what the participant said in Chinese.

16. *她..先 掀开 那张画儿, 然后 她..拿..拿 了 那个 画儿,...她..拿
    she...first uncover that picture then she...take...take ASP that picture...she...take
    了 那个画儿 挂 着 在 墙 上, 她 拿 着… 拿 起来. (G3.P18)
    ASP that picture hang DUR at wall LOC she take DUR take RVC (up)

    First she uncovered the picture, and then took... took that picture... She took that picture hanging on the wall. She took... picked it up.

The individual differences in G3 are also reflected in the standard deviations in the production data shown in Table 16, which indicate that G3's mean production score was the highest among the learner groups without the nonproducers.

Table 16. Mean production scores without nonproducers

group	# of participants	mean score
G1	12	3.0
G2	18	3.0
G3	13	3.6
native	20	6.1

Another interesting observation about the differences among the learner groups was that 52% of the participants in G1, 52% in G2, and 67% in G3 had no prior experience in learning foreign languages. Research has shown that the experience of learning one foreign language can facilitate the learning of another one (e.g., Nation & McLaughlin, 1986). The fact that more people in G3 did not have prior foreign-language learning experience may have contributed to their lack of better mastery of the *ba* construction than the other two groups, despite the fact that they had studied Chinese 15 or 30 weeks longer than the other two groups in the same program. The effect of prior language-learning experience on the learning of additional languages merits further research.

Explanations for weak developmental trends

The cross-sectional design of this study involving learners of three proficiency levels aimed at capturing possible developmental trends. However, the developmental trends were not striking, leading to three possible explanations. First, the basis for distinguishing the three levels, namely, the number of weeks that the learners had been in the program, probably did not truly represent their proficiency. The ideal procedure would have been to establish individual oral proficiency levels according to standardized tests, such as the Oral Proficiency Interview, although this was not feasible with the students at the DLI. Second, the differences among the three learner groups in terms of the weeks that they had been in the program were probably not great enough to have caused measureable differences in their command of the *ba* construction.

Third, the results might be related to the curriculum at the DLI. Because the students at the DLI learn in a foreign-language environment without opportunities to interact with NSs in natural settings, their only source of input was from the teachers and teaching materials. Therefore, the point at which the *ba* construction is introduced in the curriculum and how it is practiced and consolidated afterwards could have made a difference in the learners' performance. If the students did not have constant opportunities to practice using the *ba* construction throughout the program, they might perform better on tasks involving *ba* just after learning it, as opposed to later, when they had not been intensely practicing this structure for a while. This could make it appear that students at a higher level were less proficient than students at lower levels. For example, after G3.P17 completed his production task, he said that describing the actions was too easy for students at his level because they were doing much more "sophisticated stuff," such as focusing on authentic materials from China, including newspapers, TV programs, and so on. If true, this could explain why G3's performance on the *ba* construction was a little "rusty": The *ba* construction investigated is not likely to appear in those media very often. The teachers' response to my follow-up questionnaire confirmed that the *ba* construction was introduced during the 18th and 19th weeks and was practiced intensively at that time. Afterwards, however, they moved on to other structures and only occasionally revisited the *ba* construction. If the practice was not enough for the students to internalize the structure, then spending a longer period of time in the program does not necessarily translate into superior command of the structure. This can be explained by cognitive approaches to second-language acquisition.

According to cognitive psychology, learning takes at least two stages: New knowledge is first stored in working memory. It is eventually transferred into long-term memory (e.g., Gathercole & Baddeley, 1994). The new knowledge is called "declarative knowledge," and the knowledge that is eventually stored in long-term memory is called "procedural knowledge" (Anderson, 1989). The crucial link between the two kinds of memory or the two types of knowledge is sometimes called *rehearsal*, constant practice of the new knowledge that finds its way into working memory. Applying this to the learning of a new grammatical pattern, such as the *ba* construction, means that when it is first introduced in the curriculum, it is new knowledge, the declarative knowledge in working memory. With practice, it is stored in long-term memory and can be used freely at the learner's disposal. However, the rehearsal takes time, and the frequency of the *ba* construction in the input is also crucial for learners to internalize it in their interlanguage systems (Schmidt, 1990). Because the learners at the DLI study Chinese in a foreign-language environment without natural input from sources other than their classes, the teachers need to enhance the input to make the *ba* construction more salient to the learners, and they need give the learners ample opportunities to practice to internalize the structure.

Pedagogical implications

What counts as acquisition?

The discrepancy between the production and grammaticality-judgment results is very interesting. Grammaticality judgment is the main method of eliciting data from NSs in linguistic research, while production is widely used in L2 acquisition research. Grammaticality judgment arguably taps into linguistic competence, while production taps into linguistic performance (Sorace, 1996). In this study, the learners were almost as good as the NSs in their judgments. Does this mean that they have the same competence as NSs? Probably not. This raises the issue of productive knowledge and receptive knowledge. The learners in this study were able to tell whether certain *ba* sentences were correct, but they were still not ready to use them on their own. This shows that they already have some receptive knowledge about this construction in their developing interlanguage systems, but their productive knowledge is still not as fully developed as that of a NS. This means that teachers, on the one hand, should not lose heart when students are not ready to freely use a new structure on their own. On the other hand, a way should be found to facilitate their transition from passive, receptive knowledge to active, productive knowledge.

Focusing on form

The communicative approach has been the mainstream approach in classroom foreign-language teaching in North America for more than two decades. Some extreme advocates of this approach have even eliminated the teaching of grammar altogether in favor of communication in the classroom. However, several years' of total immersion programs in Canada have shown that without grammar instruction, input and communication alone tend to produce fluent but grammatically inaccurate or even fossilized speakers of the L2 (e.g., Doughty & Williams, 1998). In response to this, a number of researchers have suggested focus on form in the classroom (e.g., Doughty & Williams; Long, 1996). As Long suggested, linguistic form should be focused on in the second-language classroom in communicative contexts. This can be done in two ways: proactive or reactive. The proactive way means that teachers anticipate problems ahead of time and explain a structure to students before it is introduced. The reactive way means the teachers find ways to address a problem after they find that students have trouble with certain structures. Some researchers suggest that the proactive way should be used with linguistic forms that are purely formal (e.g., Harley, 1998), such as the English third-person singular marker *s*. Because these forms do not affect meaningful communication, learners might never realize that they have problems with them. On the other hand, forms that are communicatively salient should be handled in the reactive way (e.g., Lightbown & Spada, 1990) because learners might notice problems in such forms if they affect their communication.

In the case of the Chinese *ba* construction, both the proactive and reactive methods are needed. The results of this study confirmed teachers' experiences that the *ba* construction is difficult to acquire. Therefore, teachers should draw students' attention to it before introducing it. After the students have been exposed to it, they should be given many opportunities to practice it. If they show problems with it, teachers should address the problems in an efficient and timely manner. Teachers might also need to explicitly ask the students to produce the *ba* construction because there is always an SVO alternative.

Conclusion and directions for further research

This study found that classroom learners of Chinese as a second language can acquire knowledge of the complexity constraint on the *ba* VP, reflected in the participants' overall accurate judgments of the *ba* sentences containing RVC or *le* and those without RVC or *le*. They judged *ba* sentences that satisfied the complexity constraint on the *ba* VP (+RVC/+*le*) better than those that did not (−RVC/−*le*). Their production was still predictably lower than that of the NSs, but when they did produce the *ba* construction, they rarely committed errors using bare verbs, thus indicating that they had some knowledge of the complexity constraint on the *ba* VP. The fact that their production was low confirms findings from other studies that the *ba* construction is difficult to acquire. Therefore, more attention should be paid to it in the classroom, and students should be given more opportunities to practice using it.

However, unlike students who take Chinese at other postsecondary institutions in the US, the students of Chinese at the DLI have to take two language aptitude tests before being admitted to the program. This means that all of the participants had been carefully selected for their program at the DLI. This fact could potentially limit the power to generalize the results of this study.

For further research, because the students at the DLI were highly selected, whether the same patterns can be found in other student populations needs to be determined. Better defined groups of learners should be studied for possible developmental trends. Even though the students at the DLI went through a rigorous selection process and studied in an intensive environment, their production of the *ba* construction was still very low. Therefore, higher-level learners, for example, learners who have studied Chinese for several years and have lived in a Chinese-speaking region, should be studied to probe the possible ceiling.

References

Anderson, J. R. (1989). Practice, working memory, and the ACT theory of skills acquisition: A comment on Carlson, Sullivan, and Schieder. *Journal of Learning, Memory, and Cognition, 15*, 527–530.

Bender, E. (2000). The syntax of Mandarin BA: Reconsidering the verbal analysis. *Journal of East Asian Linguistics, 9*, 105–145.

Chen, G. T. (1983). The *ba* construction: A topic and comment approach. *Journal of the Chinese Language Teachers Association, 18*, 17–29.

Cheung, H. (1992). *The acquisition of ba in Mandarin.* Unpublished doctoral dissertation, University of Kansas, Lawrence.

Doughty, C., & Williams, J. (1998). Pedagogical choices in focus on form. In C. Doughty & J. Williams (Eds.), *Focus on form in classroom second language acquisition* (pp. 97–261). Cambridge, England: Cambridge University Press.

Erbaugh, M. (1982). *Coming to order: Natural selection and the origin of syntax in the Mandarin speaking child.* Unpublished doctoral dissertation, University of California, Berkeley.

Fahn, R.-L. S. (1993). *The acquisition of Mandarin Chinese* ba *construction.* Unpublished doctoral dissertation, University of Hawai'i, Honolulu.

Feng, S. (2001). Prosodically constrained bare-verb in *ba* construction. *Journal of Chinese Linguistics, 29*, 243–280.

Gathercole, S. E., & Baddeley, A. D. (1994). *Working memory and language.* Hove, England: Lawrence Erlbaum.

Goodall, G. (1990). X'-internal word order in Mandarin Chinese and universal grammar. *Linguistics, 28*, 241–261.

Gropen, J., Pinker, S., Hollander, M., & Goldberg, R. (1991). Affectedness and direct objects: The role of lexical semantics in the acquisition of verb argument structure. *Cognition, 41*, 153–195.

Halliday, M. A. K. (1994). *An introduction to functional grammar* (2nd ed.). London: Edward Arnold.

Harley, B. (1998). The role of focus-on-form tasks in promoting child L2 acquisition. In C. Doughty & J. Williams (Eds.), *Focus on form in classroom second language acquisition* (pp. 156–174). Cambridge, England: Cambridge University Press.

Huang, C.-T. J. (1982). *Logical relations in Chinese and the theory of grammar.* Unpublished doctoral dissertation, Massachusetts Institute of Technology, Cambridge.

Huang, C.-T. J. (1989). Pro-drop in Chinese: A generalized control theory. In O. Jaeggli & K. J. Safir (Eds.), *The null subject parameter* (pp. 185–214). Dordrecht, the Netherlands: Kluwer.

Huang, C.-T. J. (1992). Complex predicates in control. In R. K. Larson, S. Iatridou, U. Lahiri, & J. Higginbotham (Eds.), *Control and grammar* (pp. 109–147). Dordrecht, the Netherlands: Kluwer Academic Press.

Jin, H. G. (1992). Pragmatization and the L2 acquisition of Chinese BA constructions. *Journal of the Chinese Language Teachers Association, 28*(3), 33–52.

Li, A. Y.-H. (1985). *Abstract case in Chinese.* Unpublished doctoral dissertation, University of Southern California, Los Angeles.

Li, C. N., & Thompson, S. A. (1981). *Mandarin Chinese: A functional reference grammar.* Berkley and Los Angeles: University of California Press.

Li, P. (1993). The acquisition of the *zai* and *ba* constructions in Mandarin Chinese. In J. C. P. Liang & R. P. E. Sybesma (Eds.), *From classical 'Fú' to 'Three inches high': Studies on Chinese in honor of Erik Zürcher* (pp. 103–120). Leuven/Apeldoorn, the Netherlands: Garant Publishers.

Lightbown, P., & Spada, N. (1990). Focus on form and corrective feedback in communicative language teaching: Effects on second language learning. *Studies in Second Language Acquisition, 12*(4), 429–448.

Liu, F. H. (1997). An aspectual analysis of BA. *Journal of East Asian Linguistics, 6,* 51–99.

Long, M. (1996). The role of the linguistic environment in second language acquisition. In W. C. Ritchie & T. K. Bhatia (Eds.), *Handbook of second language acquisition* (pp. 413–468). San Diego, CA: Academic Press.

Nation, R., & McLaughlin, B. (1986). Experts and novices: An information-processing approach to the 'good language learner' problem. *Applied Psycholinguistics, 7,* 41–56.

Pinker, S. (1984). *Language learnability and language development.* Cambridge, MA: Harvard University Press.

Ross, C. (1991). Coverbs and category distinction in Mandarin Chinese. *Journal of Chinese Linguistics, 19,* 79–115.

Schmidt, R. (1990). The role of consciousness in second language learning. *Applied Linguistics, 11,* 17–46.

Sorace, A. (1996). The use of acceptability judgments in second language acquisition research. In W. C. Ritchie & T. K. Bhatia (Eds.), *Handbook of second language acquisition* (pp. 375–409). San Diego, CA: Academic Press.

Sun, C. (1995). Transitivity, the BA construction and its history. *Journal of Chinese Linguistics, 23,* 159–194.

Sybesma, R. (1999). *The Mandarin VP.* Norwell, MA: Kluwer.

Thompson, S. A. (1973). Transitivity and some problems with the *ba* construction in Mandarin Chinese. *Journal of Chinese Linguistics, 1,* 208–227.

Travis, L. (1984). *Parameters and effects of word order variation.* Unpublished doctoral dissertation, Massachusetts Institute of Technology, Cambridge.

Tsao, F. (1987). A topic-comment approach to the *ba*-construction. *Journal of Chinese Linguistics, 15,* 1–54.

Wang, L. (1947). *Zhongguo xiandai yufa [A modern grammar of Chinese].* Shanghai, China: Zhonghua Shuju.

Yang, G. (2004). The systemic theory of process types applied to the Bǎ construction in Chinese. *Journal of the Chinese Language Teachers Association, 39*(2), 49–84.

Yong, S. (1993). *The aspectual phenomena of the BA construction.* Unpublished doctoral dissertation, University of Wisconsin, Madison.

Zou, K. (1993). The syntax of the Chinese BA construction. *Linguistics, 31,* 715–736.

Appendix A: Production

(In the order that the action pairs appeared in the experiment.)

1. *chi* (1): to eat (model)
    he (1): to drink
    fan (4): meal
    shui (3): water
2. *zhan* (4): to stand (practice 1)
    kai (1): to open
    men (2): door
3. *da (3) kai (1)*: to open (practice 2)
    dao (4): to pour
    shui (3) ping (2): water bottle
    shui (3): water
4. *xi* (3): to wash (pretest)
    zuo (4): to sit
    shou (3): hand
5. *xian* (1) *kai* (1): to uncover (RVC)
    na (2): to take
    hua (4): picture
6. *kan* (4): to watch (le)
    guan (1): to turn off
    dian (4) *shi* (4): TV
7. *zou (3) jin (4)*: to enter (filler)
    zuo (4): to sit
    fang (2) jian (1): room
8. *du* (2): to read (le)
    si (1): to tear
    xin (4): letter
9. *xi* (3): to wash (RVC)
    ca (1): to wipe
    shou (3): hand
10. *jiao* (1): to water (filler)
    kai (1): to open
    hua (1): flower
    men (2): door
11. *dao* (4): to pour (le)
    chi (1): to eat/take (medicine)
    yao (4): pill
12. *he* (1): to drink (filler)
    chi (1): to eat
    shui (3): water
    fan (4): meal
13. *zhu* (3): to boil (RVC)
    na (2): to take
    mian (4) tiao (2): noodle
14. *kan* (4): to look (filler)
    kan (4) jian (4): to see
    zuo (3) you (4): left and right
    di (4) tu (2): map
15. *fa (1) xian (4)*: to discover (le)
    xi (3): to wash
    ping (2) guo (3): apple
16. *zhao (3) dao (4)*: to find (RVC)
    dian (3): to light
    la (4) zhu (2): candle
17. *zhan* (4): to stand (filler)
    zou (3): to walk
    men (2) kou (3): door
18. *fan (1) kai (1)*: to open (le)
    reng (1): to throw
    shu (1): book
19. *na* (2): to take (RVC)
    dai (4): to wear
    yan (3) jing (4): glasses

Appendix B: Grammaticality judgments

(喝: to drink) (水: water)

1.
   tā hē shuǐ
   a. 她喝水
   tā shuǐ le hē
   b. 她水了喝
   tā zhèngzài hē shuǐ
   c. 她正在喝水
   tā hē le shuǐ
   d. 她喝了水
   shuǐ hē tā
   e. 水喝她
   shuǐ le   tā hē
   f. 水了她喝

(开: to open) (门: door)

2.
   mén kāi le tā
   a. 门开了她
   mén kāi tā
   b. 门开她
   tā kāi le mén
   c. 她开了门
   tā le mén kāi
   d. 她了门开
   tā mén kāi
   e. 她门开
   tā kāi mén
   f. 她开门

(擦: to wipe) (手: hand)

3.
   tā cā shǒu
   a. 她擦手
   tā bǎ shǒu cā gānjing
   b. 她把手擦干净
   tā shǒu cā gānjing
   c. 她手擦干净
   tā shǒu cā
   d. 她手擦
   tā cā gānjing shǒu
   e. 她擦干净手
   tā bǎ shǒu cā
   f. 她把手擦

(扔: to throw) (书: book)

4.
   tā shū rēng le
   a. 她书扔了
   tā rēng le shū
   b. 她扔了书
   tā bǎ shū rēng
   c. 她把书扔
   tā rēng shū
   d. 她扔书
   tā bǎ shū rēng le
   e. 她把书扔了
   tā shū rēng
   f. 她书扔

(点: to light) (蜡烛: candle)

5.
   tā làzhú diǎn
   a. 她蜡烛点
   tā diǎn qǐlai làzhú
   b. 她点起来蜡烛
   tā bǎ làzhú diǎn
   c. 她把蜡烛点
   tā diǎn làzhú
   d. 她点蜡烛
   tā làzhú diǎn qǐlai
   e. 她蜡烛点起来
   tā bǎ làzhú diǎn qǐlai

f. 她把蜡烛点起来

(关: to turn off) (电视: TV)

6.
tā bǎ diànshì guān.

a. 她把电视关

   guān le tā diànshì

b. 关了她电视

   tā diànshì guān le

c. 她电视关了

   tā bǎ diànshì guān le

d. 她把电视关了

   tā guān diànshì

e. 她关电视

   tā diànshì guān

f. 她电视关

(拿: to take) (画: picture)

7.
tā huà ná

a. 她画拿

   tā bǎ huà ná

b. 她把画拿

   tā ná huà

c. 她拿画

   tā huà ná xiàlai

d. 她画拿下来

   tā xiàlai ná huà

e. 她下来拿画

   tā bǎ huà ná xiàlai

f. 她把画拿下来

(撕: to tear) (信: letter)

8.
tā bǎ xìn sī le

a. 她把信撕了

   tā xìn sī

b. 她信撕

   tā sī xìn

c. 她撕信

   tā sī le xìn

d. 她撕了信

   tā bǎ xìn sī

e. 她把信撕

   tā xìn sī le

f. 她信撕了

(戴: to wear) (眼镜: glasses)

9.
tā yǎnjìng dài shang

a. 她眼镜戴上

   tā bǎ yǎnjìng dài

b. 她把眼镜戴

   tā dài yǎnjìng

c. 她戴眼镜

   tā yǎnjìng dài

d. 她眼镜戴

   tā dài shang yǎnjìng

e. 她戴上眼镜

   tā bǎ yǎnjìng dài shang

f. .她把眼镜戴上

(吃: to eat) (药: pill)

10.
tā chī yào

a. 她吃药

   tā yào chī le

b. 她药吃了

   tā chī le yào

c. 她吃了药

   tā yào chī

d. 她药吃

   tā bǎ yào chī le

e. 她把药吃了

   tā bǎ yào chī

f. 她把药吃

Language Attrition in Grammar and Receptive Skills in Mandarin Chinese

Miao-fen Tseng
University of Virginia

Possible decreased proficiency in grammar, listening, and reading after a summer break was investigated in light of literature on language-attrition hypotheses in the psychological, neurolinguistic, and sociopsychological domains. Language data were collected in two phases in which participants completed a 1st-year Chinese language course and began a 2nd-year course while completing self-assessments to indicate their confidence levels. A t-test showed that significant language loss occurred in grammar, but not in listening and reading. The finding that language loss in reading skills was not statistically significant was consistent with J. J. Hayden's (2003) findings, while the participants' self-assessments revealed more of a perceived loss in productive over receptive skills. Overall, the participants tended to overestimate loss in all language skills except for grammar. Pedagogical implications and directions for further research are addressed.

本研究根据语言流失研究之心理学、神经语言学、以及社会心理语言学领域之理论假设，探讨已完成大学初级中文课程而开始学习中级课程之学习者在暑期三个月之后，其语法、听力、及阅读能力可能产生的语言流失现象与学习者自我信心评估之关系。有关语言流失现象的研究，无论是第一外语或第二外语的研究，多半集中在其它外语方面的研究，中文方面的参考文献极少。本文以Hayden于2003年发表的研究报告为基础，扩大其语言技能研究范围，包括语法，阅读以及听力能力三方面前测与后测的研究，并加入学习者对各项语言技能之自我信心程度评估。主要研究目的乃在探讨学习者三方面语言技能前测与后测的结果，观察暑期结束三个月后，语言水平是否有下降的倾向，也就是是否有语言流失的现象，并比较分析暑期结束后语言实测水平与学习者之自我评估，观察学习者信心程度与实际语言水平之间的关系，是否对语言流失情况做正确的自我评估。语料的收集分为两个阶段，第一个阶段是大学两个学期初级中文即将修毕之际，第二个阶段是中级中文第一学期开始修习之际，语料的分析，辅以学习者自我评估之语言信心程度，做对应性的讨论。T测试的统计分析显示，语法部份的前测与后测结果具显着差异,而听力和阅读部份的前测与后测结果不具显着差异,阅读能力未呈现显着差异的发现肯定Hayden于2003年的研究结果。学习者自我信心评估的分析显示,说写能力的信心流失比听读能力的信心流失多,除了语法以外,大部份学习者对各项语言技能的语言流失程度有高估的倾向。换言之,由于暑期三个月学习中文间断,学习者在暑期过后对于暑期之前习得之语言技能普遍存在缺乏信心之现象。这项研究结果与Hansen-Strain (1993), Weltens (1989) , de Bot和Weltens (1995) 的推论一致, 认为学习者由于短期或长期语言学习中断等心理因素而有高估语言流失的倾向, 对自我各项语言技能水平普遍缺乏信心。此缺乏信心之现象可能与学习者心理层面等因素有关, 并不完全与语言实际测试结果相符。根据讯息恢复假设 (the retrieval failure hypothesis), 讯息存留假设 (the saving hypothesis) , 以及再学习理论架设 (the relearning hypothesis) , 暑期中断学习可能造成的语言流失应该是短暂现象, 经常使用或练习, 即能恢复原来习得的技能, 这对教学实践有相当程度的啓發作用。教师应该正面鼓励学生, 培养他们 "我能" 的积极学习动机和态度。文章最后, 作者提出未來語言流失與信心程度研究方向与重点, 殷切期待口语语料分析尽快完成, 与学习者对口语能力方面的自我评估相互比较, 辅助并充实本文研究结果。

Language attrition in grammar and receptive skills in Mandarin Chinese

The importance of research on language attrition was not formally acknowledged until the University of Pennsylvania organized a conference on the topic in 1980 (Lambert & Freed, 1982). Language attrition, which is the loss of one's first or second language or a foreign language, manifests itself at individual and societal levels in the sociolinguistic, psychological, neurological, and linguistic domains (Jiménez, 2003). In the acquisition of a second or foreign language, language attrition refers to "the loss of proficiency" due to "lack of use over time" (Gardner, Lalonde, & MacPherson, 1985, p. 519). Using this definition, this study investigated the phenomenon of reduced proficiency in Mandarin Chinese over a summer break during which Chinese as a foreign language (CFL) learners did not use the language.

Literature review

The psychological domain has six hypotheses concerning language attrition in a second or foreign language. Three hypotheses—retrieval failure, saving, and relearning—all support the notion that acquired knowledge is never lost but only temporarily inaccessible due to infrequent use (Cohen, 1989; Hansen, 1980; MacLeod, 1988; Nelson, 1978, 1985; Yukawa, 1997). According to the saving hypothesis, different levels of memory require different levels of reactivation; that is to say, production needs a high level of activation, whereas a lower level of reactivation is sufficient for recognition. The regression hypothesis suggests that the path of language attrition is actually disproportionate to acquisition on a "first learned, last forgotten" basis (Jakobson, 1941). Several studies have tested this hypothesis and shown that the reverse order holds true (Berman & Olshtain, 1983; Cohen, 1975; Hansen, 1980, 1999; Hayashi, 1999). Some evidence supporting this hypothesis also demonstrates that receptive skills precede productive skills in acquisition and that the reverse seems to be true in attrition (Bahrick, 1984; Weltens, 1989). The inverse hypothesis posits that the higher the degree of attainment, the lower the degree of attrition (Vechter, Lapkin, & Argue, 1990). Counterevidence, however, reports that the amount of forgotten information is relatively constant for second-language (L2) learners at different levels of proficiency (Bahrick). Neisser's (1984) threshold hypothesis supports the inverse of Bahrick's hypothesis and proposes that in Bahrick's study, the overall proficiency of the participants must have passed a "critical threshold point."

The impact of hypotheses outside of the psychological domain cannot be overlooked. The neurolinguistic approach argues that language change is a consequence of neural plasticity (Yoshitomi, 1999). At the sociopsychological level, motivation and attitude have been identified as having very important indirect influences on language maintenance (Gardner, Lalonde, Moorcroft, & Evers, 1987). With regard to a learner's confidence level, researchers have also found that learners tend to assume that they have lost more than they actually have. That is, a learner's self-assessment of language loss usually exceeds test-measured results. One interpretation of this phenomenon is that decreased language use results in a marked lack of confidence in learner language ability as reflected in their self-assessments. In a study by Hansen-Strain (1993), high school students of Japanese presumed a significant loss of their language proficiency, whereas no significant language loss was found in terms of their use of morphology before and after a summer break. Weltens' (1989) study demonstrated a similar finding whereby adult learners of French believed that their proficiency decreased tremendously, while the results of the test data indicated otherwise. Such a discrepancy between test results and self-assessment, according to de Bot & Weltens (1995), may be due to learners' awareness of their slowed retrieval pace that can lead them to believe that their language proficiency has been reduced.

Current study[1]

Research in language attrition has mainly focused on languages other than Mandarin Chinese, and investigations of attrition among learners of Mandarin Chinese as a foreign language is crucial due to the uniqueness of Mandarin's phonetics, linguistic features, and writing system. Hayden (2003) investigated whether CFL learners who had completed 1st- and 2nd-year Chinese courses had reduced reading skills after a summer break. Despite no significant differences, he noted some attrition.

Extending Hayden's (2003) pioneering study, this project aims to enrich existing findings in Mandarin Chinese by examining attrition in grammar and receptive skills[2] as it pertains to learners' self-assessments of their confidence levels after a summer break. The results of the study will shed valuable light on the current literature in language attrition. The pedagogical implications derived from the results will be helpful for CFL educators in understanding the phenomenon of language attrition in Mandarin Chinese.

This study examined learners' experiences during the "incubation period" identified by Gardner (1982), which coincides with the "retention interval" identified by Bahrick (1984). Prior to this period is the *activation period*, where 1st-year language learning takes place, and following it is another activation period in which 2nd-year language learning occurs together with the relearning, that is, review, of 1st-year Chinese.

The language skills investigated in this study are grammar and receptive skills, that is, listening and reading. The self-assessment was of the same language areas. The research questions are as follows:

1. Do grammar, listening, and reading skills suffer any attrition after a 3-month summer break?

---

[1] This chapter was made possible by the Jiede Research Grant awarded by the Jiede Empirical Research Committee in 2005.

[2] The scope of the project includes the analysis of both receptive and productive skills. The results of the analysis of receptive skills are reported in this chapter; the discussion of the productive skill of speaking will be documented separately.

2. Do students' self-assessments of their language skills coincide with the results of tests on grammar, listening, and reading?

Method

The participants were nonheritage learners who took 1st-year Chinese in the fall of 2004 and the spring of 2005 and took 2nd-year Chinese in the fall of 2005 after a summer break. The instructional hours for 1st- and 2nd-year Chinese were the same: 50 minutes per class per day, five classes per week, 15 weeks per semester, and two semesters per academic year, for a total of 125 instructional hours per year. Toward the end of the spring semester of 2004, 31 1st-year Chinese learners volunteered to participate in the first phase of the study. The instructional materials were *Integrated Chinese* (1997) and supplementary and authentic materials. Approximately 750 characters were introduced.

Upon finishing the 1st-year course, the participants were expected to complete the Chinese Proficiency Test[3] (CPT) and an Oral Proficiency Interview (OPI). The CPT included sections in grammar, listening, and reading. The OPI followed the guidelines created by the American Council on the Teaching of Foreign Languages. After a 3-month break, the same tests were given to the same students who were taking 2nd-year Chinese during the first 2 weeks of the fall semester of 2005[4] A questionnaire was added to the tests that asked the learners to self-assess their confidence levels in different language skills. Of the 31 participants, 5 learned Chinese in a formal or informal setting over the summer break and were therefore excluded from the study. Another 9 participants did not continue to participate in the study due to their unavailability or withdrawal from the course. Consequently, only 17 students participated in the second phase of the study. Of them, 10 were male, and 7 were female. Their ages ranged from 18 to 24, with a mean age of 19.12 years.

The CPT, a multiple-choice test, was scored by the Center for Applied Linguistics. To control for an order effect, the sections in the CPT were administered in a different order for each participant. The participants were required to not discuss the pretest, which they completed before the summer. They were not informed that they would be asked to take a posttest until the beginning of the fall semester of 2005. A t-test was performed to examine if significant differences existed between the two groups of scores, that is, the scores collected prior to and after the summer break for skills in grammar, listening, and reading.

Results and discussion

This section begins with the analysis of the test scores of the pretest and the posttest of the CPT. It then documents the results of the questionnaire on the participants' confidence levels in different language skills.

---

[3] The CPT was used to replace the Computer Adaptive Test for Reading Chinese (CATRC) because the participants in this study did not have access to CATRC, which is a Macintosh-only HyperCard application. The CATRC can be accessible through http://EALL.hawaii.edu/yao/catrc. Because the CPT used in this study includes a listening section, the Chinese Computerized Adaptive Listening Comprehension Test (CCALT) was not used in this study. The CCALT can be accessed through http://www.ccalt.com/index.php.

[4] Like 1st-year Chinese, the major instructional materials used in 2nd-year Chinese were Integrated Chinese (Liu, Yao, Shi, & Bi, 1997) and supplementary and authentic materials.

Pretest and posttest of the CPT

Table 1: Results of the t-test in grammar, listening, and reading and total scores

category	grammar	listening	reading	total
mean of pretest	20.24	37.29	41.24	98.76
mean of posttest	18.76	37.06	40.65	96.47
SD of pretest	2.36	3.70	3.85	8.78
SD of posttest	2.62	3.98	5.92	11.70
p	.008	.6684	.434	.0926

note: p<.05

The results of the t-test of the completed CPT that was administered in the pretest and posttest stages is shown in Table 1. The maximum score on the CPT is 125 points: 25 for grammar, 50 for listening, and 50 for reading. As shown in the table, as compared to the means of the pretest scores, the means of the posttest scores in grammar, listening, and reading all decreased slightly, as did the mean of the total score. Obviously, the participants' language proficiency decreased to some extent after the summer break. The standard deviation of the posttest increased in grammar, listening, reading, and total scores. This indicates more variability in scores on the posttest. Despite the slight decrease of the mean of the posttest in grammar, listening, reading, and total scores, the p value reveals a significant difference in grammar scores only, not in listening, reading, or total scores. Statistically, the participants' language proficiency in grammar significantly decreased, but their overall language proficiency did not significantly decrease, nor did their language proficiency in the discrete language skills of listening and reading. The finding that language ability in reading did not significantly decrease coincides with the findings of Hayden's (2003) study, in which Yao's (1993) Computer Adaptive Test for Reading Chinese was used as a measure.

Results of the questionnaire on participants' confidence levels

The questionnaire was intended to elicit information about participants' self-assessment of loss in different language skills after a summer break. The items were divided into two categories: direct and indirect statements of confidence loss in different language skills. An example of a direct statement of confidence loss is, "I feel that I have lost confidence in my overall grammaticality judgment ability after a summer break." Indirect statements on confidence loss always had key phrases such as "I feel that I have forgotten…," "I feel that I cannot…," "I feel that my ability decreases…," and "I feel that I am unable to …." All of the items had a 5-point scale, with 1 labeled "least agree," and 5 labeled "strongly agree." For the convenience of discussion, the average value of each item will be called the agreement index. The maximum agreement index is 5, and the minimum agreement index is 1. All of the items on the questionnaire were regrouped and are summarized in the following three tables. The results of the direct statements are summarized in Table 2, and the results of the indirect statements are summarized in Tables 3 and 4.

Table 2. Agreement indexes of confidence loss in language skills

category	grammar	listening	speaking	reading	writing
agreement index	3.24	3.82	4.0	2.71	3.94

The agreement indexes all exceed 3 in items pertaining to self-assessment of confidence loss except for that of reading skills, as indicated in Table 2. The agreement indexes are, from the highest to the lowest, speaking, writing, listening, grammar, and reading. The productive skills of speaking and writing have agreement indexes equal or close to 4. The receptive skills of listening and reading have noticeably divergent agreement indexes. The agreement index of confidence loss in listening skills is close to 4, while that of reading skills is the lowest in the table. The second-lowest agreement index is that of grammar.

Table 3. Agreement indexes of decreased ability in language skills

category	grammar	listening	speaking	reading	writing
agreement index	3.71	3.53	3.94	2.94	3.89

Participants' agreement indexes of decreased ability in language skills in indirect statements are shown in Table 3. Consistent with what is shown in Table 2, the agreement indexes all exceed 3 in items related to self-assessment of decreased ability in both productive and receptive skills except for that of reading skills. Slightly different from what is shown in Table 2, the agreement indexes from the highest to the lowest in Table 3 are speaking, writing, grammar, listening, and reading. Despite the order being different, the agreement indexes of the productive skills remain higher than those of the receptive skills, and the lowest agreement index is that of reading skills. Reading skills has the lowest agreement index, which is a possible indicator of language loss as perceived by the participants.

Taking Tables 2 and 3 together yields that, generally speaking, the students agreed that they had lost more confidence in speaking and writing than in listening, grammar, and reading over the summer break. They perceived that the productive skills, speaking and writing, suffered more attrition, while the receptive skills suffered less. Reading is the area that suffered the least attrition according to the participants' self-assessments. A very interesting result that deserves further attention is that in the participants' self-assessments of confidence loss, the agreement index of listening was higher than that of grammar, whereas in their self-assessment of decreased ability, the agreement index of grammar was closer to that of listening. This indicates that overall, the participants perceived that they had lost more confidence in listening than in grammar.

Table 4. Agreement indexes of decreased ability in discrete items associated with speaking

categories	vocabulary	phrases	structures	pronunciation
agreement index	4.35	4	3.65	3.47

To further understand the factors that might have impacted the participants' perceived speaking abilities, the questionnaire also elicited the participants' assessments of their use of vocabulary, phrases, structures, and pronunciation in speaking. For example, a question that asked about vocabulary was, "I feel that I have forgotten some vocabulary and cannot use them in speaking as well as I did in Chinese 102." The questions about phrases, structures, and pronunciation in speaking were delivered in a similar way on the questionnaire.

The agreement indexes of decreased ability in discrete items associated with speaking skills are shown in Table 4. The agreement indexes, from the highest to the lowest, are those of vocabulary, phrases, structures, and pronunciation. According to the participants' self-assessments, pronunciation seems to have the least impact on their decreased abilities in speaking and may suffer the least attrition. Vocabulary and phrases may be more closely associated with the decreased ability in speaking than the use of structures.

This can be justified by observing what L2 learners tend to focus on while speaking. During oral communication, L2 learners tend to focus on meaning rather than form. To convey intended meaning, they rely more heavily on vocabulary and expressions than on structures or grammar. When a speaker is unable to recall vocabulary and expressions to express what he or she intends to say, he or she easily senses failure or communication breakdown. Unlike vocabulary and expressions, the appropriate use of structures may not be of such great concern to learners for oral communication.

A closer look at the relationship between test scores and self-assessed confidence levels

As far as productive skills are concerned, the participants' assessments of their confidence loss and decreased abilities in speaking and writing all have higher agreement indexes than those of grammar and the receptive skills of listening and reading.

Determining whether the test scores coincide with participants' perceptions requires further analysis of recorded speech and written data. Bahrick's (1984) and Weltens' (1989) findings support one of the notions in the regression hypothesis: that productive skills precede receptive skills in language loss. That is, a reduced ability in productive skills may be noticed earlier than a reduced ability in receptive skills, and productive skills may suffer more loss than receptive skills. Whether this hypothesis holds true for the acquisition of Mandarin Chinese as a foreign language is beyond the scope of this chapter and requires further analysis of OPI data.

This chapter reported on three language areas: grammar and the two receptive skills of listening and reading. The participants seemed to overestimate their attrition in the two receptive skills of listening and reading, and the only language area in which the posttest scores agreed with the self-assessment was that of grammar. That is, the participants' did not appropriately assess their language abilities in listening and reading, but their self-assessments coincided with their significantly lower performances in grammar after the summer break.

The agreement indices of the participants' self-assessments of the three language areas showed that the participants tended to overestimate their losses. This phenomenon was demonstrated by the elicited-agreement indexes, which all exceeded 3 except for reading. Even though the indexes of the self-assessed language losses and decreased abilities in reading were less than 3, the values that were close to 3 but toward the extreme of "strongly agree" still indicated the participants' perceptions of losses in reading ability. This agrees with the results of several psychological studies (i.e., Hansen-Strain, 1993; Weltens, 1989; de Bot & Weltens, 1995) that learners have a tendency to underestimate their maintenance of language proficiency. This indicates their lack of confidence in what they can do after a certain period of not using the target language.

Pedagogical implications

The analysis of listening and reading abilities based on the pretest and posttest scores indicates no significant language loss. This is consistent with the findings reported in Hayden's (2003) study of reading development in Mandarin Chinese, Hansen-Strain's (1993) study of the use of Japanese morphology, and Weltens' (1989) study of language proficiency in French. According to the retrieval-failure, saving, and relearning hypotheses, language loss is a temporary phenomenon, and learned language skills are accessible through frequent use. Moderate language loss can be reversed through reactivating memory. Effective review and instruction help learners to reactivate memory. This helps more for information that is temporarily lost after a short interval than that lost after a long interval. The interval of a summer break is considered relatively short, and reviewing would therefore be effective for retrieving information lost over that period of time.

Keeping this argument in mind, although the participants' language abilities in listening and reading may have decreased to a certain degree, such a decrease is moderate and should not be treated as a threat or a barrier to studying in a more advanced course after the summer. In fact, the prevalent assumption that language proficiency decreases after a summer may be associated more with psychological mentality than with linguistic factors. Psychologically, students may falsely believe that after a summer break, they have lost much of what they learned before the summer. The results of this study provide evidence that this assumption is false. What is lost is much less than was imagined and assumed. Even though grammar skills are noticeably lost, what is lost linguistically can be easily remedied through effective instruction.

In light of the study of motivation and attitude conducted by Gardner, Lalonde, Moorcroft, and Evers (1987), this study echoes a need to emphasize and reinforce a "can-do" attitude, as addressed in Hayden's (2003) study.

Teachers should therefore make students aware that even though language loss might occur in reading and listening after a summer, the loss is not statistically significant and might be much smaller than they assume. This loss, then, should not and will not affect their overall language proficiency and continued growth in a more advanced language course. In this regard, teachers are reminded to use a normal pace in developing students' reading and listening skills. Significant curricular adjustment by slowing the pace to add additional review sessions for these two language areas does not seem to be urgently needed when a 2nd-year Chinese language course begins. However, helping students build confidence in their reading and listening abilities at the beginning of 2nd-year language instruction seems to be important to consider.

Unlike reading and listening skills, statistically significant loss does occur in grammar. Strategically, teachers are highly encouraged to include grammar review sessions at the beginning of 2nd-year Chinese language courses or during the courses. Grammatical structures taught in the 1st-year language course can be either independently taught in a meaningful, authentic, communicative context at the beginning of the 2nd-year course or be spirally recycled and integrated into new lessons. This prepares students for a smooth transition from a solid grasp of grammatical structures at the elementary level to a more challenging phase of grammar learning at the intermediate level. While teaching grammar, teachers should always keep in mind that grammar instruction should be kept at a minimum in accordance with the principles of the communicative approach, and when grammar is taught, it should always be taught in a communicative context. Teaching grammar without context has been proven to be the least effective method of teaching grammar and is therefore not highly recommended.

Conclusion

Noticeable attrition in language skills was found in grammar only, not in listening and reading. The loss in grammar that occurred after a summer break is assumed to be temporary and can be remedied with effective mediated instruction during the first several weeks of class at the intermediate level. However, it is uncertain whether language loss in grammar can be attributed to a lack of effectiveness in grammar instruction at the 1st-year level. This paper does not document how grammar was taught in the 1st-year Chinese language course and therefore lacks the legitimacy to claim that ineffectiveness grammar instruction played a role in determining the significantly lower posttest scores. The only statistically significant finding dealing with grammar can serve as an indicator for further research to investigate the universality and applicability of the indicator to Mandarin Chinese and other foreign languages. Further studies should consider the way grammar is taught to further validate the results found in this study. It would also be useful to enlarge the subject pool at the learner levels used and extend the research to the 3rd- and 4th-year levels for longitudinal or cross-sectional studies with the same length of summer break. Different research designs are also needed to test the hypotheses mentioned in the literature review. Further analysis will enhance our understanding of whether learners' self-assessments of the productive skill of speaking appropriately reflects their sustained language proficiency after a summer break.

References

Bahrick, H. P. (1984). Fifty years of second language attrition: Implications for programmatic research. *Modern Language Journal, 68*, 105–111.

Berman, R. A., & Olshtain, E. (1983). Features of first language transfer in second language attrition. *Applied Linguistics, 4*(3), 222–234.

Cohen, A. D. (1975). Forgetting a foreign language. *Language Learning, 25*, 127–138.

Cohen, A. D. (1989). Attrition in the productive lexicon of two Portuguese third language speakers. *Studies in Second Language Acquisition, 11*, 135–149.

de Bot, K., & Weltens, B. (1995). Foreign language attrition. *Annual Review of Applied Linguistics, 15*, 151–164.

Gardner, R. C. (1982). Social factors in language retention. In R. D. Lambert & B. Freed (Eds.), *The loss of language skills* (pp. 24–39). Rowley, MA: Newbury House.

Gardner, R. C., Lalonde, R. N., & MacPherson, J. (1985). Social factors in second language attrition. *Language Learning, 35*, 519–540.

Gardner, R. C., Lalonde, R. N., Moorcroft, R., & Evers, F. T. (1987). Second language attrition: The role of motivation and use. *Journal of Language and Social Psychology, 6*, 29–47.

Hansen, L. (1980). *Learning and forgetting a second language: The acquisition, loss and reacquisition of Hindi-Urdu negative structures by English-speaking children*. Unpublished doctoral dissertation, University of California, Berkeley.

Hansen, L. (1999). Not a total loss: The attrition of Japanese negation over these decades. In L. Hansen (Ed.), *Second language attrition in Japanese contexts* (pp. 142–153). New York: Oxford University Press.

Hansen-Strain, L. (1993). The attrition of Japanese negation by English-speaking adults [Abstract]. AILA 10th World Congress of Applied Linguistics, Amsterdam, *Conference Abstracts*, p. 114.

Hayashi, B. (1999). Testing the regression hypothesis: The remains of the Japanese negation system in Micronesia. In L. Hansen (Ed.), *Second language attrition in Japanese contexts* (pp. 154–168). Oxford, England: Oxford University Press.

Hayden, J. J. (2003). Shocking our students to the next level: Language loss and some implications for teaching Chinese as a foreign language. *Journal of the Chinese Language Teachers Association, 38*(3), 1–20.

Jakobson, R. (1941). *Kindersparache, Aphasie und allgemeine Lautgesetze* [Child language, aphasia, and phonological universals]. The Hague, the Netherlands: Mouton Publishers.

Jiménez, A. (2003). *Linguistic and psychological dimensions of second language attrition during and after a study abroad experience*. Unpublished doctoral dissertation, University of Michigan, Ann Arbor.

Lambert, R. D., & Freed, B. F. (Eds.). (1982). *The loss of language skills*. Rowley, MA: Newbury House.

Liu, Y., Yao, T., Shi, Y., & Bi, N. (1997). *Integrated Chinese*. Boston: Cheng & Tsui Company.

MacLeod, C. M. (1988). Forgetting but not gone: Savings for pictures and words in long-term memory. *Journal of Experimental Psychology: Human Learning and Memory, 42*(2), 195–212.

Nelson, T. O. (1978). Detecting small amounts of information in memory: Savings for nonrecognized items. *Journal of Experimental Psychology: Human Learning and Memory, 4*(5), 453–468.

Nelson, T. O. (1985). Ebbinghaus's contribution to the measurement of retention: Savings during relearning. *Journal of Experimental Psychology: Human Learning and Memory, 11*(3), 472–479.

Neisser, U. (1984). Interpreting Harry Bahrick's discovery: What confers immunity against forgetting? *Journal of Experimental Psychology: General, 113*, 32–35.

Vechter, A., Lapkin, S., & Argue, V. (1990). Second language retention: A summary of the issues. *The Canadian Modern Language Review, 46*(2), 189–203.

Weltens, B. (1989). *The attrition of French as a foreign language*. Dordrecht, the Netherlands: Fori.

Yoshitomi, A. (1999). On the loss of ELS of Japanese returnee children. In L. Hansen (Ed.), *Second language attrition in Japanese contexts* (pp. 80–112). Oxford, England: Oxford University Press.

Yukawa, E. (1997). L1 Japanese attrition of a 5 year-old bilingual child. *Japan Journal of Multilingualism and Multiculturalism, 3*(1), 1–22.

Analysis of Radical Knowledge Development Among Beginning CFL Learners

Helen H. Shen
University of Iowa

Quantitative and qualitative approaches were used to investigate beginning college students' learning behaviors in mastering Chinese semantic radicals. The investigation focused on four areas: determining the difficulty level of mastering the three linguistic components of a radical (sound, shape, and meaning), examining the types of difficulties that the learners were facing in learning radicals, finding the types of learning and teaching methods that learners considered most effective, and generalizing the learners' views on the importance of radical knowledge for character learning in general. The results show that the beginning learners considered the sounds and shapes of radicals to be much more difficult to learn than their meanings. This observation was consistent with their performance on radical tests. Among various instructional methods, the students consider these five to be effective: a combination of aural, oral, and visual repetition and review; explaining the etymology of the radical along with its origin and its historical development; relating radicals to character learning; taking quizzes and tests on radical knowledge; and using games and activities in learning radicals. The results indicated that 93% of the participants considered radical knowledge helpful to learn Chinese characters in a number of ways. Pedagogical implications are briefly discussed.

认知心理对中文阅读加工过程的研究表明，在阅读过程中存在着多层次的认知加工，即包括部首、汉字、词三种水平的加工。而对部首的加工出现在汉字心理表征激活之前 (Taft & Zhu, 1997)。因此部首 (而不是笔画) 被认为是汉字词认知的基本单元 (Chen, Allport, & Marshalls, 1996)。进一步的研究表明，读者对部首的熟悉度影响着对合体字识别的速度 (Huang, 1984)。这些研究不仅充分表明了部首知识在汉语学习中的重要性，也对汉语作为二语教学带来了挑战。汉语工作者迫切需要找到如下问题的答案: 从认知角度来说，学生是如何学习部首的? 部首教学的最有效的途径和方法是什么? 本研究将从定量和定性两个方面对汉语作为二语的初级学习者的部首学习行为和看法进行调查分析。具体地说，通过观察和分析初级学习者在一年的时间里掌握100个高频率部首的过程来回答这样几个问题：1. 对初级学生来说，部首的音、形、义三者，哪个因素最难掌握？2. 学生在掌握部首的这三个因素中所面临的困难是什么？3. 学生认为什么样的教和学的方法对部首学习最为有效？4. 在何种程度上,学生认为部首有利于汉字学习？

本研究的参与者是美国中西部一所大学的65名非华裔的一年级中文学习者。该校的中文部要求学生在一年的时间里学会100个高频率部首。这里提到的100高频部首是根据[汉语大词典]中部首出现在所有合体字中的频率以及部首出现在三千常用汉字中的频率统计而成。学生每学期学习50个部首。50个部首分为5个教学单元，每单元学习10个部首。该研究所使用的测量工具是部首测验和部首学习调查表。部首测验分为四次，每学期期中和期末各测一次。每次测验只包括前次测验后新学的部首。测验要求学生写出每一部首的音 (拼音)、形、义。部首学习调查在一年级第二学期期末进行，要求学生回答四个部首学习方面的问题。第一个问题是要求学生在10分点的语义区分量表上分别对部首音、形、义三者的学习难度进行甄别。第二个问题要求学生选择音、形、义三者，哪一项最难学并回答为什么。第三个问题要求学生回答部首知识对汉字学习是否有帮助，无论回答是与否，都要解释为什么。即为什么部首知识对学习汉字有帮助或没有帮助。第四个问题要求学生识别何种教和学方法 (正在使用的) 对部首学习最有帮助并解释为什么。

本研究的主要发现是，一、初级学习者认为部首的音和形要比义的记忆难得多，这一看法与他们的考试结果一致。对部首测验结果的方差分析表明学生对义的记忆显著地比音和形要好。定性分析的结果表明，学生学习部首的发音的主要困难在于不能区别四声声调；无法找到音—形之间联系；无法将部首的发音与母语的发音相联系。关于部首字形的学习，学生认为最困难的是对不同笔画的区分尤其是对那些形似的部首的区分并记住它们。二、在定性分析的基础上，作者发现学生认为至少有五种部首教学的方法是有效的。赞同视、听、说三者结合的教学方法最为有效的人数为最多。三、93%的学生认为部首知识有助于汉字学习，主要体现在部首帮助对合体字的形、义和音的理解和记忆。作者对本研究的结果进行了理论分析并提出了教学法的建议。

Research into the cognitive processing of Chinese reading texts has revealed that Chinese words are processed at a submorphemic (radical) level during reading. That is, in reading Chinese characters, radicals are processed before character-level representations are activated (Taft & Zhu, 1997), and radicals, rather than strokes, are the functional orthographic units in Chinese word recognition (Chen, Allport, & Marshalls, 1996). In addition, the degree of familiarity a reader has with the radical within a compound character affects the speed of recognizing the compound character as a whole (Huang, 1984). These results suggest that radicals play an important role in learning Chinese characters, which further suggests that the study of Chinese radicals should be an integrated part of Chinese instruction. Classroom teachers are searching for the answers to fundamental questions such as the following: How do students learn individual radicals? What are the difficulties learners might encounter in learning radicals? What kinds of teaching or learning methods are effective for learning radicals? This study aims to search for answers to these questions by examining the behaviors of nonnative beginning Chinese learners for learning radicals.

What are Chinese radicals?

Chinese radicals are the smallest meaningful orthographic units in compound characters, also referred to as *submorphemes*. According to their orthographic functions, radicals can be classified as phonetic or semantic. A phonetic radical cues the pronunciation of a compound character, and a semantic radical signifies the meaning. All phonetic radicals in compound characters are themselves standalone characters, but when they function as phonetic radicals in compound characters, they lose their meanings as independent characters. Take the compound character 湖 (lake), for example. The right side of this character, 胡 (hú), serves as a phonetic radical for 湖 and indicates the pronunciation of 湖 (hú), but 胡 as an independent character has several meanings, such as *non-han nationalities, concoct,* or *moustache.* Due to the historical evolution of Chinese phonology, in modern Chinese, only about 26% of these phonetic radicals can be considered reliable cues to the pronunciation of compound characters without considering tonal differences (Fan, Gao, & Ao, 1984).

Semantic radicals, historically, are all integral characters. Take again the character 湖 as an example: The left part of the character, 氵 (water), is a semantic radical. However, 氵 by itself originally was an independent character that was written 沝 in oracle bone inscriptions. About 200 semantic radicals are used in the 7,000 characters listed in 现代汉语通用字表 (Statistics on Commonly Used Chinese Characters, 1998). These semantic radicals usually suggest a general category of meaning in compound characters rather than a precise meaning. That is, the radical 氵 in 湖 suggests only that 湖 is related to water but not the exact meaning—*lake*. Due to the linguistic complexity of compound characters, one character containing a semantic radical can have multiple meanings, while some semantic radicals also serve as phonetic radicals in compound characters (e.g., 土 [earth, soil, or ground] is a semantic radical, but it serves as a phonetic radical in the character 吐 [to spit]). Consequently, computing the reliability rate of all semantic radicals in cueing meanings for the compounds is a rather a difficult task. So far, no complete statistics have been reported. Nonetheless, the reliability rate of semantic radicals to cue the meanings of compound characters is estimated to be much higher than phonetic radicals' abilities to cue the pronunciations of compound characters. For example, according to Jin (1985), more than 90% of compounds with the semantic radical 手 (hand) have their meanings related to the hand or to the action of the hand.

Relationship between semantic-radical knowledge and character learning

Due to the orthographic functions of semantic radicals in compound characters, readers' knowledge of semantic radicals can be assumed to play a significant role in successful character recognition. Studies of skilled Chinese readers have verified this assumption. Radical knowledge has been reported to affect character recognition in a number of ways. First, the semantic transparency of a radical in a target character facilitates recognizing the meaning of the character (Feldman & Siok, 1999). Second, the position of a radical in a specific character can affect the speed and accuracy of character recognition (Fang & Wu, 1989; Feldman & Siok, 1997, 1999a; Hoosain, 1991; Kess & Miyamoto, 1999; Li & Chen, 1997, 1999; Peng, Li, & Yang, 1997; Zhou & Marslen-Wilson, 1999). Third, the frequency of a radical and the number of radicals in a specific character affect the time needed to process the character (Peng & Wang, 1997).

The studies mentioned above examined the role of radical knowledge in character recognition among skilled readers, but how does radical knowledge affect character learning among native Chinese learners? A study by Shu and Anderson (1997) of 220 first, third, and fifth graders in mainland China showed that native Chinese children at the third-grade level and above were able to decompose characters into radicals and to derive meaning from unfamiliar characters using the semantic radicals. A study by Ko and Wu (2003) was conducted in Taiwan of second- to fifth-grade students, with 11–17 students in each grade level. The participants were asked to complete a lexical-decision task for two-character words under two kinds of conditions: phonetic regular and consistent conditions and phonetic irregular and inconsistent conditions. The results indicated that second and third graders began to demonstrate knowledge of how to use radicals to infer character meanings, with this skill stabilizing in fourth graders. That is, from the fourth grade onwards, the students were able to make full use of radical information in character recognition.

What is the role of radical knowledge in facilitating character learning among nonnative learners of Chinese? A few studies have been conducted to address this issue. A study by Taft and Chung (1999) investigated whether the internal radical structure of Chinese compound characters helped beginning learners to memorize the characters. The participants were English-speaking novice Chinese learners at an Australian college. During the experiment, the participants were asked to learn 24 characters. The participants were divided into four groups, with each group under one of four conditions for character learning. The conditions varied from a total lack of introducing radical knowledge to the participants to introducing radicals that appeared in the 24 target characters at different learning intervals. The results showed that the participants used their radical knowledge to recall the meanings of the characters, but they performed best under the condition where radical knowledge was provided during the initial presentation of a character.

Another study investigated the role of radical knowledge and its relation to both character recognition and character production for beginning and intermediate learners of Chinese (Shen, 2000). The participants were two groups of nonnative learners from 1st- and 2nd-year college Chinese classes. Each group was asked to complete a radical-knowledge test and two radical-knowledge application tests. The results showed that in each group, the students with good radical knowledge performed significantly better on the radical-knowledge application tests than did students with poor radical knowledge. Jackson, Everson, and Ke (2003) investigated adult beginning learners' awareness of and ability to use the orthographic structure of semantic-phonetic compounds by analyzing data collected from weekly classroom observations, testing results, interviews with an instructor, and an analysis of a textbook. They concluded that some learners were able to use semantic radical knowledge to identify the meanings of some novel characters by the end of the 1st year of instruction. Shen and Ke (2007) investigated learners' radical awareness and its effect on word acquisition by studying 140 participants from three learning levels and found a moderate correlation across learning levels between students' knowledge of Chinese characters and their skills in applying radical knowledge to character learning.

To summarize, studies investigating the relationship between radical knowledge and character learning among skilled readers, native learners, and nonnative learners have provided strong evidence that radical knowledge facilitates character learning. No studies thus far, however, have been conducted to investigate how Chinese radicals are actually acquired in the classroom learning environment

The present study was designed to investigate nonnative beginning students' learning behaviors in the study of Chinese semantic radicals. By observing the beginning learners' mastery of 100 high-frequency semantic radicals during 1 year, the researcher sought the answers to the following questions:

1. Among the three linguistic components of sound, shape, and meaning, which do students consider the most difficult to learn?
2. How do students' views of difficulty levels in radical learning account for their actual performances?

3. What specific difficulties do beginning learners face in terms of mastering these three linguistic components?
4. What kind of teaching and learning methods do the learners consider most effective for learning radicals?
5. To what extent do students consider radical knowledge to be helpful in learning characters?

The results of this study will hopefully yield insights into how radical knowledge is acquired and contribute to more effective ways of teaching radicals to students of Chinese as a foreign language.

Background in radical instruction

This study was conducted at a Midwestern university during the 2005–2006 academic year. According to the Chinese instruction plan of this university, 1st-year students were introduced to 100 high-frequency semantic radicals (see Appendix A). Students were required to learn 50 radicals in the first semester and another 50 in the second semester. The 50 radicals were divided into five instructional units, each containing 10 radicals. During each instructional period (about 15–20 minutes), 10 radicals were introduced. In the class, the instructor guided the students to learn the sounds, meanings, and shapes of the radicals. When presenting the meanings and shapes of the radicals, the instructor explained the etymology of each radical and illustrated the evolution from the pictograph form to the modern script.

After 15–20 minutes of radical instruction, the students were introduced to new characters in the lesson. All introduced radicals (including previously introduced radicals) appearing in the new characters were highlighted with different colors either on PowerPoint presentations or on vocabulary cards to attract the students' attention to the radicals. The instructor also asked the students to name the radicals in the compound character and explain how the meanings of the radicals could be related to the overall character meaning whenever there was such a connection. In the next few days' of classroom instruction, the radicals were reviewed together with the characters. The radical tests were incorporated into the weekly quizzes and monthly exams. Before the week of the monthly exam was a review session that included radicals as part of the content. During this session, the instructor designed activities to guide students in reviewing the three linguistic components (sound, shape, and meaning) of the radicals and recognizing the radicals in novel characters.

Methods

Participants

The participants were 65 nonnative college learners of Chinese enrolled in a 1st-year Chinese class. Their ages ranged from 19 to 26; 42 were male, and 23 were female. None of the participants had any Asian language background before starting their 1st year of Chinese.

Instruments

Radical tests
The purpose of these tests was to find out if the students had mastered the radicals that were introduced to them. Each test contained two forms: Form 1 required the students to provide sounds (in pinyin) and meanings (in English) for the list of radicals that had been introduced to them, and Form 2 required the students to write the radicals based

on the given meanings and sounds (see Appendix B). There were four tests in all; two tests contained 20 radicals each, and the other two, 30 radicals each. Altogether, the four tests covered the 100 semantic radicals that had been introduced during the 1-year learning period.

Radical-learning survey

The purpose of this survey was to investigate the students' cognitive behaviors and study preferences when learning radicals. The survey contained four questions (see Appendix C). Question 1 used a 10-point semantic differential scale to ask students to rate the difficulty level involved in learning the three linguistic components—sound, shape, and meaning—of radicals. Question 2 asked students to first circle the most difficult linguistic component among sound, shape, and meaning of a radical, then to provide a verbal description of why a certain linguistic component was the most difficult to learn. Question 3 was designed to find out to what extent (if any) radical knowledge helped students to learn characters. To achieve this, students were asked to first circle either *yes* or *no*, then required to explain why or why not. Question 4 required students to identify the kinds of teaching and learning methods that were most helpful to them for learning radicals.

Data collection and scoring

The four radical tests were administered during 1 year. Each semester, two radical tests were administered. The first test contained 20 radicals, and the second, 30 radicals. Data were collected during the monthly exam period; thus, the radical tests were treated as part of the monthly exam content. If a student correctly identified the sound, shape, and meaning of the radical, 3 points were awarded, and 1 point was given for separately identifying sound, shape, or meaning. A radical learning survey was administered at the end of the 1st year of Chinese language study. The survey took about 20 minutes for the students to complete.

Interrater reliability

To answer research questions 2, 3, and 4, the students' verbal responses were collected for analysis. During the process of classifying the responses into certain categories, interrater reliability tests were conducted to ensure the accuracy of the classifications. In this study, a five-step procedure was adopted for the interrater reliability check.

1. The researcher served as first rater to classify the participants' verbal responses into categories based on emerging patterns of the response items (for details, please see the qualitative analysis part of the Analysis and Results section).

2. The second rater (another instructor who taught 5th-year Chinese in the program) independently examined the classification made by the first rater, marked the items with which she disagreed, and provided written comments on the areas of disagreement. The interrater agreement at this step was 91%.

3. The first rater then read the comments provided by the second rater and revised the classification of the items where she concurred with the second rater's judgments and provided feedback on the items with which she disagreed.

4. The second rater read the revised classification and conducted a second round of interrater reliability analysis, that is, repeated step two. The interrater agreement for the second round analysis was 98%.

5. Based on the second-round comments of the second rater, the first rater then discussed any discrepancies with the second rater until both raters reached 100%

agreement. A second revision then was made on the classification based on the discussion. The classification categories presented in the qualitative analysis section of this study is the version with 100% interrater agreement.

Analysis and results

Among the three linguistic components of a radical (sound, shape, and meaning), which did the students consider most difficult to learn?

To answer this question, two pieces of information were collected: the students' views on which linguistic component is the most difficult to learn as indicated by the radical-learning survey and their performance on the four radical tests.

Question 1 from the radical-learning survey required that students rate the difficulty level of each linguistic component on a 10-point semantic differential scale, with 1 being the least difficult and 10 being the most difficult. Judging from the descriptive data (Table 1), the students considered sound to be the most difficult component to learn, with an overall mean of 5. Next was the shape, with an overall mean of 4.92. The least difficult component was the meaning, with an overall mean of 3.44. A one-way analysis of variance (ANOVA) was performed to determine whether these means were significantly different. The overall one-way ANOVA indicated a significant difference between means, $F(2, 192)=9.97$, $p<.000$. A posthoc group comparisons (Tukey) test showed that there was a statistically significant difference between sound and meaning and between shape and meaning but no significant difference between sound and shape (Table 1). The results suggest that these learners considered the sounds and shapes of radicals to be equally difficult to learn, while both sounds and shapes were considered to be more difficult to learn than meanings.

Table 1. ANOVA on posthoc group comparisons (Tukey) on students' views of difficulty levels in learning three linguistic components of radicals ($N=65$)

item	M	SD	GC		p
sound	5.12	2.32	1	2	.877
				3	.000*
shape	4.92	2.62	2	3	.001*
meaning	3.45	2.03	3		

note: GC=group comparison; *$p<.05$

How did the students' views of difficulty levels in radical learning account for their actual performance?

Next examined was the consistency of the students' views of the difficulty levels of learning the three linguistic components (as measured on the 10-point semantic differential scale) and their actual performance on the radical tests. A one-way ANOVA followed by posthoc (Tukey) multiple comparison tests were again conducted on the results of the four radical tests. The results of the overall analysis and the follow-up posthoc multiple comparisons for each radical test are reported in Table 2. The last section of Table 2 shows the group performance on the four tests combined. This section shows a significant main effect for the overall analysis, $F(2, 192)=5.678$, $p=.004$. The descriptive data showed that the participants' performance on meaning was the best, with a mean of 80.64. The second best was sound, with a mean of 73.09, and the performance on shape had the lowest mean of 69.37. The ANOVA on the posthoc group comparisons confirmed that meaning was the least difficult component to learn: The posthoc test detected a statistically significant difference between shape and meaning. Although the group mean scores indicated that students' performance on sound was higher than that on shape (73.09 vs. 69.37), no statistically significant difference was observed between sound and shape. This observation is consistent with the results of radical tests 1–3. Thus, the students' self-assessment of the learning difficulty level for each linguistic component was highly consistent with their actual performance on the radical tests. That is, in the beginning stages, learning the sound and shape of a radical is much more difficult than learning its meaning.

Note that in Test 4, there was no statistically significant difference in performance between sound, shape, and meaning. This could simply be due to the fact that for this particular test (this was the last test in the 1st-year curriculum), students put more effort into memorizing sounds and shapes to achieve higher grades. This could also reflect the progress that students made in mastering learning methods by the end of their 1st year of study. For instance, at this stage of their learning, memorizing sounds and shapes might no longer have been as difficult as learning meanings. If this is true, then a similar pattern should be observed in subsequent radical tests in the 2nd year. A separate study is needed to investigate at which point students consider learning the sound and shape of a radical to be as easy as learning the meaning of a radical.

Table 2. ANOVA on overall analysis and posthoc (Tukey) multiple comparisons of four radical tests (N=65)

item	M	SD	GC		p
	Radical test 1, overall $F(2, 192)=7.697$, $p=.001$				
sound	19.80	6.99	1	2	.206
				3	.073
shape	17.84	7.17	2	3	.000*
meaning	22.32	5.25	3		
	Radical test 2, overall $F(2, 192)=3.672$, $p=.027$				
item	M	SD	GC		p
sound	14.06	6.30	1	2	.699
				3	.160
shape	13.23	6.26	2	3	.024*
meaning	15.95	4.94	3		
	Radical test 3, overall $F(2, 192)=3.671$, $p=.027$				
item	M	SD	GC		p
sound	20.29	8.32	1	2	.302
				3	.441

shape	18.18	8.35	2	3	.020*
meaning	22.03	7.61	3		

Radical test 4, overall F(2, 192)=.971, p=.40					
item	M	SD	GC		p
sound	18.94	6.94	1	2	.543
				3	.418
shape	20.11	5.90	2	3	.976
meaning	20.34	6.07			

Radical test (1–4), overall F(2, 192)=5.678, p=.004					
item	M	SD	GC		p
sound	73.09	21.02	1	2	.520
				3	.071
shape	69.37	21.16	2	3	.003*
meaning	80.64	15.61			

note: Overall F (2, 192) =5.678, p=.004*; GC=group comparisons; * p<.05

What difficulties did the beginning learners face in terms of mastering the three linguistic components—sound, shape, and meaning—of a radical?

The second question in the radical learning survey was designed to answer this question. All of the participants' responses to Question 2 were collected and sorted into three categories: difficulties in learning sounds, shapes, and meanings. The invalid responses were removed from each category of the initial list. Those invalid responses included providing no explanation for the choice, such as, "I do not know," and "I am not clear," and providing no specific information pertaining to how it is difficult, such as, "Sound in general is difficult to catch," and "I usually forget them." Thus, 54 valid responses were obtained for the three categories: difficulty in learning sounds (30 responses), shapes (19 responses), and meanings (5 responses).

For each category, the response items were further classified into several types based on the nature of difficulty. For the difficulty in learning sound, six types of difficulties were identified (Table 3). Among them, five were considered major difficulties (reported by more than 5% of the participants). The first type of difficulty was discriminating and memorizing tones, which accounted for 16.67% of the total responses. The second type was that students felt that they could not find connections between the pronunciation of a radical and its meaning or shape (16.67%). The third type was discriminating between similar sounds or accurately producing certain sounds (9.26%). Some students also reported that they were not able to relate the sound of a radical to their native language (5.55%) and that they did not have enough opportunities to encounter the radicals after initially learning them (5.55%).

Table 3. Students' difficulties in learning sounds of radicals (54 Responses)

SOUND

55.55% of the students reported that sound was the most difficult component to learn.

type of difficulty	sample responses
difficulty discriminating and memorizing tones (17%)	The exact tones of Chinese words are difficult for me.
	The tone can be confusing and hard to differentiate. Also I have the most trouble pronouncing the different tones.
	It is difficult to remember the tones, the pinyin is relatively easy, but trying to remember tones is difficult.
lack of connections from the sound to the meaning or shape (17%)	The way the shapes of the radicals are reflects the meaning of radical itself, but the Chinese sound of it is more difficult to connect.
	For the most part, sound is almost irrelevant to the shape or meaning of the character.
	The sounds have no direct connection to the shape or meaning, so it is hard to remember them.
difficulty discriminating similar sounds and accurately producing certain sounds (9%)	I have trouble hearing the difference between Chinese sounds.
	Many are the same.
	I get very tongue twisted and cannot make some of the sounds right.
inability to relate sounds to one's native language (6%)	Because Chinese has a lot of sounds which don't exist in my language. So they are quite difficult to pronounce.
	The sounds are not familiar to me.
lack of practice (6%)	It is not used in Chinese class often, so I often will forget the sound of the radical after a while.
	I never use it.
poor mastery of pinyin (2%)	Because I feel I never really got a grasp on the first 2 weeks in Romanization and pinyin.

Two major difficulties were identified in learning the shape of a radical (Table 4). About 35% of the students reported that they had great difficulty discriminating and memorizing graphically similar radicals. Usually, similarly shaped radicals share most strokes but differ in one or two strokes. This indicates that the students had difficulty identifying the dissimilarities of these one or two strokes. About 9% of the students considered the difficulty to be caused by a lack of opportunities or time to practice.

Table 4. Students' difficulties in learning shapes of radicals (54 responses)

SHAPE

35% of the students reported that shape was the most difficult component to learn.

type of difficulty	sample responses
difficulty discriminating and memorizing strokes in a radical (22%)	A lot of times, the radicals are similar to each other. I want to make sure I'm writing them correctly.
	It is especially difficult when you have two radicals that look almost the same.
	Because there is a lot of strokes to remember.
lack of practice (9%)	Just a lot of simple shapes that can be difficult to remember and take a lot of time
	It is hard to learn because you have to practice it more and a lot of times I can picture a character in my head but can't write it.
inability to relate the shape to the sound and meaning (4%)	It is easy to connect a sound and meaning with a radical, but when confronted with a foreign radical, it is possible to guess its meaning. With a meaning and sound, who knows what its radical look like?
	I have a hard time putting the shape with the sound in my head.

Only a few responses reported meaning as the most difficult component to learn (Table 5). The major difficulty reported was that the similarity in shapes and sounds of some radicals affected memorizing their meanings (6%). That is, students felt that it was more difficult to memorize the meanings of radicals that had similar shapes or pronunciations but totally different meanings because psychologically, one would expect that a radical with a sound or shape similar to a target radical would also have a similar meaning.

Table 5. Students' difficulties in learning meanings of radicals (54 responses)

MEANING

9% of the students reported that meaning was the most difficult component to learn.

type of difficulty	sample responses
effect of similarity in shapes and sounds of radicals on memorization of meanings (6%)	Many have similar shapes, but different meanings.
	Connecting the meaning to the shape and not confusing it with another shape is difficult.
effect of amount of input on memorization of meaning (4%)	Many radicals are similar in shape and sound yet the meaning is different so often time, I will get the meaning confused.
	Because of the large amount of meanings needed to be learned and the lack of relation they have.

What kind of teaching and learning methods did the learners consider most effective in radical learning?

The students' responses were collected to the survey question, "What kind(s) of current teaching and learning method(s) are most helpful to you in learning radicals?" Vague responses such as "I think the way teaching is going is effective" or "Everything that was done was effective" were removed from the list because these answers provided no detailed information pertaining to the topic. Then, the list of responses was further classified into five types based on the nature of the responses, which are presented below.

The first of the five types was a combination of aural, oral, and visual repetition and review, which accounted for 38% of the responses. The next was explaining the etymology of the radical, that is, its origin and historical development. About 27% of the participants considered this to be the most effective method. The third most effective method, reported by 15% of the participants, was relating radicals to character learning. This included asking students to identify semantic radicals in a new character and to find the connections of this radical to the meaning or sound of the character. Taking quizzes and tests on radical knowledge was considered to be the most effective method by 13% of the students. About 8% of the participants considered using games and activities in class to be the most helpful method for learning radicals. The participants' responses to each of the five methods are shown in Table 6.

Table 6. The most effective radical teaching and learning methods reported (60 responses)

type of method	sample response
aural, oral, and visual repetition and review (38%)	Going over them multiple times. I learn better through repeated exposure.
	Vocal repetition with whole class.
	Constant repetition and practice writing, reading, and speaking the radicals.
	More review of older radicals. More in class writing activities.
explanation of the etymology of the radical (its origin and development; 27%)	I like the way you explain the pictorial meaning.
	[Explaining] concepts like origin.
	It helps me when you explain the meaning of the radical on the board by drawing pictures.
relation of radicals to character learning (13%)	Asking students about what radicals are in certain character/words. If we often come across the radicals and actually test us, we would remember the meaning, shape and tone of the radicals.
	Application to characters we know.
	It's very useful when you point out which radicals make up particular characters, because it's easy to forget them unless you use them often.
quizzes and tests (13%)	I like the way we do the tests.
	Testing is most helpful, because it forces me to memorize them.
	More quizzes so I have more motivation to study them and more focus on writing characters.
games and class activities (8%)	Games=good.
	Maybe some more games would be useful in learning and making it fun.
	I remember one day in first semester when the class drew pictures on the board and other classmates wrote what they thought the corresponding radical was – that was a lot of fun, and it helped.

To what extent did the students consider radical knowledge to be helpful in learning characters?

A total of 60 valid responses were collected for this question, and 93% of the participants provided a positive answer to this question (Table 7). A further analysis of the students' positive responses indicated that more than half of the students (53%) believed that radical knowledge helped them to understand the meanings and sounds of compound characters. Radical knowledge helped them to better memorize the physical structures of compound characters, according to 34% of the participants. Because radicals are parts of compound characters, if students were familiar with the component radicals in a novel character, they would be able to decompose the character into radicals to facilitate memorization. Only about 7% of the participants reported that radical knowledge was not useful in character learning. Their major complaint was that they could not relate a radical's meaning to a character containing the radical or that they never tried to use a radical's meaning to figure out the meaning of a character that contained it. Note that for morphologically opaque characters, a meaningful connection between the character and the radical within it is hard to determine. These students seemed to be either discouraged when they did not find a radical-character connection or were not motivated to actively use radical knowledge in character learning.

Table 7. Students' responses to the usefulness of radical knowledge to character learning (60 responses)

type of response	sample response
Radical knowledge is helpful for learning characters/words (93%).	
help in understanding meanings or sounds of compound characters (53%)	It builds a basis for the meaning of the character.
	Radicals have meanings, so I think they help learning characters.
	Radicals appear in all characters. The radicals that you recognize in the character can help you get an idea of the meaning of the character before even knowing what it is.
	It gives me a clue to the meaning and/or possibly the sound.
help in learning graphic structure of the character (37%)	It helps you memorize characters better if you know the parts to them at first.
	It helps you further learn more complex characters, as most Chinese characters I've learned have at least one of the radicals.
	It helps me break down characters to their components, which makes it easier to learn than stroke to stroke.
help in using a Chinese dictionary (3%)	It makes it easier to use a dictionary.
	Learning radicals is essential to me for translating text via dictionaries.
Radical knowledge is not helpful for learning characters/words. (6.67%).	
inability to find connections between radicals and character learning	Often the radical meaning has nothing to do with character learning.
	I don't find a connection between knowing radicals and learning characters.
	I don't really because most do not work for me but some do such as (shui) 氵, then I know it was something to do with water.

Discussion and pedagogical implications

This study investigated beginning learners' behaviors while learning 100 high-frequency semantic radicals and yielded the following meaningful findings. First, the beginning learners considered the sounds and shapes of radicals to be much more difficult to learn than their meanings. This observation was consistent with their performance on radical tests. The data indicate that the major difficulties that the participants experienced in learning sounds included having problems discriminating tones and memorizing them, finding no clues to connect a sound to its graphic structure or meaning, and having difficulty in producing similar sounds or some particular sounds and relating the sounds to one's native language. For learning the graphic structure of radicals, students reported that the primary difficulty was in discriminating and memorizing the strokes. These difficulties are mainly caused by the drastic linguistic differences between the students' native language and Chinese, which in turn forces a cognitive restructuring for learning Chinese radicals. Graphically, Chinese radicals originated from pictographs without sound-script correspondences; thus, learners cannot rely on a written symbol to decipher its sound. Phonologically, in Chinese, each syllable can be read using four different tones, another linguistic feature that is absent in English. In terms of graphic structures, Chinese characters use strokes as building blocks. Learners cannot find any similarities between using strokes to write characters and using Roman letters to write English; rather, they quite often refer to writing Chinese characters as "drawing characters." Interestingly, they see the commonality between using strokes to paint a picture and to write Chinese characters. Historically, Chinese radicals are logographic writing that is rich in meaning-to-script connection, but the strokes of modern Chinese radicals are straightened, and their graphic structures squared, which makes it difficult to find visual connections between meaning and shape. Thus, learners of Chinese are facing dual cognitive difficulties in learning the sounds and shapes of radicals. That is, on the one hand, they need to expend a great deal of cognitive effort to suppress the interference from their existing, well-developed cognitive structure that is used to learn their native language, such as the alphabetic principle, intonation principle, and letter-string principle. On the other hand, they need to develop a new cognitive structure or a new 'language processor' (Pienemann, 2005) that is suitable to learn a language with a tone-based pronunciation system and a stroke-based writing system.

From a curriculum-design perspective, to alleviate students' difficulties in learning the sounds and shapes of radicals, students should have a good mastery of the pinyin system and character strokes before moving on to learn radicals. Why do students find it especially difficult to recall a target radical with similar sound, tone, or graph to previously learned radicals? From the perspective of *competition theory* (Anderson, Bjork, & Bjork, 1994; Watkins, 1979), interference is assumed to arise when the retrieval cue normally used to access a target radical becomes associated with additional memory items such as radicals with similar sounds, tones, and shapes. Under such conditions, successfully connecting a retrieval cue to a target radical depends not only on how strongly that cue is related to the target radical, but also on whether the cue is related to other similar radicals in memory. When a retrieval cue is linked to more than one radical in memory, the similar radicals are assumed to compete with the target radical for access to the learner's conscious awareness.

To help students establish a strong association between the retrieval cue and the target radical that will win the competition among similar associations, quality and amount of practice are essential factors. For learning pinyin, one issue is that some current beginning-level Chinese textbooks neither explain how individual pinyin sounds are actually produced nor provide enough pinyin exercises for practice. Under such circumstances, classroom teachers need to provide supplemental materials to increase conceptual understanding of the differences and similarities among Chinese sounds and tones and provide extensive drills to ensure students' mastery of the pinyin system. With regard to the mastery of the strokes used to write Chinese characters, observing students' errors in radical writing has shown that nonnative beginning learners have great difficulty distinguishing the differences between strokes written in a similar manner, such as 一, ⌒, and ⇁ when they are together with other strokes to form a radical. Apparently, beginning learners are insensitive to the importance of adding or dropping a stroke in a radical or to the subtle differences between strokes in a radical. This does not mean that beginning learners cannot visually discriminate the differences from one stroke to another or from one graphic structure to another; rather, the difficulty comes because their minds are so used to perceiving Roman letters that it is difficult for them to develop a new perceptual structure. To help students establish the concept of a stroke, it is important that students are allowed sufficient time and practice on individual strokes until they reach a level of automaticity in producing them and that teaching activities are designed that require students to recognize and name individual strokes used in the different radicals.

A second finding is that students consider five types of learning and teaching methods most effective. Among them, aural, oral, and visual repetition and review was embraced by 38% of the participants. This confirms an important concept from human cognition about verbal memory—rehearsal. Classroom instructors may all agree with the view that forgetting is the enemy of learning and that learners have to fight constantly against forgetting before knowledge is registered in long-term memory. Not all instructors, however, are aware of the critical role of repetition and review in knowledge acquisition and how it takes effect. Some instructors are reluctant to use classroom time for repetition and review. They consider it a waste of class time. Others are in favor of heavy repetition on a single item within one time slot. For example, students are required to sound out a new character or word many times. Studies from cognitive science indicate that neither of these views is accurate.

Forgetting is a result of different types of interference during the learning process. The major kinds of interferences in learning are retroactive and proactive (Bjork & Bjork, 1996). Retroactive interference refers to the situation where an individual can no longer recall the target radicals during a test due to the interference of learning new radicals and other material after initially learning the target radicals. Proactive interference refers to the situation where an individual can no longer recall the target radicals during a test due to inference from previous learned radicals or other related material. To resist interference, practice (repetition and review) of learned materials is an essential approach to keep the materials from being forgotten. Studies on forgetting suggest that the most effective practice is spaced practice, which is to repeat or review materials in distributed time slots rather than conducting massed practice in which repetitions are made in a single time slot (Greene, 1989). One main reason provided by the voluntary-attention hypothesis (Dempster, 1987; Hintzman, 1974, 1976; Magliero, 1983) is that students treat massed repetition as a rest opportunity, and they pay less attention to the target item that is being repeated many times. Spaced practice makes the practice less redundant and provides more opportunities for learners to access previously encoded target items.

In addition to repetition and review, explaining the etymology of radicals (their origins and development), relating radicals to character learning, and using games and activities in class were all considered effective methods by the students. These approaches allowed the students to make meaningful connections between new learning materials and their existing knowledge. This increased the depth of cognitive processing and enhanced memorization.

The data also indicate that about 13% of the students considered having quizzes and tests to be the most effective learning method. The students seemed unafraid of tests; rather, they praised them and benefited from the tests with enhanced radical learning. Many instructors consider quizzes and exams to be only assessment tools to evaluate students' learning results, not means of promoting learning. Studies show that intervening tests act primarily as additional study and review opportunities and that they improve memory performance by increasing the amount of cognitive processing that learners devote to particular items (Dempster & Perkins, 1993). Therefore, intervening quizzes and tests should be viewed as part of regular instruction and a review tool to improve learning, especially at the beginning level. When instructors analyze the results of quizzes and tests with their students, they should direct the students' attention to the items that they failed to recall and explore why this happened, rather than only informing the students of how many points they earned on the test.

The third finding was that the overwhelming majority of the beginning learners (93%) considered radical knowledge to be a help in learning characters for a number of reasons. For instance, students reported that radical knowledge helped them learn the meanings and sounds of compound characters and to learn the graphic structure of characters. This shows that a solid mastery of radical knowledge at the beginning stage of learning is an important component that leads to effective character learning in subsequent years. Unfortunately, not many textbooks provide lessons for the teaching and learning of radicals. Instructors must make an effort to see to it that radical learning becomes an integral part of Chinese language curriculum, so providing radical lessons either prior to or during character learning is an important step for character instruction.

References

Anderson, M. C., Bjork, R. A., & Bjork, E. L. (1994). Remembering can cause forgetting: Retrieval dynamics in long-term memory. *Journal of Experimental Psychology: Learning, Memory, and Cognition, 20,* 1063–1087.

Bjork, E. L., & Bjork, R. A. (1996). *Memory.* New York: Academic Press.

Chen, Y.-P., Allport, D. A., & Marshalls, J. C. (1996). What are the functional orthographic units in Chinese word recognition: The stroke or the stroke pattern? *The Quarterly Journal of Experimental Psychology, 49A,* 1024–1043.

汉语大字典 [Chinese character dictionary]. (1995). Wuhan, China: 湖北辞书出版社, 四川辞书出版社 [Hubei Dictionary Publisher and Sichuan Dictionary Publisher].

Dempster, F. N. (1987). Effects of variable encoding and spaced presentations on vocabulary learning. *Journal of Educational Psychology, 79,* 162–170.

Dempster, F. N., & Perkins, P. G. (1993). Revitalizing classroom assessment: Using tests to promote learning. *Journal of Instructional Psychology, 20,* 197–203.

Fan, K. Y., Gao, J. L., & Ao, X. P. (1984). Pronunciation principles of Chinese characters and alphabetic script.中国文字改革 *[Chinese Character Reform], 3,* 23–27.

Fang, S.-P., & Wu, P. (1989). Illusory conjunctions in the perception of Chinese characters. *Journal of Experimental Psychology, 15,* 434–447.

Feldman, L. B., & Siok, W. W. T. (1997). The role of component function in visual recognition of Chinese characters. *Journal of Experimental Psychology: Learning, Memory, and Cognition, 23,* 776–781.

Feldman, L. B., & Siok, W. W. T. (1999). Semantic radicals contribute to the visual identification of Chinese characters. *Journal of Memory and Language, 40,* 559–576.

Greene, R. L. (1989). Spacing effects in memory: Evidence for a two-process account. *Journal of Experimental Psychology: Learning, Memory, and Cognition, 15,* 371–377.

Hintzman, D. L. (1974). Theoretical implications of the spacing effect. In R. L. Solso (Ed.), *Theories in cognitive psychology:* The Loyola Symposium (pp. 77–99). Potomac, MD: Erlbaum.

Hintzman, D. L. (1976). Repetition and memory. In G. H. Bower (Ed.), *The psychology of learning and motivation: Advances in research and theory* (Vol. 10, pp. 47–91). New York: Academic Press.

Hoosain, R. (1991). *Psycholinguistic implications for linguistic relativity: A case study of Chinese*. Hillsdale, NJ: Lawrence Erlbaum Associates.

Huang, J. T. (1984). Visual integration process in recognizing fragmented Chinese characters. In H. S. R. Gao & R. Hoosian (Eds.), *Linguistics, psychology, and the Chinese language* (pp. 46–54). Hong Kong: Hong Kong University Press.

Jackson, N., Everson, M., & Ke, C. (2003). Beginning readers' awareness of the orthographic structure of semantic-phonetic compounds: Lessons from a study of learners of Chinese as a foreign language. In C. McBride-Chang & H.-C. Chen (Eds.), *Reading development in Chinese children* (pp. 142–153). Westport, CT: Praeger Publishers.

Jin, J.-H. (1985). 从静态与动态相结合的角度看待汉字 [Analyzing Chinese characters from both static and dynamic perspectives]. 中国文字改革 *[Chinese Language Reform]*, 5, 13–15.

Kess, J. F., & Miyamoto, T. (1999). *The Japanese mental lexicon*. Philadelphia: John Benjamins Publishing Company.

Ko, H., & Wu, C. F. (2003). The role of character components in reading Chinese. In C. McBride-Chang & H.-C. Chen (Eds.), *Reading development in Chinese children* (pp. 73–79). Westport, CT: Praeger Publishers.

Li, H., & Chen, H.-C. (1997). Processing of radicals in Chinese character recognition. In H.-C. Chen (Ed.), *Cognitive processing of Chinese and related Asian languages* (pp. 141–160). Hong Kong: The Chinese University Press.

Li, H., & Chen, H.-C. (1999). Radical processing in Chinese character recognition: Evidence from lexical decision. *Psychologia, 42*, 199–208.

Magliero, A. (1983). Pupil dilations following pairs of identical words and related to-be-remembered words. *Memory & Cognition, 11*, 609–615.

Peng, D.-L., Li, Y.-P., & Yang, H. (1997). Orthographic processing in the identification of Chinese characters. In H.-C. Chen (Ed.), Cognitive processing of Chinese and related Asian languages (pp. 85–108). Hong Kong: The Chinese University Press.

Peng, R., & Wang, C. (1997). Basic processing unit of Chinese character recognition: Evidence from stroke number effect and radical number effect. *Acta Psychologica Sinica, 29*, 8–15.

Pienemann, M. (2005). Language processing capacity. In C. J. Doughty & M. H. Long (Eds.), The handbook of second language acquisition (pp. 679–714). Malden, MA: Blackwell Publishing.

Shen, H. H. (2000). Radical knowledge and character learning among learners of Chinese as a foreign language. 语言研究 [Linguistic Studies], *June*, 85–93.

Shen, H. H., & Ke, C. (2007) An Investigation of radical awareness and word acquisition among non-native learners of Chinese. *Modern Language Journal, 91*, 97–111.

Shu, H., & Anderson, R. C. (1997). Role of radical awareness in the character and word acquisition of Chinese children. *Reading Research Quarterly, 32*, 78–89.

现代汉语通用字表 [Statistics on Commonly Used Chinese Characters]. (1998). Beijing, China: 语文出版社 [Linguistics Publisher].

Taft, M., & Zhu, X. (1997). Submorphemic processing in reading Chinese. *Journal of Experimental Psychology: Learning, Memory, and Cognition, 23*, 761–775.

Taft, M., & Chung, K. (1999). Using radicals in teaching Chinese characters to second language learners. *Psychologia, 42,* 243–251.

Watkins, M. J. (1979). Engrams as cuegrams and forgetting as cue-overload: A cueing approach to the structure of memory. In C. R. Puff (Ed.), *The structure of memory* (pp. 347–372). New York: Academic Press.

Zhou, X., & Marslen-Wilson, W. (1999). Sublexical processing in reading Chinese. In J. Wang, A. W. Inhoff, & H.-C. Chen (Eds.), *Reading Chinese script: A cognitive analysis* (pp. 37–64). Mahwah, NJ: Lawrence Erlbaum Associates, Inc.

Appendix A: 100 high-frequency Chinese radicals

no.	radical	no.	radical	no.	radical	no.	radical
1	水(氵)	26	禾	51	示(礻)	76	立
2	艸(艹)	27	辵(辶)	52	彡	77	白
3	木	28	犬(犭)	53	隹	78	殳
4	口	29	玉(王)	54	田	79	身
5	手(扌)	30	食(饣)	55	毛	80	又
6	心(忄)	31	邑(阝)	56	欠	81	冫
7	金(钅)	32	車(车)	57	歹	82	子
8	人	33	頁(页)	58	風(风)	83	亠
9	蟲(虫)	34	刀(刂)	59	齒(齿)	84	止
10	言(讠)	35	阜(阝)	60	羽	85	尤(尢)
11	糸(纟)	36	門(门)	61	耳	86	矢
12	竹(⺮)	37	革	62	骨	87	八
13	鳥(鸟)	38	巾	63	見(见)	88	匸
14	土	39	貝(贝)	64	弓	89	爪
15	月	40	宀	65	瓦	90	斤
16	女	41	雨	66	尸	91	夕
17	山	42	酉	67	力	92	厶
18	火(灬)	43	舟	68	大	93	兒(儿)
19	魚(鱼)	44	广	69	网	94	十
20	足(⻊)	45	穴	70	角	95	小
21	疒	46	攴(攵)	71	羊	96	辛
22	石	47	米	72	囗	97	舌
23	衣(衤)	48	彳	73	厂	98	寸
24	馬(马)	49	走	74	戈	99	一
25	日	50	牛	75	皿	100	卩

Appendix B: Sample radical tests

Radical test (1–20), form 1

姓名: _____

Write out the pinyin and meaning according to the radical given.

no.	radical	pinyin	meaning	no.	radical	pinyin	meaning
1	水 (氵)			11	糸 (纟)		
2	艹			12	竹 (⺮)		
3	木			13	鳥 (鸟)		
4	口			14	土		
5	手 (扌)			15	月		
6	心			16	女		
7	金 (钅)			17	山		
8	人 (亻)			18	火 (灬)		
9	蟲 (虫)			19	魚 (鱼)		
10	言 (讠)			20	足 (⻊)		

Radical test (1–20), form 2

姓名: _____

no.	radical	pinyin	meaning	no.	radical	pinyin	meaning
1		shuǐ	water	11		mì	silk
2		cǎo	grass	12		zhú	bamboo
3		mù	wood	13		niǎo	bird
4		kǒu	mouth	14		tǔ	soil; earth
5		shǒu	hand	15		yuè	moon; meat
6		xīn	heart	16		nǚ	female
7		jīn	gold	17		shān	mountain
8		rén	person	18		huǒ	fire
9		chóng	insect	19		yú	fish
10		yán	speech	20		zú	foot

Appendix C: Chinese radical-learning survey (spring 2006)

Name _____ Chinese Class Level _____

Dear student: The purpose of this survey is to help us find out more efficient ways of teaching and learning Chinese radicals (not characters). So, telling your true feeling is important. Thank you for your cooperation.

1. Please rate the difficulty level of learning the three linguistic components of radicals from the 10-point scale below:

   Learning the sound of a radical is

   Least difficult most difficult

   1   2   3   4   5   6   7   8   9   10

   Learning the shape of a radical is

   Least difficult most difficult

   1   2   3   4   5   6   7   8   9   10

   Learning the meaning of a radical is

   Least difficult most difficult

   1   2   3   4   5   6   7   8   9   10

2. Please circle one from the following choices that fits your situation best.

   In general, I consider the most difficult linguistic component to learn in a radical is

   1) sound 2) shape 3) meaning

   Please explain in detail why this linguistic component is relatively difficult to learn.

3. Do you think that radical knowledge helps you learn characters? yes no

   Regardless of whether you choose "yes" or "no," please explain why.

4. What kind(s) of current teaching and learning method(s) are most helpful to you in learning radicals?

词汇熟悉度、词性和语言水平对欧美学习者汉语词汇联想的影响[1]

NFLRC

The Effects of Word-Knowledge Depth, Part of Speech, and Proficiency Level on Word Association Among Learners of Chinese as a Second Language

Chan Lü
Loyola Marymount University, Los Angeles, California

本文的主要目的是考察词汇熟悉度、词性以及语言水平对汉语作为第二语言的欧美初级和中级学习者词汇联想的影响,以及讨论在不同语言水平的学习者心理词典中,不同熟悉度、不同词性的词在心理词典中的表征结构。研究中我们以三种熟悉度(熟悉、较熟悉、不熟悉)、三种词性(名词、动词、形容词)的汉语双音节词为材料,采用词汇联想的范式,以四个不同的反应方式(聚合反应、组合反应、语音反应和无关反应)作为因变量加以考察。实验结果表明,汉语学习者的心理词典的发展与英语学习者心理词典的发展并不相同,其经历的并不是一个由"语音主导"到"意义主导"的过程,而是一个由杂乱无章的结构逐渐发展为一个意义主导的结构。词汇熟悉度是影响学习者心理词典结构的一个重要因素。熟悉词和较熟悉词在学习者心理词典中多以聚合和组合的方式存在,而不熟悉词多以语音和无关联想的方式存在。不同语言水平的学习者的心理词典的结构不同。对于初级学习者来说,无关和语音联想占据主要位置,而对于中级学习者来说,无关联想大量减少,聚合和组合联想的数量有了很大的提高,他们的语音联想在数量上也多于初级学习者。在初、中级汉语学习者的心理词典中,名词之间的联系最强,形容词和动词次之。较之初级学习者,中级学习者的词性意识已有了较大的发展。

The influences of depth of word knowledge, part of speech, and proficiency level on a word-association test were empirically examined among English-speaking learners of

---

[1] 本文是作者在北京语言大学硕士论文的基础上修改而成。作者感谢北京语言大学对外汉语研究中心江新教授的悉心指点。

Lü, C. (2010). The effects of word-knowledge depth, part of speech, and proficiency level on word association among learners of Chinese as a second language. In M. E. Everson & H. H. Shen (Eds.), *Research among learners of Chinese as a foreign language* (Chinese Language Teachers Association Monograph Series, Vol. 4). (pp. 67–91). Honolulu: University of Hawai'i, National Foreign Language Resource Center.

Chinese as a second language. The purpose was to explore the organization of Chinese learners' mental lexicons and its changes as proficiency developed. More specifically, the representational structures of words with different depths of knowledge and parts of speech were examined in the mental lexicons of learners at different proficiency levels. A word-association test was used, and 90 disyllabic Chinese words with 3 depths of knowledge (familiar, less familiar, and unfamiliar) and 3 parts of speech (nouns, verbs, and adjectives) were used as the stimuli. The depths of knowledge were rated by learners of Chinese from the same pool as the subjects. The results suggest that different depths of word knowledge, parts of speech, and proficiency levels influenced the way that the words were represented and connected in the mental lexicons. The mental lexicons of the learners are suggested to have evolved from sound- to meaning-oriented, which meant that individual words in a mental lexicon were connected in a more organized and meaning-related way as students came to know individual words better while becoming more proficient. However, the shift of sound to meaning exhibited a pattern different from the findings of previous studies on ESL learners.

Implications for vocabulary instruction are discussed. The focuses of vocabulary teaching are suggested to be strategically different when teaching students at different proficiency levels because of the ever-changing word association in their mental lexicons. Teachers should attend to the associational changes to more efficiently facilitate vocabulary learning.

问题的提出和选题意义

问题的缘起

在与留学生的日常交往和教学活动中我们经常会遇到这样的问题：当你说到一个字或词时，学生会马上联想到另一个字或词。如，一初级水平的美国学生在听见"散步"时，问：是不是"打伞"的"伞"？诸如此类的问题还有很多。我们认为，这些现象不仅仅说明汉语同音字词、近义字词较多，给学习者的学习造成了一定的困难，更重要的是，这个简单的词汇联想也许揭示了不同语言水平的第二语言学习者的心理词典和母语者的心理词典在组织方式上的不同。那么，这种组织方式上的差异究竟何在？同时，我们知道，一个学习者对不同的词的掌握程度是不同的，学习者的词汇习得始终是在一个不断深化的过程中，那么，不同掌握程度的词在心理词典中的表征方式有何不同？学习者是如何逐渐习得一个词的不同方面的知识的？这些都是本文所关心的问题。

选题意义

首先，在语言教学和应用语言学研究的领域内，相比语法、语音和话语研究而言，词汇习得在很长一段时间内被二语习得(SLA)研究者们所忽略。Richards (1976) 指出了应用语言学在整体上对词汇习得重视不够而过于注重句法发展的趋势。但在最近的几十年内，第二语言教师逐渐意识到词汇知识对于语法习得、话语理解等的重要性 (Ellis, 1997), SLA研究者对词汇习得的兴趣也与日俱增，有关词汇习得的研究无论在深度还是广度上都明显增长 (Koda, 1997)，词汇教学法也从语言学在词汇研究上的理论进展、以学习者为中心的交际化教学的趋势及心理语言学对心理词典的研究中获益颇丰 (Carter & McCarthy, 1988)。

因此，从二十世纪八十年代中期开始，研究者日益关注词汇习得，关于双语者心理词典、词汇习得、词汇存储、词汇提取及词汇使用的实证研究也逐渐增多。但是，在我们所关心的词汇习得的心理语言学研究中，关于词汇习得、词汇加工的研究要远多于对于词汇表征的研究 (Jiang, 2000)。但任何二语习得的理论都不能缺少"表征"这一环，正如Levelt (1989) 指出，我们无法独立地研究加工和表征。而目前，虽然第二语言词汇习得研究方兴未艾数十年,但我们仍然缺乏一个能够解释第二语言习得过程中词汇发展和表征的特征的模型(Jiang, 2000)。

同时,在关于心理词典的研究领域之内,认知心理学家一直关心的问题是"同一表征"或"独立表征","语音中介"还是"语义中介"。认知心理学家们虽然对双语者的心理词典有较为深入、细致的研究,但能对我们进行二语教学有直接指导作用的,还只是少数。完全以学习汉语的外国留学生为参试者的心理词典研究,目前还不多见。且这些研究大多集中在对静态表征的研究,缺乏对动态的词汇发展过程与词汇表征相结合的研究。而了解处于不同学习阶段的学习者心理词典内部词汇发展的动态过程,对于语言教师来说是非常有益的,因为这能帮助我们判断学生究竟是否习得了这个词汇。习得一个词汇远远不只是知道这个词的意思和词性,Richards (1976) 和Nation (1990, p. 31) 曾详细论述要完全掌握一个词,应该掌握关于该词哪些方面的知识。它们包括该词的口语形式、书面语形式和语法形式的变化,该词的搭配和用法,该词的词频、语域限制、概念和意义及该词与相关词的联系。

如果关于一个词的上述词汇知识都能被掌握,那么学习者就能像母语者一样流利自如地使用这个词。当然,对于母语者来说,他们也不一定完全掌握了他们知道的词的所有上述方面的知识,有很多低频词的上述方面的知识并不是产出型的 (productive),而是接受型的 (receptive)。对于他们掌握得最好的那方面的词,他们的词汇知识处于由接受到产出的渐变线的不同位置上。第二语言学习者也可能掌握不同方面的词汇知识。在形式、意义、语法方面的知识可能最先习得,但在搭配、语域限制等方面的知识可能永远也无法完全习得。虽然如此,上述词汇知识的不同方面只是一个描述性的列表,无法解释学习者习得一个词汇不同方面知识的习得过程,而且也无法解释这些词汇知识之间是如何内在关联的。但是,目前没有一个公认的词汇习得模型 (Schmitt & Meara, 1997),各家也只是分别做了某一方面的研究而没有揭示其中的内在关联。因此,本文研究的目的除了比较不同语言水平的学习者心理词典的异同之外,也希望能在构建一个词汇习得的解释性模型的道路上更进一步。但是,在一个研究中,我们无法探讨所有词汇知识之间的联系,因此本文将研究对象限定在其中的两方面:语法知识和词汇联想知识。

迄今为止,研究者采用了许多不同的方法来探索心理词典的结构和组织,而词汇联想测验是其中相对古老但很直接又简单易操作的一种。从Francis Galton (1879–1880) 使用第一个词汇联想测验开始,母语研究者以及随后的第二语言习得研究者便开始广泛采用这一研究范式。最基本的词汇联想测验就是向参试者呈现一个刺激词,然后让他尽可能快地说出他所想到的第一个词。我们的假设是,这种没有经过深思熟虑所给出的自动反应反映了参试者心理词典中与刺激词联系最强的那些词,因此词汇联想测验也被广泛用于语义记忆的研究当中。通过分析这些联想词,我们能够得到关于心理词典中词汇之间的联系的线索,即心理词典的组织结构。虽然这些联想词不一定都能象语言的其它方面问题那样用既定的规则来解释,但在经历了一个多世纪的研究之后我们对这种行为已经能有较为合理的解释。参试者在联想测验上的行为表现出来的高度的系统性是先前所有研究的起点 (Aitchison, 2003)。在英语母语研究领域,Kent和Rosanoff (1910) 词表是出现较早的一个标准化的词汇联想词表,虽然它最初是用于研究精神病患者的心理词典,但后来的研究者也将其用于对正常人的研究,流传甚广。较有影响的还有Russell和Jenkins (1954) 根据美国明尼苏达大学学生的词汇联想测试编订的联想常模以及Postman & Keppel (1970) 的词汇联想测试常模。有的研究者甚至认为,如果一个关于心理词汇的研究项目没有使用词汇联想测验,那么它将面临一个效度证明的问题 (Singleton, 1999, p. 208)。因此本文决定采用词汇联想测验的范式来研究不同语言水平的参试者对不同掌握程度的词在词汇联想测验上反应的差异,试图发现一些规律化的差异并解释其产生原因。

文献回顾

有关母语词汇联想研究

母语者反应类型"组合—聚合的转变"

一般说来,研究者比较关心词汇联想测验中三种类型的反应:聚合反应 (paradigmatic response)、组合反应 (syntagmatic response) 以及语音反应 (phonological或clang response)。聚合反应指的是那些和刺激词词性相同的反应,如,dog-cat。组合反应是那些与刺激词有线性句法关系或搭配关系的反应,如,dog-bite。而语音反应是那些仅与刺激词语音相近,而没有任何明显的语义关系的反应,如,dog-bog (Nelson, 1977)。许多研究者一致发现,成人的反应大多为聚合反应,而儿童大多为组合反应。在五到九岁的时候,儿童的反应模式逐渐和成人趋于一致,即发生所谓的"组合—聚合转变 (syntagmatic-paradigmatic shift)"。Brown和Berko (1960)、Ervin (1961)、Entwisle (1966) 以及Palermo (1971) 都比较了不同年龄的母语者 (native speakers, NSs) 在反应模式上的差异。这些研究都发现,年龄越大,聚合反应的比例就越高,而语音反应所占的比例逐渐降低。研究者也使用了不同的语言学或心理语言学的理论来解释这些现象。主要的理论有古典的关联理论,认为联想的结果之所以会如此,是因为反应和刺激词经常是一起出现的。但这种理论有其明显的漏洞,因为这虽然能较好地解释组合反应的结果,但很难说明为什么也会存在大量的聚合反应 (Nelson, 1977)。随后出现的还有语言结构理论 (McNeil, 1966)。这一理论是基于 Chomsky (1965)、Katz和Fodor (1963) 的语言理论之上的,认为心理词典中每个词条都是由决定其意义的特征、出现在特定位置的语法优先权以及使用的选择性限制等决定的,而儿童在学习这些词的时候,是逐渐习得这些特征的。Clifton (1967) 进一步将这个理论发展为"基于特征的"(feature-based) 匹配假设,认为组合反应是将语境特征与一个词的内在特征相匹配,而聚合反应则是将一个词与整个集合的特征相匹配。还有的研究者认为这是儿童逐渐学会将心理词典中的词按词类整合归类的结果 (Brown & Berko, 1960s)。也有人认为,这种反应类型的转变只是现有知识的重组或对信息的不同使用的结果,而不是对关于词的句法类别的语义特征的新信息的习得使然,这种变化也许是儿童概念组织 (conceptual organization) 的变化或者仅是对词汇联想作业性质的理解的变化,而词汇联想测验告诉我们的是,在不同的年龄段,与一种概念相关的不同方面的信息在这个时候最为显著 (Nelson, 1977)。

在母语习得的过程中,儿童的认知发展与语言水平的发展是密不可分的,并且前者对后者有很大影响,因此在解释"组合—聚合转变"的时候,研究者很难明确区分,到底是什么原因使然。那么对于认知发展已经比较成熟的第二语言学习者来说,如果也观察到了这一转变,又应该如何解释呢?在接下来的章节中我们将继续讨论这个问题。

母语者对不同词性、词频词反应的差异

先前的研究除了发现年龄对反应类型的影响之外,还发现参试者对不同词性的词的反应也有明显的差异。Brown和Berko (1960) 发现,人们对不同词性的词给出的同类反应 (homogeneous即聚合反应) 按比例由少到多的顺序依次为:形容词、不及物动词、及物动词、副词、名词。Fillenbaum和Jones (1965) 的发现也与此一致。Entwisle (1966) 发现,当刺激词为名词时,所有年龄组的参试者的聚合反应的比例都相当高,而从小学一年级到三年级,参试者对形容词、动词、代词的聚合反应也逐渐增加。这些实验都说明,在母语者的心理词典中,不同词性的词之间的关系紧密程度是不一样的,名词之间的关系最为紧密,而动词、形容词之间的关系则稍微松散 (Hotpof, 1980, 转引自Aitchison, 2003, p. 105),因为名词所受的句法限制较少,而动词和形容词则因其与句子的句法之间关系复杂而使得词之间的关系较为疏散 (Bird, Howard, & Franklin, 2000)。

Deese (1962) 则发现了词频的影响。他发现,组合反应的多少仅与形容词的频率有关,对动词、副词、低频形容词的反应主要由线性句法关系决定。词汇关系在对名词做出反应时更为重要,即高频形容词和名词容易诱发出聚合反应,动词、副词及低频形容词诱发出的组合反应和聚合反应是差不多的。

Stolz和Tiffany (1972) 研究了成人母语者参试者对高频词和低频词的反应。他们认为，如果儿童从无关反应 (unrelated) 到逻辑反应 (即聚合反应) 的变化是因为习得了更多词汇以及它们之间的关系的缘故的话，那么这种变化也应该存在于成人对于熟悉和不熟悉词的形容词的反应当中。他们发现，逻辑反应的比例随熟悉度的增加而增加，但同时，句法反应的比例 (即组合反应) 也增加了，只是无关反应的比例下降了。

这些词汇联想研究的结果说明，母语者的心理词典中词汇的组织方式因词性、词频的不同而不同。那么第二语言学习者情况又如何呢？在不同语言水平的学习者的心理词典中，词性，词频又是如何影响其词汇组织方式的呢？是否还存在其它可能的影响因素呢？第二语言习得的研究者和心理语言学家们在第二语言学习者词汇联想测验上发现了与母语者相似或相异的结果，并以此作为研究第二语言学习者心理词典组织结构的途径之一。

有关第二语言学习者的词汇联想研究

第二语言学习者的心理词典

第二语言学习者在学习过程中，会建立起一个与母语语言系统共存的目的语语言系统。研究者也一直致力于建立一个第二语言的心理词典结构模型，但研究结果并不一致，目前普遍的观点是，第二语言心理词典与第一语言的心理词典基本上是不同的。Channell (1990) 回顾了对第一语言和第二语言的大量研究后总结道："第二言学习者的心理词典与母语者的心理词典相似处极少"。Meara (1982, 1984) 在一项大型的Birbeck (e.g., Meara, 1982, 1984) 项目中进行了一系列的词汇联想测验后认为，"有很好的理由相信，第二语言学习者的心理词典和母语者的心理词典存在显著差异" (Meara, 1984, p. 231; Singleton, 1999, p. 131)。Meara (1984) 指出，第一，母语者心理词典中词汇之间的联结比第二语言学习者的稳定；第二，第二语言学习者心理词典的词汇联结中语音起主导作用；第三，第二语言学习者心理词典中词汇的语义联结呈一种系统性变化的趋势。也有研究者从词汇发展的角度出发，认为学习者的心理词典是处于一个不断发展的过程当中的，学习者和母语者的心理词典并非完全不同，前者在很大程度上受到"词汇知识熟悉度"的影响。这就是Wolter (2001) 所提出的"个体词熟悉度" (Depth of Individual Word Knowledge, DIWK) 模型。反映在词汇联想测验上，即不同的熟悉度的词的词汇联想反应模式呈现出系统性不同，关于这一点，在后面将会更详细地阐述。

第二语言学习者的词汇联想测验研究也力图发现：1.语言水平的变化是否也会如母语者的年龄变化一样，导致"组合-聚合转变"的产生？这种变化的产生是否能做为语言水平提高的一种标志？2.反应类型是否受到词频、词性的影响？3.学习者掌握程度不同的词在词汇联想测验上的反应类型是否有类型化的差异？4.第二语言学习者和母语者对掌握不同熟悉度的词的反应类型异同何在，以及这些反应了二者的心理词典组织结构上的何种差异？需要指出的是，我们做词汇联想研究的最主要的目的，并不仅仅在于观察参试者的反应类型究竟如何，而是在于揭示心理词典中词之间的最真实的无意识联系，并由此帮助我们更好地理解学习者的心理词典。

英语作为第二语言学习者 (ESL) 反应类型的转变

Cunningham (1990) 使用两组以爱尔兰语为第二语言的小学生作为参试者，一组为接受英语输入较多，仅在爱尔兰语课上使用爱尔兰语，另一组则仅在英语课上接受英语输入，其它时间均接受爱尔兰语输入。结果发现，接受目的语输入较多的参试者产生的语音反应较少，而聚合反应则相对较多。

Kudo & Thagard (1999) 对25个日本ESL学习者进行了一次词汇联想测验。实验刺激词表为Kent-Rosanoff (1910) 词表，研究者根据参试者的托福分数将他们分为450分以下组、450－550分组以及550以上组。他们发现，三组之间并不存在显著的组合–聚合转变的差异，所有参试者的聚合反应均多于组合反应，且语音反应非常少。他们认为，这是实验将聚合反应定义太广，组合反应定义太窄的结果，同时他们认为，仅根据组合和聚合反应的分类来研究词汇组织的复杂性有些太过简单。

Söderman (1993) 的研究是一个被后来的研究者广泛引用的研究。实验考察的是参试者对常用词的词汇联想。参试者的母语分别为芬兰语和瑞士语,目的语为英语。实验者按照他们所处的年级将他们按语言水平分为从初级、中级、中高级以及高级四个不同的组。在使用英语常用词的自由联想测验的第一个实验中,对实验结果的组合/聚合反应的方差分析发现,语言水平主效应显著,但后三组之间语言水平主效应不显著,即后三组学习者聚合反应的比例比初级组学习者显著得多,而后三组之间在聚合反应上的差异不大。

这些研究说明,ESL学习者在学习过程中,随语言水平的提高而发生的 "组合-聚合转变" 也许是存在的,但语言水平并非 "组合-聚合转变" 产生的必然原因。

词频对英语作为第二语言学习者 (ESL) 词汇联想反应的影响

Söderman (1993) 的第二个实验使用了由相同数量的高频和低频形容词组成的词表,共64个词。参试者是根据计算机化的Swansea 词汇测验 (Meara, 1990) 的分数选拔出来的28个高级ESL学习者以及相同数量的英语母语者 (NS),他们是大学教师或学生。对组合/聚合反应的方差分析的结果显示,语言水平主效应不显著,ESL和NS的组合反应和聚合反应并没有显著差异。但频率主效应非常显著,两组对低频词的聚合反应比对高频词的显著减少。同时,语言水平和频率的交互作用不显著,即两组参试者在高频/低频词上的组合/聚合反应没有差别。对异常反应的方差分析却发现,语言水平主效应显著,高级ESL所产生的异常反应比NS多得多。频率效应同样非常显著,参试者在低频词上产生的异常反应比高频词要多得多。同时,语言水平和频率的交互作用也很显著,说明两组在高频词上的反应没有显著差异,但在低频词上的反应差异显著。且学习者持异常反应的越多,他们在词汇机上考的成绩就越低。Söderman (1993) 认为,虽然在ESL学习者中发现了反应类型转变存在的证据,但不一定就是学习者语言水平的原因使然,且他认为所谓的 "组合–聚合" 反应的转变在实验结果中体现得并不是非常明确,因为实验发现,高级学习者的反应,特别是对低频词的反应中也存在许多语音及无关反应,而初级学习者的反应中也有相当数量的聚合反应。因此,他认为应将该现象与每个词在心理词典中的发展相联系,而不是将其与心理词典整体的发展相联系。虽然每个词在心理词典中发生转变的时间是不一样的,但所经历的发展路径可能大体相同。词汇联想测验得到的结果只是参试者因对不同词的掌握程度不同而产生不同的反应。因此作者认为 "组合–聚合转变" 这个术语并不适合ESL,而应该使用一个更加普遍的 "反应类型的转变" 的概念,即由语音及无关反应到聚合反应的转变。而且作者不赞同反应类型转变仅仅就是年龄和语言水平变化的结果。但Söderman在文章中并没有说明,这个大体相同的发展路径究竟应该是怎样的。在他的实验二中,他使用的刺激词均为形容词,而没有其它词性的词,因此未能对学习者的心理词典进行更为完整的描述,这都是后继研究值得注意的地方。同时我们认为,利用母语者词频做为二语习得研究中的一个变量是否恰当还有待进一步考证,因为词频的高低并不一定就代表学习者掌握程度的好坏,而如果说反应类型与一个词条被整合到学习者心理词典中的程度有关的话,那么实验变量就应该是整合程度 (或说学习者的掌握程度) 而不是词频。

因此,在Söderman (1993) 假设的基础上,Wolter提出了 "个体词熟悉度" (DIWK, 见图1) 模型 (Wolter, 2001)。该研究继续探讨了每个词的词汇熟悉度与其在词汇联想测验上反应类型的关系,即词汇熟悉度决定特定词被整合到心理词典中去的程度,并体现在词汇联想的反应类型上。作者使用的是听–说法连续 (audio-oral continuous) 词汇联想测验,然后请参试者对刺激词按照VKS (vocabulary knowledge scale, Wesche & Paribakht, 1996) 进行词汇熟悉度评分,并以这个数据结果作为词汇熟悉度的标准。参试者是13名日本ESL参试者以及9个英语NSs。他并没有将ESL的语言水平作为一个变量,ESL参试者的语言水平大体相同。实验发现,从整体上来看,NSs的聚合反应比语音及无关反应要多,词汇联想测验结果的模式和VKS分数的模式相一致,但两组的反应特别是在熟悉词上的反应存在较大差异。首先,两组对不熟悉词 (在VKS测验中分数为1和2的词,简称VKS1, VKS2, 以下类推。) 的反应模式相同; 第二, ESL参试者在中等熟悉的词 (VKS3) 上产生了大量的语音及无关类型的反应; 第三, 在对熟悉词 (VKS5) 的反应中, NSs的组合反应少, 聚合反应多, 而ESL恰好相反。作者发现, 在对熟悉词的反应中, ESL参试者的组合联想所占比例很大, 说明在ESL参试者心理词典中, 组合联想占据主要位置。如果按照先前的观点, 组合主导的心理词典不如聚合主导的心理词典, 那么, 为什么组合联想占心理词典主要位置的学习者也能够成功地使用这些产出型词汇? 这说明第二语言学习者的心理词典只是在结构上与母语者的心理词典有所差异, 但功能上并不一定不如后者。在DIWK模型中, 心理词典被看作是由掌握得很好的"核心词"和处于不同掌握层次的"外围词"共同组成的整体。用它可以清楚地解释词汇联想实验的结果: 心理词典中某个词的词汇联想模式取决于该词所处的位置。位于核心圈的词易形成聚合联想, 距核心圈稍远一点的词易形成组合联想, 而位于外围圈的词易形成语音联想。但这并不意味着处于核心圈的词只有聚合联想, 而是说它的聚合联想比组合联想和语音联想强。同理, 被掌握程度为中等的词可能同时存在组合联想和语音联想, 只不过组合联想比语音联想强。

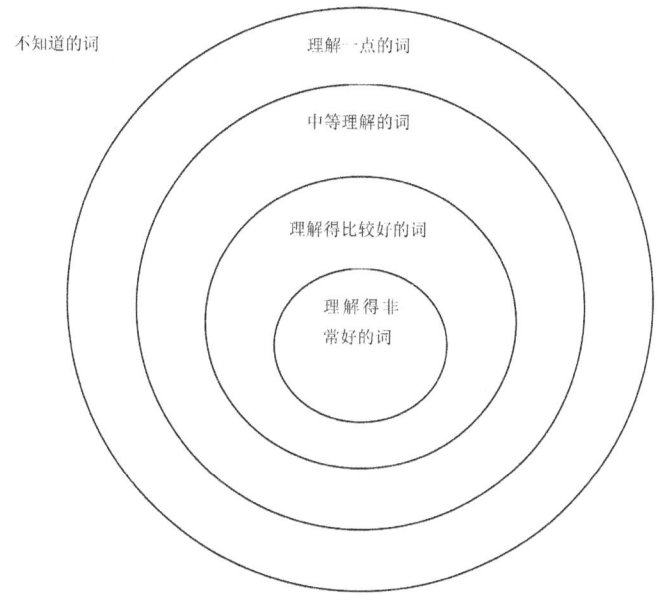

图一. DIWK模型, Wolter (2001)。

同时, Wolter (2001) 还对以前的研究提出了一些质疑。他发现, 过去的研究虽然证明了组合—聚合转变的存在, 但它们几乎都只关注聚合反应比例在不同参试组之间的差异, 而并没有仔细考虑组合反应的问题。早期关于母语儿童词汇发展的研究 (Brown & Berko, 1960; Ervin, 1961; Palermo, 1971; Piper & Leicester, 1980) 几乎对组合反应都没有清楚地界定并对其进行独立的分析。仅有Ervin在他的研究中结合词汇联想测验使用了另一种测验, 即要求不同年龄的参试者从两个规定联想 (一个为组合联想, 另一个为聚合联想) 中选择一个。他发现, 聚合联想随年龄的增大而增加, 但这并不意味着组合反应的减少, 而是语音反应和无关反应的减少。Söderman (1993) 确实清楚地界定并分析了参试者的组合反应, 但各组组合反应的平均比例并不存在显著差异。Wolter认为, 所谓的组合—聚合反应的转变实际上是一个错误的命名, 研究者发现的不过是从语义缺乏到语义丰富的转变。因此, 现有研究并不能证明, 学习者的组合主导的心理词典就不能与母语者的聚合主导的心理词典在同一个水平上运作。为此, 作者提出了一个词汇知识"熟悉度—广度"模型及一个心理词典的发展模型, 即, 在心理词典中, 处于边缘地位的词的词汇熟悉度是决定其在大脑中与其它词联系的关键因素, 而对于那些已经很熟悉的词来说, 词汇量则更为重要。对于母语者和学习者来说, 反应类型是与词汇知识熟悉度息息相关的, 作者认为, 第二语言学习者的心理词典中的每个词是从语音和其它非语义联系主导的状态逐渐向组合

(句法) 或聚合联系主导的状态推进的。需要指出的是, Wolter的研究虽然考察了词汇熟悉度 (在他的文章里称词汇知识深度), 但是, 我们对他得出词汇深度的方法有质疑。根据Wolter (2001), 他的词汇深度的评定是在词汇联想之后立即进行。这样先前的词汇联想不可避免地对深度评定产生影响。比如, 因为实验时间控制得比较严格, 参试者未能在规定时间内对刺激词作出合理联想, 对该词给出语音或者无关反应。但之后参试者又回忆起了这个词, 在随后的深度测验中却将该词评定为"熟悉"。那么这样就有可能会威胁到词汇深度评定的可信度, 最终威胁实验的结果。

词性对ESL反应类型的影响

在目前所见的关于第二语言学习的词汇联想研究中, 很少有将词性作为一个自变量加以研究的, 似乎研究者并不关心心理词典中不同词性的词的表征和习得问题。但基于母语研究我们认为, 词性对于第二语言学习者的反应类型应该是有影响的, 不同词性的词在心理词典中表征应该有所不同。

Piper和Leicester (1980) 发现初级日本ESL、高级日本ESL参试者和英语母语者参试者的平均聚合反应的比例存在显著差异。结果发现, 当刺激词为动词、形容词的时候, 母语者的聚合反应要明显多于高级组, 而高级组的聚合反应又要显著多于初级组参试者。但当刺激词为名词时, 三组参试者的反应没有显著差异。他们认为这说明ESL学习者和母语儿童一样, 较其它词性的词来说, 名词的反应转变发生较早。

综上, 我们发现, 先前所述的影响母语者词汇联想的变量, 如年龄 (语言水平)、词性、词频等, 也是影响第二语言学习者词汇联想的重要变量, 但是, 我们仍然需要澄清一个问题, 即, 母语者的词频并不适用于第二语言学习者。因为无论选词的语料库多么丰富, 也无法确定我们的参试者是否一定认识这些词, 这也是我们本文实验为何要从参试者的现学教材中选取刺激词的原因之一。

关于汉语的词汇联想研究

目前所见的关于汉语词汇联想的研究, 无论是母语者还是第二语言汉语学习者 (CSL) 的, 都屈指可数。还没有看到汉语的象Kent-Rosanoff (1910) 词表那样的一个标准化词表, 或者一个可以参照的词汇联想标准, 词汇联想研究似乎没有受到研究者的关注。Jiang (2002) 应该说是目前所见在汉语作为第二语言习得领域的第一篇关于词汇联想研究的文献。该实验根据自然教学班将参试者分为初级 (10人)、中级 (13人)、中高级 (14人) 及高级 (11人) 四组, 并使用了一个12人的NS组作为对照。刺激词表是作者翻译成中文的Kent-Rosanoff词表。实验方式为听—说形式。结果发现, 聚合反应的比例确实随着语言水平的提高而提高, 但从中级到高级组并没有显著的转变发生, 显著差异只存在于初级组和初级以上组之间, 这与Söderman (1993) 的发现有相似之处。而从初级组到母语组, 语音反应逐渐减少, 但语音反应的比例在各组中都非常之高。先前的实验虽然也观察到了语音反应的存在, 但只是相对很小的一部分。"无关 (other)" 类的反应的情况有些复杂。实验发现, 初级、中级、高级及母语者的无关反应是依次减少的, 但中高级的"无关"类反应却在五组中是最高的。而"无反应 (no response)" 的比例总体上是随着语言水平的提高而降低的。但该实验也存在明显的不足。首先, 实验所用的刺激词均为高频词, 对于所有的参试者来说, 其掌握程度可能相当, 即词汇特征的表征在所有的参试者的心理词典中可能是类似的。而学习者的语言水平逐渐提高, 他们对词的掌握也越好, 因为词汇的掌握不是"全或无 (all or none)" 情况, 学习者对不同的词汇掌握的程度是不同的。这就是所谓的"词汇熟悉度"(可以通过词汇知识量表测量, Wesche & Paribakht, 1996), 研究者认为词汇熟悉度对心理词典中词汇的表征有很大的影响, 如, 学习者在词汇联想测验上对不同词汇的反应类型的不同 (Söderman 1993; Wolter, 2001)。其次, Jiang (2002) 所使用的刺激词基本上是Kent和Rosanoff (1910) 词表的中文翻译, 没有考虑对词汇音节数、平衡词性等无关变量的控制。虽然作者对词表进行了一些处理, 但我们仍然不知道这些词与学习者所学过的词是否相对应, 也许正是因为词表词汇选择的问题才造成测试中"无反应"类反应的出现。且英语母语研究所用的词表应该是无法代替汉语二语习得的词表的。同时,该词表仅仅包含名词和形容词，因此要对学习者的心理词典做一个更全面的描述，仅有这些词性的词还是不够的。其三，研究仅仅计算了不同组不同反应的百分比，但并没有对这些结果做进一步的统计分析，因此我们并不知道，该实验中语言水平及其它变量是否具有统计学意义上的显著效应。基于上述问题，在对词汇熟悉度、词性和学习者与语言水平加以控制的基础上，本文通过词汇联想测验对汉语作为第二语言的学习者的心理词典进行了进一步的研究。

实验研究

实验假设

在前人研究的基础上，本研究试图进一步考察如下问题：

1. 汉语学习者是否也会产生"组合—聚合转变"，以及这一转变是否与语言水平相关？
2. 词汇熟悉度对汉语学习者词汇联想反应的模式是否有系统性的影响，如果有，那么这种影响的表现形式是怎样的？学习者掌握得很好的词和掌握得不好的词在反应模式上有何差异？
3. 不同语言水平的学习者在词汇联想反应模式上是否有显著的差异？
4. 参试者对于不同词性的词的反应模式有何不同？
5. 词性和语言水平是如何共同影响词汇联想的？
6. 这些差异如何反应出不同语言水平的学习者的心理词典的结构差异？

由此提出三点假设：

1. 随着语言水平的提高，语音反应和无关反应逐渐减少，聚合反应和组合反应逐渐增多，但"组合-聚合"的转变不一定会产生，
2. 词汇熟悉度（即Wolter (2001) 所提出的"词汇知识深度"）语言水平和词性都会影响汉语学习者词汇联想反应的模式，学习者的反应模式随这些因素的变化而呈现出系统性的变化。
3. 语言水平不同，心理词典的结构也不同。

方法

实验设计
本研究包括一个参试者间变量（语言水平：初级，中级汉语学习者）和两个参试者内变量（词汇熟悉度：分为1、2、3三个等级；刺激词的词性：名词、动词、形容词）。

参试者
参试者包括北京语言大学速成学院进修系留学生，共22人，分别来自B (初级) /C (中级) 两个语言水平的自然班，每组11人。初级水平学生学习汉语时间为半年左右，中级水平学生学习汉语时间为一年半以上。视力或矫正视力正常。所有参试者均是自愿参加实验，实验结束后获得少量报酬。他们的母语均为拼音文字，分别来自美国、英国、法国、德国、土耳其、瑞士、俄罗斯、加拿大、秘鲁。华裔学生未参加本实验。

实验材料
所有的刺激词分为两部分，一部分从北京语言大学速成学院2004年秋季二十周班所使用的教材（北京语言大学出版社《汉语口语速成：基础篇/提高篇》、《速成汉语初级教程：综合课本》、《汉语听力速成：基础篇/提高篇》）中选出，另一部分是[汉语水平考试汉字和词汇等级大纲]的丙丁级词汇，这是为了保证进行词汇熟悉度评定的词中既有学生熟悉的词，也有学生完全不熟悉的词。

首先我们选取了共300个汉语双音节合成词作为词汇熟悉度评定的刺激词，其中，名词、动词、形容词各100个。这300个词先由与本研究的参试者来自同一学习环境的另一组学生进

行词汇熟悉度的评定。这些学生亦来自北京语言大学速成学院进修系B (初级组) /C (中级组) 两个语言水平的自然班,包括初级组学生15人,中级组学生12人。他们的母语均为拼音文字。因为所需进行词汇熟悉度评定的词数量较多,因此分为三次评定。每次100个词,时间为半个小时。根据词汇熟悉度量表 (见表2) ,学生在规定的时间内完成对所给词的评定。

在词汇熟悉度评定结束后,实验者统计每个学生评定的每个词词汇熟悉度的结果,取学生对每个词的评分的平均值,然后根据平均值将这些词分为三个等级 (等级标准的描述见后)。随后,在每个等级中随机选择三种词性的词各10个。这样一共生成90个刺激词,这些词即用于词汇联想测验的刺激词 (见表一)。

表一. 词汇联想测验刺激词分配表

词汇熟悉度等级	名词 (个)	动词 (个)	形容词 (个)
VKS1不熟悉词	10	10	10
VKS2较熟悉词	10	10	10
VKS3熟悉词	10	10	10

与先前的研究相比,在与刺激词有关的变量的控制上,本文采用更为严格和科学的步骤。首先,我们选择的都是双音节词,这样就避免了由于词汇音节多少这样的无关变量对实验带来的可能的影响。其次,本文考察了不同词性的影响,这是先前第二语言的词汇联想研究所没有研究的问题。Söderman (1993) 的实验二的刺激词全部是形容词,但是在形容词上得到的结果未必能推广到其它的词性上去。

其次本文考虑到了不同熟悉度对参试者词汇联想的可能的影响。刺激词部分为参试者的教科书中已学词汇,部分为未学词汇,同时,我们根据词汇熟悉度评定的结果作为我们界定词汇熟悉度的标准,这样保证了我们对词汇熟悉度这一变量的界定的有效性。

分类标准

词汇熟悉度量表的等级描述和分级标准

Wesche & Paribakht (1996) 将学习者自我报告用的Vocabulary Knowledge Scale (VKS词汇知识量表) 分为五个等级:

VKS1: 我不记得曾经我学过这个词。

VKS2: 我以前见过这个词,但是我不知道它的意思。

VKS3: 我以前见过这个词,我想它的意思是 (请给出同义词或者翻译)。

VKS4: 我认识这个词,它的意思是 (请给出同义词或者翻译)。

VKS5: 我能用这个词造句

(如果选做这一部分,请同时也给出同义词或者翻译)。

同时他们对分数做出了解释:

VKS1: 学习者完全不认识这个词。

VKS2: 这个词看起来熟悉但是不知道它的意思。

VKS3: 学习者能正确地给出它的同义词或翻译。

VKS4: 学习者能在一个句子中恰当地运用这个词的语义。

VKS5: 学习者在一个句子里正确地运用了这个词的语义,而且没有语法错误。

本人在暑假的预测实验中采用了这个标准。参试者为某大学暑期项目二年级 (8人) 和三年级 (10人) 的美国学生。刺激词均为当时所用教材中出现的所学过的词,选择标准及方法与本文"实验材料"部分所述相同。预测实验结果显示，VKS的五级分类过于细致，我们发现反应在学生提交的问卷中，几乎很少出现如Wesche和Paribakht (1996)中所提出的VKS3及VKS4级的词。学生的答卷显示，出现最多的情况是VKS2，即似曾相识，但无法唤起词义，而学生一旦唤起一词的词义，那么就能够基本正确地使用该词。因此，我们在此将词汇知识评定量表稍做调整，简化为三个等级：

表二. 词汇知识评定量表

熟悉度等级	评分	等级描述
不熟悉	1	我完全不认识这个词
较熟悉	2	我见过这个词，但是我不记得它是什么意思
熟 悉	3	我认识这个词，我可以用它造句(或组成短语)

如上文所述，在词汇熟悉度评定结束之后，我们先将所有学生对每个词词汇熟悉度的评分取平均值，然后按照四舍五入的原则，将所有的词分成三个等级。

词汇联想测验的反应类型的分类标准

前人对词汇联想反应的分类已有既定的标准，即，聚合反应指的是那些和刺激词属于同一个词类的反应，如，dog-cat；组合反应是那些与刺激词有线性句法关系或搭配关系的反应，如，dog-bite；语音反应是那些仅与刺激词语音相近，而没有任何明显的语义关系的反应，如，dog-bog；无关反应是那些与刺激词既无语意联系，也没有语音联系的反应 (Nelson, 1977)。

在采取该标准之外，考虑到汉语词汇的特殊性质 (双/多音节)，参考Jiang (2002) 我们还预测了几种可能的情况 (因本实验所用的刺激词均为双字词，故在此我们将一个词的第一个字称为前字，第二个字成为后字。)：

根据前字或后字的音进行联想，例如：彩色—菜单，合唱—非常，等；我们将此类归入语音 (clang) 反应。

根据前字或后字的意进行联想的，例如：水饺—杯子等；我们将此类归入无关 (other) 反应。

施测过程

实验采取个别测试的方式进行。在一段指导语和三到五次练习之后，主试将90个词以听觉形式呈现给参试者，并要求他们尽可能快地 (10秒之内) 说出所想到的第一个词，参试者所有的反应均被录音。超过10秒的反应均计为无效反应。

实验设备

Toshiba Satellite 2410手提电脑一台。所有刺激词均事先录制在电脑中，在实测过程中通过Windows Media Player播放给参试者。

实验结果

聚合反应

参试者对不同熟悉度、不同词性的词的聚合反应的百分比见表三和图二。

表三. 参试者对不同熟悉度、不同词性的刺激词的聚合反应的百分比表

	不熟悉词 (30个)			较熟悉词 (30个)			熟悉词 (30个)		
	名词	动词	形容词	名词	动词	形容词	名词	动词	形容词
初级	2%	0	4%	31%	16%	13%	25%	31%	34%
中级	17%	16%	13%	42%	25%	34%	62%	41%	46%

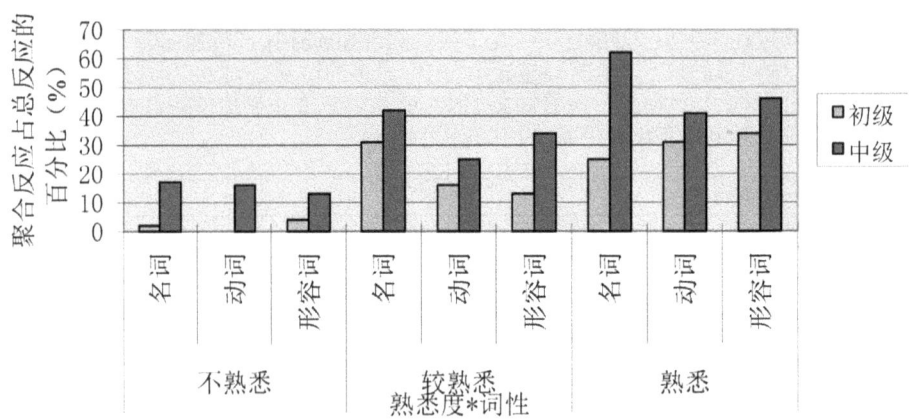

图二. 参试者对不同熟悉度、不同词性的刺激词的聚合反应。

方差分析结果显示,词汇熟悉度主效应显著 [$F(2, 40)=50.425, p<.01$]。事后多重比较结果显示,不熟悉词,较熟悉词以及熟悉词三者的两两之间的差异均达到显著水平 ($p=.001, .001, .002$),从不熟悉到熟悉词,聚合反应的数量显著增多。

词性主效应显著 [$F(2, 40)=11.704, p<.01$]。事后多重比较结果显示,在所诱发出的聚合反应的数量上,名词与动词,动词与形容词,动词与形容词三者两两之间的差异也达到显著水平 ($p=.001, .017, .018$),参试者在名词上产生的聚合反应最多,其次为形容词,最后为动词。且名词和动词之间的聚合反应的差异比动词与形容词之间的差异要大。

语言水平主效应显著 [$F(1, 20)=12.929, p<.01$]。这表明两个语言水平的参试者产生的聚合反应在数量上有显著差异,中级水平的参试者聚合反应显著多于初级水平参试者。

词汇熟悉度和语言水平交互作用不显著 [$F(2, 40)=0.628, p>.05$]。这说明,熟悉度对两组参试者产生聚合反应的影响模式是相同的。无论是初级还是中级参试者,聚合反应的数量都随词汇熟悉度的提高而增多。

词性和语言水平交互作用显著 [$F(2, 40)=3.597, p<.05$]。词性在两个语言水平上的简单效应分析发现,词性的影响只在中级组水平上显著 [$F(2, 40)=14.14, p<.01$],中级组产生聚合反应由多到少的顺序为:名词>形容词>动词,而事后多重比较结果显示,名词和动词之间,名词和形容词之间差异显著 ($p=.001, .017$),说明由名词诱发出来的聚合反应都显著多于形容词和动词。而动词和形容词之间的差异并不显著 ($p=.767$),说明由形容词诱发出的聚合反应并没有显著多于动词的。初级组对三种词性的刺激词产生的聚合反应并没有显著差异 [$F(2, 40)=1.16, p>.05$]。

词汇熟悉度和词性交互作用显著 [$F(4, 80)=3.187, p<.01$]。词汇熟悉度在词性三个水平上的简单效应分析发现,在词性的三个水平上,词汇熟悉度的简单效应均达到显著水平 [$F(2, 42)=39.12, p<.01; F(2, 42)=27.01, p<.01; F(2, 42)=23.76, p<.01$]。而词性在词汇熟悉度三个水平上的简单效应分析发现,当刺激词为不熟悉词和熟悉词时,词性的作用不显著 [$F(2, 42)=0.28, p>.05; F(2, 42)=1.58, p>.05$]。只有当刺激词为较熟悉词时,词性的作用才达到显著性水平 [$F(2, 42)=13.39, p<.01$]。

词汇熟悉度,词性和语言水平三因素交互作用显著 [$F(4, 80)=5.121, p<.01$]。简单效应分析发现:

当刺激词为不熟悉词时,无论是名词、动词还是形容词,语言水平的简单效应均达到显著水平 [$F(1, 20)=19.013, p<.01; F(1, 20)=14.336, p<.01; F(1, 20)=7.143, p<.05$],中级水平参试者对低熟悉度的三种词性的产生的聚合反应均比初级水平参试者要多。

当刺激词为较熟悉词时, 对于形容词来说, 两个语言水平的参试者的聚合反应在数量上的差异达到显著水平 [$F(1, 20)=6.799, p<.05$], 中级水平参试者产生的聚合反应显著多于初级水平参试者。对于名词和动词来说, 两个语言水平的参试者产生的聚合反应在数量上的差异都不显著 [$F(1, 20)=2.939, p>.05; F(1, 20)=1.845, p>.05$]。

当刺激词为熟悉词时, 对于名词来说, 两个语言水平参试者的聚合反应在数量上的差异达到显著水平 [$F(1, 20)=36.036, p<.01$], 在该水平上, 中级水平的参试者产生的聚合反应显著多于初级水平参试者。而当刺激词为动词和形容词时, 两个语言水平的参试者产生的聚合反应在数量上的差异都不显著 [$F(1, 20)=1.378, p>.05; F(1, 20)=1.604, p>.05$]。

综上所述, 随着熟悉度的提高, 两组参试者的聚合反应都显著增多, 中级水平的参试者产生的聚合反应比初级水平的显著要多。词性对中级水平的参试者有显著的影响, 中级水平的参试者对名词产生的聚合反应比对动词和形容词的要多, 而词性对初级水平的参试者没有显著的影响。当刺激词为不熟悉词时, 中级水平的参试者对三种词性的刺激词的聚合反应比初级水平的参试者显著要多; 当刺激词为较熟悉的词时, 中级水平的参试者仅在形容词比初级水平的多, 而他们对于名词和动词的聚合反应没有显著差异; 当刺激词为熟悉词时, 中级水平的参试者对名词的聚合反应比初级水平参试者显著要多, 而对动词和形容词的聚合反应没有显著差异。

组合反应

参试者对不同熟悉度、不同词性的词的组合反应的百分比见表四和图三。

表四. 参试者对不同熟悉度、不同词性的刺激词的组合反应的百分比表 (%)

	不熟悉词 (30个)			较熟悉词 (30个)			熟悉词 (30个)		
	名词	动词	形容词	名词	动词	形容词	名词	动词	形容词
初级	0%	0%	1.8%	35%	29%	30%	41%	40%	51%
中级	6.3%	11%	8%	12%	33%	12%	28%	29%	39%

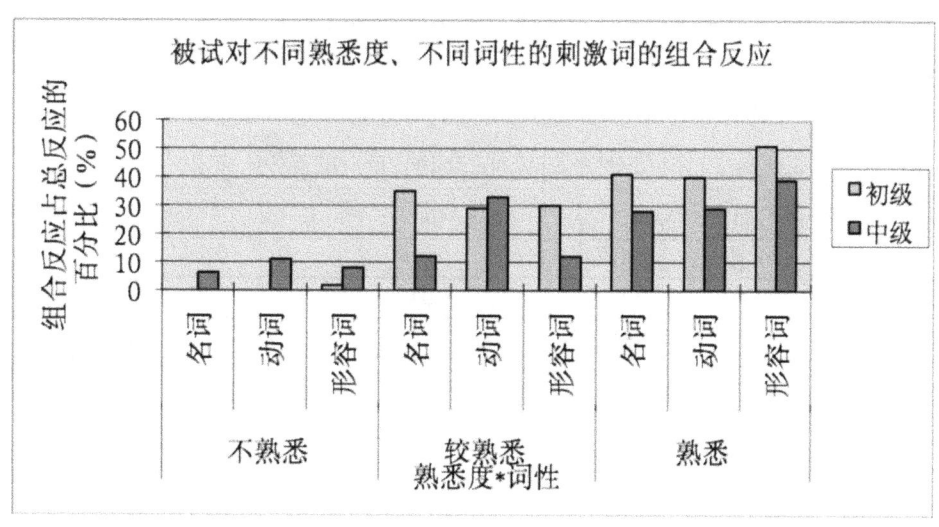

图三: 参试者对不同熟悉度、不同词性的刺激词的组合反应

图三. 参试者对不同熟悉度、不同词性的刺激词的组合反应。

方差分析显示:

词汇熟悉度主效应显著 [$F(2, 40)=77.003, p<.01$]。事后多重比较结果显示, 在组合反应的数量上, 不熟悉词, 较熟悉词以及熟悉词三者的两两之间的差异均达到显著水平 ($p=.001, .001, .002$), 从不熟悉到熟悉词, 组合反应的数量显著增多。

词性主效应不显著 [$F(2, 40)=0.988, p>.05$]。事后多重比较结果显示, 名词, 动词, 形容词三者两两之间的差异均没有达到显著水平 ($p>.05$)。

语言水平主效应不显著 [$F(1, 20)=1.180, p>.05$]。说明两个语言水平的参试者产生的组合反应在数量上没有显著差异。

词汇熟悉度和语言水平交互作用显著 [$F(2, 40)=9.016, p<.01$]。参试者组内变量"词汇熟悉度"在参试者组间变量"语言水平"两个水平上的简单效应分析发现: 词汇熟悉度的简单效应在语言水平的两个水平上均达到显著水平 [$F(2, 40)=67.04, p<.01; F(2, 40)=18.98, p<.01$]. 语言水平在词汇熟悉度三个水平上的简单效应分析发现, 仅当刺激词为不熟悉词的时候, 中级水平参试者的组合反应才显著多于初级水平参试者 [$F(1, 20)=4.94, p<.05$], 而当刺激词为较熟悉词和熟悉词时, 两组的组合反应并没有显著差异 [$F(1, 20)=3.75, p>.05; F(1, 20)=2.71, p>.05$]。

词性和语言水平交互作用不显著 [$F(2, 40)=2.278, p>.05$]。说明词性不同, 对两个语言水平的参试者产生的组合反应的数量没有显著影响。

词汇熟悉度和词性交互作用显著 [$F(4, 80)=3.486, p<.05$]。词汇熟悉度在词性三个水平上的简单效应分析发现, 在词性的三个水平上, 词汇熟悉度的简单效应均达到显著水平 [$F(2, 42)=28.05, p<.01; F(2, 42)=21.88, p<.01; F(2, 42)=37.15, p<.01$]。事后多重比较结果显示, 不熟悉词, 较熟悉词和熟悉词之间的差异均达到显著水平 ($p=.001, .001, .001$)。

词汇熟悉度, 词性和语言水平三因素交互作用不显著 [$F(4, 80)=1.669, p>.05$]。

总而言之, 随着参试者对刺激词熟悉度的提高, 组合反应的数量显著增多, 组合反应并没有随语言水平的提高而增多。仅当刺激词为不熟悉词时, 中级水平参试者的组合反应才显著多于初级水平参试者, 而当刺激词为较熟悉和熟悉词时, 两个语言水平参参试者的差异不显著。词性对组合反应的产生影响没有达到显著水平。

语音反应

参试者对不同熟悉度、不同词性的词的语音的百分比见表五和图四。

表五. 参试者对不同熟悉度、不同词性的刺激词产生语音反应的百分比表 (%)

	不熟悉词 (30个)			较熟悉词 (30个)			熟悉词 (30个)		
	名词	动词	形容词	名词	动词	形容词	名词	动词	形容词
初级	33%	63%	23%	12%	9%	18%	14%	5%	7%
中级	39%	36%	49%	28%	21%	34%	9%	20%	11%

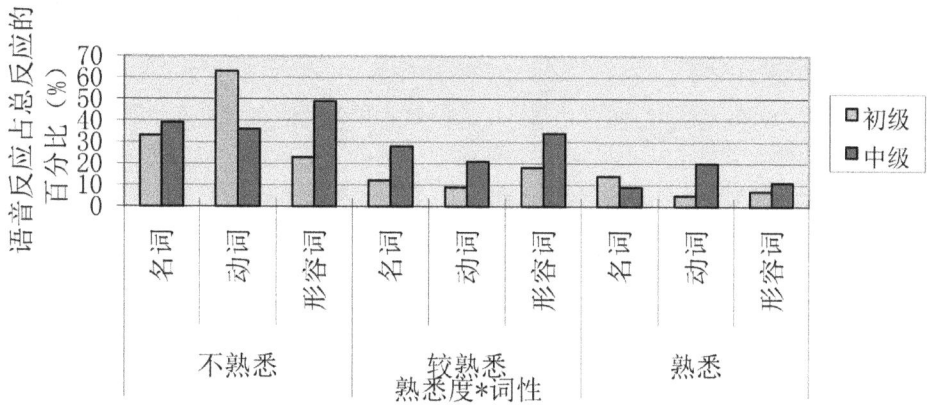

图四. 参试者对不同熟悉度、不同词性的刺激词的语音反应。

方差分析显示:

词汇熟悉度主效应显著 [$F(2, 40)=42.829, p=.001<.05$]。事后多重比较结果显示, 在所诱发出语音反应的数量上, 不熟悉词, 较熟悉词以及熟悉词三者的两两之间的差异均达到显著水平 ($p=.001, .001, .037$), 两组的语音反应在熟悉词上是最少的, 而在不熟悉词和熟悉词上的语音反应多于熟悉词。

词性主效应不显著 [$F(2, 40)=0.864, p=.429>.05$]。事后多重比较结果显示, 在所诱发出的语音反应的数量上, 名词, 动词, 形容词三者两两之间的差异均没有达到显著水平。

语言水平主效应不显著 [$F(1, 20)=1.193, p=.288>.05$]。说明两个语言水平的参试者产生的语音反应在数量上没有显著差异。

词汇熟悉度和语言水平交互作用不显著 [$F(2, 40)=2.003, p=.148>.05$]。这说明, 熟悉度对两组参试者产生语音反应的影响模式是相同的。当刺激词为不熟悉词和刺激词时参试者产生的语音反应均显著多于当刺激词为较熟悉词时的语音反应。词性和语言水平交互作用显著 [$F(2, 40)=4.696, p=.015<.05$]。词性在两个语言水平上的简单效应分析发现, 词性变量仅在初级水平上达到显著性水平 [$F(1, 20)=3.80, p<.05$], 结合图四我们发现, 初级组产生语音反应由多到少的顺序为: 形容词>动词>名词。事后多重比较结果显示, 名词和动词之间, 名词和形容词之间差异显著 ($p=.001, .017$), 说明由名词诱发出来的语音反应都显著多于形容词和动词。而动词和形容词之间的差异并不显著 ($p=.767$), 说明由形容词诱发出的语音反应并没有显著多于动词。词性变量在中级水平上不显著 [$F(2, 40)=1.76, p>.05$]。说明中级组在三类词上产生的语音反应并没有显著差异。语言水平在词性三个水平上的简单效应分析发现, 两组在三种词性水平上产生的语音反应两两之间均没有显著差异 [$F(1, 20)=0.06, p>.05; F(1, 20)=2.79, p>.05; F(1, 20)=1.63, p>.05$]。

词汇熟悉度和词性交互作用显著 [$F(4, 80)=5.56, p<.01$]。词汇熟悉度在词性三个水平上的简单效应分析发现, 在词性的三个水平上, 词汇熟悉度的简单效应均达到显著水平 [$F(2, 42)=15.49, p<.01; F(2, 42)=24.51, p<.01; F(2, 42)=15.74, p<.01$]。而词性在词汇熟悉度三个水平上的简单效应分析发现, 当刺激词为不熟悉词和熟悉词时, 词性的作用不显著 [$F(2, 42)=2.56, p>.05; F(2, 42)=0.51, p>.05$]。只有当刺激词为较熟悉词时, 词性的作用才达到显著性水平 [$F(2, 42)=8.21, p<.05$]。词汇熟悉度, 词性和语言水平三因素交互作用显著 [$F(4, 80)=10.372, p<.05$]。

对语言水平的简单效应分析发现:

当刺激词为不熟悉词时, 对于动词和形容词来说, 两个语言水平的参试者产生的语音反应在数量上的差异均达到显著水平 [$F(1, 20)=4.878, p<.05; F(1, 20)=5.343, p<.05$]。当刺激词

为不熟悉的动词时,中级水平参试者对低熟悉度产生的语音反应显著少于初级水平参试者,而当刺激词为形容词时,中级水平参试者产生的语音反应显著多于初级水平的参试者。而当刺激词为名词时,两者之间的差异不显著。

当刺激词为较熟悉词时,两个语言水平的参试者语音反应在词性变量的三个水平上的差异均未达到显著水平 [$F(1, 20)=2.852, p>.05$; $F(1, 20)=1.68, p>.05$; $F(1, 20)=3.049, p > .05$]。

当刺激词为熟悉时,对于动词来说,两个语言水平参试者语音反应在数量上的差异达到显著水平 [$F(1, 20)=6.784, p<.05$],中级水平参试者产生的语音反应显著多于初级水平参试者。而当刺激词为名词和形容词时,两个语言水平的参试者产生的聚合反应在数量上的差异并不显著 [$F(1, 20)=0.893, p>.05$; $F(1, 20)=0.69, p>.05$]。

综上所述,随着参试者语言水平的提高,语音反应并没有显著增多或减少。词性显著地影响了初级水平参试者产生语音反应,他们对形容词产生的语音反应最多,其次为动词和名词。但没有影响到中级水平的参试者。当刺激词为不熟悉词时,初级水平参试者在动词上的语音反应比中级水平的要多,而中级水平参试者在形容词上的语音反应比初级水平的多,两个语言水平的参试者在对名词的语音反应上没有差异。当刺激词为较熟悉词时,词性对两个语言水平的参试者的反应没有影响。当刺激词为熟悉词时,中级水平参试者在动词上的语音反应比初级水平参试者要多,而两者在形容词和名词的反应上没有显著差别。

无关反应

参试者对不同熟悉度、不同词性的词的语音的百分比见表六和图五。

表六. 参试者对不同熟悉度、不同词性的刺激词上产生无关反应的百分比表 (%)

	不熟悉词 (30个)			较熟悉词 (30个)			熟悉词 (30个)		
	名词	动词	形容词	名词	动词	形容词	名词	动词	形容词
初级	65%	37%	72%	22%	45%	39%	20%	25%	8%
中级	37%	36%	30%	18%	21%	21%	0.9%	10%	3.6%

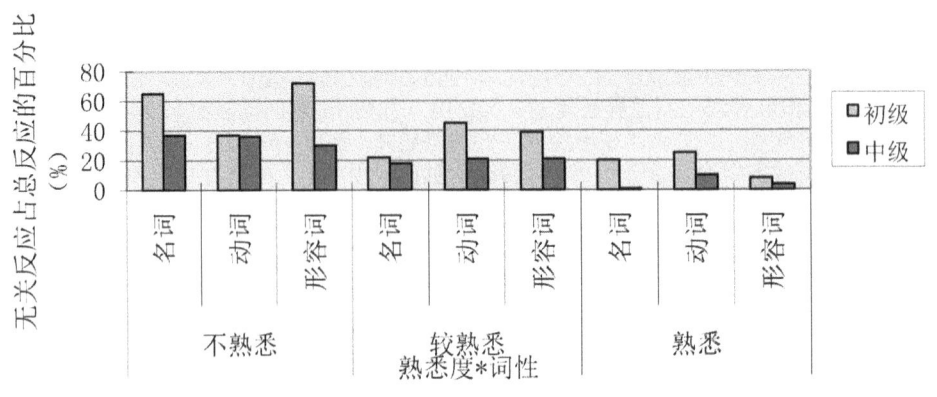

图五. 参试者对不同熟悉度、不同词性的刺激词的无关反应。

方差分析发现:

词汇熟悉度主效应显著 [$F(2, 40)=64.688, p<.01$]。事后多重比较结果显示,在所诱发出无关反应的数量上,不熟悉词,较熟悉词以及熟悉词三者的两两之间的差异均达到显著水平 ($p=.001, .001, .002$),从不熟悉到熟悉词,无关反应的数量显著减少。

词性主效应不显著 [$F(2, 40)=1.85, p>.05$]。事后多重比较结果显示，在所诱发出的无关反应的数量上，名词，动词，形容词三者两两之间的差异均未达到显著水平。

语言水平主效应显著 [$F(1, 20)=12.006, p<.01$]。说明两个语言水平的参试者产生的无关反应在数量上有显著差异，中级水平参试者的无关反应显著少于初级水平参试者。

词汇熟悉度和语言水平交互作用不显著 [$F(2, 40)=1.685, p >.05$]。这说明，熟悉度对两组参试者产生无关反应的影响模式是相同的。参试者给出无关反应的多少随词汇熟悉度的提高而减少。

词性和语言水平交互作用不显著 [$F(2, 40)=0.765, p>.05$]。这说明，词性对两个语言水平的参试者在产生无关反应时的影响模式是相同的。

词汇熟悉度和词性交互作用显著 [$F(4, 80)=7.080, p<.01$]。词汇熟悉度在词性三个水平上的简单效应分析发现，在词性的三个水平上，词汇熟悉度的简单效应均达到显著水平 [$F(2, 42)=41.58, p<.01; F(2, 42)=7.58, p<.01; F(2, 42)=32.34, p<.01$]。而词性在词汇熟悉度三个水平上的简单效应分析发现，当刺激词为不熟悉词和熟悉词时，词性的作用不显著 [$F(2, 42)=3.04, p>.05; F(2, 42)=3.21, p >.05$]。只有当刺激词为较熟悉词时，词性的作用才达到显著性水平 [$F(2, 42)=4.87, p<.05$]。

词汇熟悉度，词性和语言水平三因素交互作用显著 [$F(4, 80)=6.742, p<.05$]。对语言水平的简单效应分析发现：

当刺激词为不熟悉词时，对于名词、形容词来说，两个语言水平的参试者产生的无关反应在数量上的差异均达到显著水平 [$F(1, 20)=9.610, p<.01; F(1, 20)=16.079, p<.01$]，中级水平参试者对低熟悉度的名词和形容词产生的无关反应均比初级水平参试者显著要少。对于动词来说，两个语言水平的参试者所产生的无关反应并没有显著差异 [$F(1, 20)=0.06, p>.05$].

当刺激词为较熟悉的词时，对于名词和形容词来说，两个语言水平的参试者无关反应在数量上的差异并没有达到显著水平 [$F(1, 20)=0.352, p>.05; F(1, 20)=3.960, p>.05$]。对于动词来说，两个语言水平的参试者产生的无关反应在数量上的差异达到显著水平 [$F(1, 20)=8.322, p<.01$]，初级水平参试者产生的无关反应要显著多于中级水平参试者。

当刺激词为熟悉词时，对于名词来说，两个语言水平的参试者的无关反应在数量上的差异达到显著水平 [$F(1, 20)=36.750, p<.01$]，在该水平上，中级水平参试者产生的无关反应显著少于初级水平参试者。而对于动词和形容词来说，两个语言水平的参试者产生的无关反应在数量上的差异并不显著 [$F(1, 20)=2.357, p>.05; F(1, 20)=1.866, p>.05$]。

上述的数据表明，无关反应随词汇熟悉度的加深而显著减少，且初级水平参试者产生的无关反应比中级水平参试者产生的无关反应显著要多。但词性对两个语言水平参试者产生无关反应没有显著影响。当刺激词为不熟悉词时，初级水平参试者在名词和形容词上产生的无关反应比中级水平参试者显著要多，但两组在对动词的无关反应上没有显著差异。当刺激词为较熟悉词时，初级水平参试者对动词的无关反应显著多于中级水平的参试者，但两组在对名词和形容词的无关反应上没有显著差异。当刺激词为熟悉词时，两组在对名词的反应上差异达到显著水平，初级水平的参试者显著多于中级水平的参试者，但他们在对动词和形容词的反应上没有显著差别。

讨论

语言水平对反应类型的影响

本研究的结果并不支持前人所提出的随语言水平 (年龄) 的提高而产生"组合-聚合的转变"这一观点。从对聚合反应的分析我们可以看出，虽然中级组参试者试的聚合反应比初级组的显著要多，但初级组参试者的组合反应并没有显著的多于中级组，换句话说，中级组参试者虽然产生了大量的聚合反应，但是同时也产生了大量的组合反应，组合反应并没有随语言水平的提高而减少。减少的是无关反应。而过去的学者认为存在"组合-聚合的转变"是因为: 第一, 实验范式的差异。在前人关于"组合–聚合转变"的文献中, 使用的都是"自由联想"的实验范式, 而我们的实验采用的是"控制联想"的范式。第二, 对反应类型分类方法的差异。Brown & Berko (1960) 对反应的分类只有两种: Homogeneous (同质反应) 和Heterogeneous (异质反应)。即, 他们并不关心除这两类反应之外的其它反应, 或是这两类反应本身定义太广, 无法观察到其它不同质的反应的存在。而参考前人的研究, 我们的实验将反应分为了四类。

本研究的结果部分证明了两个互相关联的观点: Ervin (1961), Wolter (2001) 分别认为: 聚合联想随年龄的增大而增加, 但这并不意味着组合反应的减少, 而是包括语音反应和无关无意义反应的减少; "组合–聚合转变"这一术语的存在的价值值得怀疑。通过实验我们也认为, 这一转变并不能够证明学习者语言水平的提高, 其一, 参试者产生的反应是多样的, 不仅只有组合和聚合反应; 其二, 聚合反应随语言水平的提高, 其原因也是多样的, 不一定就是组合反应的减少, 事实上我们的结果也证明, 组合反应并没有随语言水平的提高而减少, 随语言水平的提高而显著减少的是无关反应。聚合和组合反应的增加, 无关反应的逐渐减少, 说明学习者的心理词典学习者由一个杂乱无章的结构逐渐进化为一个意义主导的结构。值得一提的是, 如前文所述, Meara (1982, 1984) 认为: 其一, 母语者心理词典的词汇联结比第二语言学习者心理词典的词汇联结稳定; 其二, 与母语者相比较, 第二语言学习者心理词典的组织中语音起主导作用; 其三, 与母语者相比较, 第二语言学习者心理词典中词汇的语义联结呈一种系统性变化的趋势。我们同意Meara (1984) 的第一条和第三条观点, 但是对于汉语词汇联想测验来说, "语音主导"是否适用呢? Jiang (2002) 观察到了大量的语音反应的存在, 在他的实验中, 语音反应随语言水平的提高而减少, 但我们无从得知, 在这种下降的趋势中, 语言水平的主效应是否显著。而在本实验中, 语音反应并没有随语言水平的提高而减少, 相反, 中级组参试者的语音反应要多于初级组参试者, 但是这种差异并没有达到显著水平。这种语音反应增加的现象是我们所预料到的。随着语言水平的提高, 学习者的心理词典中积累的词汇就越多, 而汉语有别于英语及其它语言的独特性之一在于, 汉语中存在着大量的同音字 (词)。因此, 在学习者能够很好地区分同音字 (词) 之前, 语言水平越高, 其产生语音反应的可能就越大。但是我们认为, 随着语言水平的进一步提高, 学习者有了区分同音字 (词) 的自觉和能力, 这种语音反应大量存在的现象便会消失。但这也是本实验的遗憾之一, 我们如能增设一个高级组, 可能会观察到, 语音反应会在中级组时达到最高, 而初级组和高级组均不如中级组的语音反应多, 语音反应线状图呈一个三角形状。但是由于条件限制, 我们未能进行这一步实验。

综上所述, 我们认为, 在汉语词汇联想测验中, 聚合反应随语言水平的提高而显著增多, 无关反应显著减少, 这说明学习者的心理词典由一个杂乱无章的结构逐渐进化为一个意义主导的结构。语音反应随语言水平的提高而提高, 虽然没有达到显著水平, 但也说明在中级阶段, 区分同音字 (词) 仍是学习者面临的一大难题, 也说明对于汉语学习者来说, 随着语言水平的提高, 心理词典的结构并不是如英语学习者的那样, 由语音主导进化为意义主导, 出现的语音反应的波峰是汉语学习者在语言水平提高过程中的必经之路。

因此, 根据本文对汉语词汇联想的结果, 我们对Wolter (2001) 的DIWK模型稍做改动: 处于核心圈内的熟悉词词容易产生聚合联想, 而距核心圈最外围的不熟悉词则容易产生无关联想, 处于核心和外围之间的较为熟悉的词, 产生的组合联想和语音联想的可能都很大, 如图六所示:

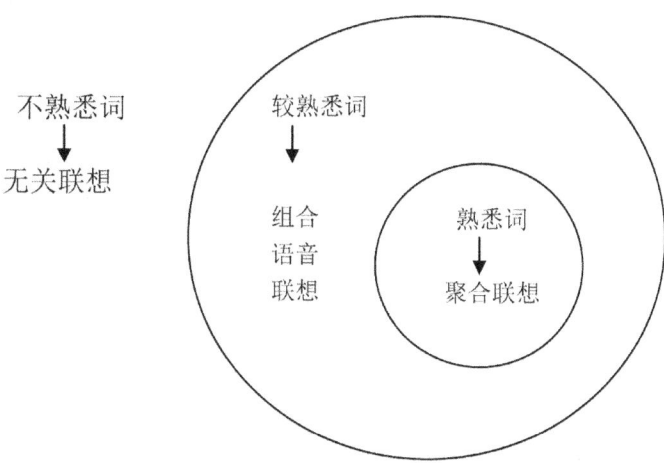

图六. 对DIWK模型的改进。

词汇熟悉度对反应类型的影响

综合参试者对不熟悉的刺激词的反应结果我们发现, 在面对不熟悉的刺激词时, 两个语言水平的参试者产生聚合反应、组合反应和无关反应的模式是大体相同的, 即, 随着语言水平的提高, 聚合和组合反应显著增多而无关反应显著减少。但随着参试者语言水平的提高, 语音反应并没有显著增多或减少。

而对于较熟悉的刺激词, 反应模式发生了一些变化: 随着语言水平的提高, 聚合反应显著增多, 无关反应显著减少, 但两个语言水平的参试者的组合反应和语音反应没有显著差别。

当刺激词为熟悉词时, 随着语言水平的提高, 聚合反应显著增多, 无关反应显著减少, 但两个语言水平的参试者的组合反应和语音反应没有显著差别。这与较熟悉词的情况是完全相同的。

我们的结果与Söderman (1993) 及Wolter (2001) 的不完全相同。首先, Söderman发现, 在产生聚合和组合反应时, 语言水平和频率的交互作用并不显著, 两组参试者在对高频/低频词产生组合/聚合反应的方式上并无区别, 而我们发现, 当刺激词为不熟悉的刺激词时, 中级水平的参试者的聚合反应和组合反应比初级水平的参试者显著要多。

我们在无关反应上得到的结果与Söderman (1993) 也不完全相似。我们没有如Söderman那样发现语言水平与词汇熟悉度之间的交互作用。他发现, 两组在高频词上的异常反应没有显著差异, 但在低频词上的反应差异显著。在本实验中我们发现, 从不熟悉词到熟悉词, 两个语言水平的参试者产生的无关反应均呈下降趋势, 且初级参试者的无关反应一直显著多于中级参试者。

产生这些差异的原因可能与Söderman (1993) 所依据的词频有关。他所使用的词频是根据Hofland和Johansson (1982) 的Word Frequencies in British and American English (见Söderman), 属于英语母语者使用的词频, 而并非根据第二语言学习者的情况编定的英语作为第二语言/外语的词频。这是在涉及词频问题的研究面临的普遍问题。而本文采用词汇知识熟悉度评定代替正是基于这一考虑, 我们认为母语者的词频是不能代替二语/外语词频的。同时, 从另一个方面来说, 我们也认为, 不能将"词频"和"词汇熟悉度"等同。而目前我们见到的明确提出"词汇熟悉度 (或曰词汇知识熟悉度)"的, 只有Wolter (2001)。但不同的是, 如, Wolter的文章中并没有比较在他定义的每个词汇深度的水平之间, 每一种类型的反应之间的差异是否显著,而只是提到非英语母语参试者在刺激词为较熟悉的词时,产生的语音反应数量为英语母语参试者的一倍。

与Wolter (2001) 相比,我们也发现了一些差异。他的文章发现,英语学习者在对熟悉词的反应中,ESL的组合联想占的比例很大,但是我们发现,在产生组合反应时,语言水平主效应并不显著,说明两个语言水平的参试者所产生的组合反应并没有区别,而词汇熟悉度的主效应显著,根据表四和图三我们发现,仅在不熟悉词上,中级组产生的组合反应多于初级组,而在较熟悉词和熟悉词上,中级组的组合反应均少于初级组。

综上,我们发现,词汇熟悉度对两个语言水平的参试者产生聚合反应和无关反应的影响模式基本上是相同的,聚合反应随词汇熟悉度的提高而显著增多,而无关反应恰好相反,它随词汇熟悉度的提高而显著减少。组合反应随词汇熟悉度的提高而显著提高,但仅在不熟悉词上随语言水平的提高而提高,中级参试者的组合反应显著多于初级参试者。在较熟悉词和熟悉词上,中级参试者的组合反应少于初级参试者,但这种差异并不显著。这个结果基本符合我们的预期。

语音反应在从不熟悉词到较熟悉词,再到熟悉词的变化过程中,经历了一个由减少到增多的过程,当参试者较熟悉刺激词时,产生的语音反应是最少的。但这些减少和增多均没有达到显著水平。

按照DIWK模型,心理词典的结构是按照词汇熟悉度(词汇知识深度,下同)组织的,随着熟悉度的加深,学习者心理词典结构表现出一种动态的发展。这种动态的发展过程也是语言信息结构的重建过程,涉及新的知识单位与已有的知识单位的联系。信息组织的重新构建使得学习者心理词典中语言知识表征结构以及不同知识单位之间的联系发生变化。如果一个词进入了心理词典的核心圈(体现为"熟悉词"),那么在使用这个词时就比较容易被激活,从而提高信息处理的效率,它与同处于核心圈内的其它词的关系也得以加强。我们与Wolter (2001) 的分歧出现在中级参试者的对于处于外围之内的那一部分词,即学习者有所了解以及了解得比较好的词。我们并没有发现中级参试者的这一部分词组合联想的截然增多,也没有发现语音联想的显著减少。我们认为这说明了两个问题:其一,组合反应没有显著增多,说明在由初级进步到中级的过程中,学习者"使用"一个词的能力并没有显著增强。这与Wolter的看法是一致的,他认为,组合反应占大多数的心理词典并不比聚合主导的心理词典要差,这至少说明学习者能有效使用这些产出型词汇。这说明我们的参试者在这个学习阶段上仍然需要将大量的"接受型"词汇转化为"产出型"词汇,使用词语的能力有待提高。其二,语音反应没有随熟悉度的提高而显著减少,说明在中级学习者的心理词典中,语音联想仍占有一席之地。这与上文论述不同语言水平的参试者产生语音反应的数量时有一些相似。当参试者语言水平未达到高级,但是高于入门阶段时,他们产生的语音反应是最多的,而当参试者对刺激词的熟悉度未达到熟悉,但并非不认识该词时,他们产生的语音反应却是最少的。为什么会出现这种情况呢?我们认为,当参试者不熟悉刺激词时,说明参试者对该词的语音形式和意义都不了解,所以只是根据语音进行联想因而产生了大量的语音反应。而当参试者较熟悉刺激词,短暂的语音输入并没有能很好地唤起该词的语音形式和意义,此时参试者对该词的概念是模糊的。当参试者对刺激词非常熟悉时,这种语音输入又激活了储存在他头脑中的相近的其它的词,于是产生了语音联想。联系到字音在语意通达中的作用,汉语母语研究者发现,字音字形的在意义通达的过程中的作用存在着一个发展转换,随着年龄的增加,母语者在意义通达过程中逐渐由对音码的依赖过渡到对形码的依赖 (Peng, Guo, & Zhang (1985); Song, Zhang, & Shu (1995)。在这里我们大胆地猜测,处于中级的汉语学习者也许还处于依赖音码以通达词义的阶段上,因此在未能有效地利用音码通达意义的时候,学习者便根据字音进行词汇联想,且学习者心理词典中储存的词汇越多,这种根据字音进行联想的可能性就越大。但是当学习者能够有效地利用音码实现意义的通达的时候,这种现象便会消失。

因此，根据本研究的对汉语词汇联想的研究结果，我们对Wolter (2001) 的DIWK模型稍做改动：处于核心圈内的熟悉词词容易产生聚合联想，而距核心圈最外围的不熟悉词则容易产生无关联想，而处于外围圈以内的那些词也最不稳定，产生的组合联想和语音联想的可能都很大。

词性对反应类型的影响

在产生聚合反应时，词性对初级组参试者的影响没有达到显著水平，而对中级组参试者的影响达到显著水平。中级组产生聚合反应由多到少的顺序为：名词>形容词>动词，而由名词诱发出来的聚合反应都显著多于形容词和动词。动词和形容词之间的差异并不显著，说明由形容词诱发出的聚合反应并没有显著多于动词。在产生语音反应时，两组参试者在名词上的语音反应没有显著差别，但在动词和形容词上有显著差别。而词性仅对初级水平的参试者有显著影响，他们在三种词性的刺激词产生语音反应多少的顺序为：形容词>动词>名词。而中级组参试者并没有受词性的显著影响。

有研究者认为，名词和动词的词性特征有较强的保持能力，而形容词的词性特征保持能力较弱 (Deese, 1962)。同时，前人的研究也说明，由语音反应和无关反应联结的两词之间的关系较松散，而由聚合反应和组合反应联结的两词之间的关系较紧密。我们的研究结果表明，在学习者的心理词典中，名词多是由聚合反应联结的，而动词和形容词多是以其它类型的反应相联结的。而词性仅在产生聚合反应时对中级水平的参试者有显著影响，对名词的聚合反应要显著多于对动词和形容词的聚合反应，而在产生其它几类反应时影响不大，说明在这个学习阶段上，学习者的词性意识已有了较显著的增强。

总结上述的分析和讨论，本研究的结果可以概括成如下几条：

1. 汉语学习者的心理词典的发展与英语学习者心理词典的发展并不相同，其经历的并不是一个由"语音主导"到"意义主导"的过程，而是一个由杂乱无章的结构逐渐进化为一个意义主导的结构。
2. 词汇熟悉度是影响学习者心理词典结构的一个重要因素。熟悉词和较熟悉词在学习者心理词典中多以聚合和组合的方式存在，而不熟悉词多以语音和无关联想的方式存在。
3. 不同的语言水平的学习者的心理词典的结构有所不同。对于初级学习者来说，无关和语音联想占据主要位置，而对于中级学习者来说，一方面聚合和组合联想的数量相对于初级学习者有了很大的提高，无关联想大量减少，但中级学习者的语音联想在数量上要多于初级学习者。
4. 在汉语学习者的心理词典中，名词之间的联系最强，形容词和动词次之。中级学习者的词性意识已有了较强的发展。

本研究对汉语作为二语词汇教学的启示

词汇联想法作为课堂词汇教学的辅助手段，虽然一直以来都在二语学习的课堂中使用，但词汇联想本身并未得到深入研究，笔者认为很大一个原因是因为词汇联想的随意性和不可控制性。但是根据本实验的结果，我们发现，词汇联想并不是完全随意且不可控制的。如果使用得当，语言教师和学习者都会获益匪浅。我们认为有以下几点值得注意：

第一，扩大词汇量的同时也要注重提高已学词汇的质量，根据学生对词汇掌握程度不同有效地引导学生进行词汇联想。我们发现，学习者对熟悉词和较熟悉的刺激词的组合反应并没有随语言水平提高而显著增多，说明学习者在句子或短语中使用这个词的能力并没有显著增强。如上文所述，Richards (1976) 和Nation (1990, p. 31) 都曾详细论述这个问题。他们认为，要完全掌握一个词，应该掌握关于该词哪些方面的知识，其中就包括了该词搭配的用法。结合本实验，我们认为，对于中级词汇教学来说，在扩大词汇量的同时，我们一定也需要保证学习者能够获得足够的关于该词搭配方面的信息，这样才能保证学习者能够使用该词，而不是掌握了很多的词，却不知道如何正确地使用。因此，一方面，为了巩固已学的词汇同时扩大学生的词汇量，我们建议对于那些认为学生已经掌握很好的词，我们可以尽可能多地引导学生给出与该词相关的其它同词性的词。而对于学生掌握得不是非常好，但对其又略知一二的词，我们应该因势利导，先引导学生给出组合联想，在学生说出这个词大部分的可能的搭配，通过这种方式让学生掌握该词的语法意义、使用频率和语域限制，再引导学生给出聚合联想，这样既练习了一个词的搭配，又巩固了学生对与该词语义相关，同一词性的词的记忆，也扩大了学生的词汇量。

第二，学习者对每种熟悉程度的词的语音反应并没有随语言水平的提高而减少，这说明，学习者知道的词越多，他们受同音字(词)干扰的可能性就越大。因此，我们认为，在中级阶段，语音教学仍值得重视，但这已不同于初级阶段的基础语音教学和正音课，而是针对那些学生易混淆的词，在语音上加以辨析。

第三，从上文的结果我们可以发现，参试者对刺激词词性的模糊判断会导致与语义无关的联想。也就是说，参试者在短时间内无法提取刺激词的词性信息，也将影响到其对语义的提取。在同一个熟悉度的水平上，我们发现由名词诱导出来的聚合反应总是显著多于动词和形容词，说明名词之间的联系最强，最稳定。而动词和形容词之间的联系就相对较弱。说明名词的提取相对容易，而动词和形容词的提取相对容易。Rodgers (1969) 也认为，词性影响词汇学习。名词最容易学，形容词次之，动词和副词最难学。这是否意味着，我们应该有意识加强动词和形容词的讲解和操练。且学习者的词性意识在初级阶段不明显，而在中级阶段逐渐明朗化，这说明我们在教学的开始阶段就应当有意识地发展学生的这种意识。

在看到本研究的种种发现的同时，我们也意识到本研究在设计上的一些局限，首先是本文在进行词汇联想测验时采用的是听觉呈现的方法，这样虽然去除了汉字字形对参试者联想可能的影响，但是对于汉语作为第二语言的研究来说，字形因素应该是比较重要的一环，使用视觉输入也许能给我们带来更多关于字词阅读和心理词典的组织结构的信息。虽然本文的研究兴趣并不在于考察字形的影响，但是笔者认为，如果用同一组刺激词，分别以视觉和听觉呈现的方式进行联想测验，再比较反应的结果，应该会有很多有趣的发现。另外，因为时间和人力的局限，本文未能使用多个评分者对参试者的反应进行分类，因此未能获得不同评分者之间的信度值，这也是本文较大的缺陷之一。虽然如此，我们相信本研究的结果对进一步的汉语作为二语的词汇联想研究会起到抛砖引玉的作用。

References

Aitchison, J. (2003). *Words in the mind: An introduction to the mental lexicon* (3rd ed.). Oxford, England: Blackwell.

Bird, H., Howard, D., & Franklin, S. (2000). Why is a verb like an inanimate object? Grammar category and semantic deficits. *Brain and Language, 72*, 246–309.

Brown, R. W., & Berko, J. (1960). Word association and the acquisition of grammar. *Child Development, 31*, 1–14.

Carter, R., & McCarthy, M. (1988). *Vocabulary and language teaching*. London: Longman.

Channell, J. (1990). Vocabulary acquisition and the mental lexicon. In J. Tomasczyk & B. Lewandowska-Tomasczyk (Eds.), *Meaning and Lexicography* (pp. 21–31). Amsterdam: Benjamins.

Chomsky, N. (1965). *Aspects of the theory of syntax*. Cambridge, MA: MIT Press.

Clifton, C. (1967). The implications of grammar for word association. In K. Salzinger & S. Salzinger (Eds.), *Research in verbal behaviour and some neuropsychological implications*. New York: Academic Press.

Cunningham, L. (1990). *L2 vocabulary: A study of the word association responses of beginning learners of Irish*. Unpublished MPhil dissertation, University of Dublin, Ireland.

Deese, J. (1962). Form class and the determinants of word association. *Journal of Verbal Learning and Behaviour, 1,* 79–84.

Ellis, R. (1997). *Second language acquisition.* Oxford, England: Oxford University Press.

Entwisle, D. R. (1966). *Word association of young children.* Baltimore: John Hopkins University Press.

Ervin, S. (1961). Changes with age in the verbal determinants of word association. *American Journal of Psychology 74,* 361–372.

Fillenbaum, S., & Jones, L. V. (1965). Grammatical contingencies in word association. *Journal of Verbal Learning and Verbal Behaviour, 4,* 248–255.

Hofland, K., & Johansson, S. (1982). *Word frequencies in British and American English.* London: Longman.

Hotpof, W. H. N. (1980). Semantic similarity as a factor in whole-word slips of the tongue. In V. Fromkin (Ed.), *Errors in linguistic performance: Slips of the tongue, ear, pen, and hand* (pp. 97–109). New York: Academic Press.

Jiang, N. (2000). Lexical representation and development in a second language. *Applied Linguistics, 21,* 47–77.

Jiang, S. (2002). Chinese word associations for English speaking learners of Chinese as a second language. *Journal of Chinese Language Teachers Association, 37,* 55–72.

Katz, J., & Fodor, J. (1963). The structure of a semantic theory. *Language, 39,* 170–210.

Kent, G. H., & Rosanoff, A. J. (1910). A study of association in insanity. *American Journal of Insanity, 67,* 317–390.

Koda, K. (1997). Orthographic knowledge in L2 lexical processing: A cross-linguistic perspective. In J. Coady & T. Huckin (Eds.), *Second language vocabulary acquisition* (pp. 39–52). New York: Cambridge.

Kudo, Y., & Thagard, D. (1999) Word association in L2 vocabulary. *University of Hawai'i Working Papers in ESL, 17,* 75–105.

Levelt, W. (1989). *Speaking: From intention to articulation.* Cambridge, MA: MIT.

McNeil, D. (1966). A study of word association. *Journal of Verbal Learning and Verbal Behaviour, 5,* 548–557.

Meara, P. (1982). Word association in a foreign language: A report on the Birkbeck vocabulary project. *Nottingham Linguistic Circular, 11,* 29–37.

Meara, P. (1984). The study of lexis in interlanguage. In A. Davies, A. Howart, & C. Criper (Eds.), *Interlanguage* (pp. 225–235). Edinburgh, Scotland: Edinburgh University Press.

Meara, P. (1990). *EFL vocabulary tests.* Swansea: Centre for Applied Language Studies, University of Wales.

Nation, P. (1990). *Teaching and learning vocabulary.* New York: Newbury House Publishers.

Nelson, K. (1977). The syntagmatic-paradigmatic shift revisited: A review of research and theory. *Psychological Bulletin, 84*(1), 93–116.

Palermo, D. S. (1971). Characteristics of word association responses obtained from children in grades one through four. *Developmental Psychology, 5,* 118–123.

Peng, D., Guo, J., & Zhang, S. (1985). 同一性判断中汉字信息的提取 [The retrieval of information of Chinese characters in making similarity judgment under recognition condition]. *Acta Psychologica Sinica, 3,* 227–233.

Piper, T. H., & Leicester, P. F. (1980). *Word association behavior as an indicator of English language proficiency.* Retrieved December, 2, 2004, from Educational Resources Information Center documents [online]. (ED 227651).

Postman, L., & Keppel, G. (1970). *Norms of word association.* New York: Academic Press.

Richards, J. C. (1976). The role of vocabulary teaching. *TESOL Quarterly, 10,* 77–89.

Rodgers, T. S. (1969). On measuring vocabulary difficulty: An analysis of item variables in learning Russian-English vocabulary pairs. *IRAL, 7,* 327–343.

Russell, W., & Jenkins, J. (1954). *The complete Minnesota norms for responses to 100 words from the Kent-Rosanoff Word Association Test* (Tech. Rep. 11, Contract N 8–ONR–66216). Office of Naval Research, University of Minnesota.

Schimitt, N., & Meara, P. (1997). Researching vocabulary through a word knowledge framework: Word associations and verbal suffixes. *Studies in Second Language Acquisition, 19,* 17–36.

Singleton, D. (1999). *Exploring the second language mental lexicon.* New York: Cambridge University Press.

Söderman, T. (1993). Word associations of foreign language learners and native speakers: Different response types and their relevance to lexical development. In B. Hammarberg (Ed.), *Problem, process, product in language learning: Papers from the Stockholm-Åbo Conference.* Stockholm: Stockholm University Department of Linguistics, 157–169.

Song, H., Zhang, H. & Shu, H. (1995). 字音、字形在中文阅读中作用的发展转换 [The developmental shift of the role of graphic code and phonetic code in Chinese reading]. Acta Psychologica Sinica, 2, 139–144.

Stolz, W. S., & Tiffany, J. (1972). The production of "child-like" word associations by adults to unfamiliar adjectives. *Journal of Verbal Learning and Verbal Behaviour, 11,* 38–46.

Wesche, M., & Paribakht, T. S. (1996). Accessing vocabulary knowledge: Depth vs. breadth. *Canadian Modern Language Review, 53,* 13–40.

Wolter, B. (2001). Comparing the L2 and L1 mental lexicon: A depth of individual word knowledge model. *Studies in Second Language Acquisition, 23,* 41–69.

附录: 词汇联想测验刺激词

附录一: 词汇联想实验用刺激词 (初级).

熟悉词, 共30个, 每种词性各10个:
名词: 成绩、电话、机票、京剧、开水、秋天、嗓子、衣柜、邮局、中药。
动词: 帮助、保存、了解、告诉、决定、旅行、认识、喜欢、预报、准备。
形容词: 安心、便宜、不错、聪明、方便、干净、厉害、美好、努力、油腻。

较熟悉词, 共30个, 每种词性各10个:
名词: 包装、电扇、父亲、歌曲、工资、机场、季节、路口、门口、气温。
动词: 兑换、改变、改进、关心、练习、庆祝、消除、训练、游览、看望。
形容词: 充分、古老、国营、清淡、辛苦、严格、要紧、整齐、专心、超重。

不熟悉词, 共30个, 每种词性各10个:
名词: 保姆、赤道、规章、记号、决赛、昆虫、廉价、缺口、深浅、行政。
动词: 辩护、歌颂、寒暄、贿赂、嫉妒、建造、落地、冒进、狭持、注射。
形容词: 单独、豪华、缓慢、急躁、难免、勤奋、太平、无知、罗索、寂寞。

附录二: 词汇联想实验用刺激词 (中级).

熟悉词, 共30个, 每种词性各10个:
名词: 事情、话题、小说、孝心、飞机、空气、阿姨、课本、绿茶、书包。
动词: 发生、锻炼、成为、出发、到达、看望、关照、强调、打听、适合。
形容词: 丰富、有名、高级、清淡、拿手、努力、亲爱、国产、美好、新鲜。

较熟悉词, 共30个, 每种词性各10个:
名词: 收据、阅读、微笑、美术、草坪、啤酒、朝代、比价、家务、友情。
动词: 播送、管理、保存、庆祝、坚持、改进、讨厌、打扰、珍惜、治疗。
形容词: 痛快、平等、急忙、要紧、相同、急性、仔细、悠久、及时、充分。

不熟悉词, 共30个, 每种词性各10个:
名词: 声势、主食、老家、难民、橡皮、金额、骨肉、期刊、人参、柠檬。
动词: 断绝、发布、离别、交涉、聘请、拥有、好转、亏待、查明、吵闹。
形容词: 优惠、高档、慷慨、匆匆、晴朗、超级、狼狈、幸运、笔直、深奥。

刺激词来源:
郭志良 (1996). 汉语速成初级教程: 综合课本, 北京语言文化大学出版社。
国家汉办 (1992). 汉语水平词汇与汉字等级大纲, 北京语言学院出版社。
马箭飞 (2003). 汉语口语速成基础篇、提高篇, 北京语言大学出版社。
毛悦 (2002). 汉语听力速成基础篇、提高篇, 北京语言大学出版社。

See How They Read: An Investigation Into the Cognitive and Metacognitive Strategies of Nonnative Readers of Chinese

Cecilia Chang
Williams College, Williamstown, Massachusetts

The development of Chinese as a foreign language (CFL) reading ability was investigated[1] by examining the discourse processing strategies of college CFL readers at three proficiency levels—after 1, 2, and 3 years of Chinese language study—and the relationship of the strategies to comprehension performance. Participants of each proficiency level read a test passage appropriate for their current linguistic ability and recalled what they read by writing in English. They also filled out a questionnaire designed to probe their cognitive and metacognitive abilities when processing a Chinese text. Correlations were used to test for relationships between reading activities and recall performance while cross tabulations were used to reveal the differences in strategy uses across proficiency levels and among more- and less-proficient readers within each proficiency level.

The results showed that readers at higher proficiency levels engaged in more global-level processing activities than readers at lower proficiency levels. This trend of moving from local to global processing as proficiency increased was particularly prominent in the intralevel comparisons of more- and less-proficient readers. Correlations, on the other hand, failed to produce a clearly discernable pattern of development across proficiency levels. Implications to future studies and curriculum design for CFL reading are discussed.

本文透過CFL學生在閱讀時使用的篇章訊息處理策略及其與閱讀理解之間的關係探討CFL學生閱讀能力的發展形態。測試文章為南加州大學中文系所使用的進階閱讀系列中的一篇關於漢字歷史的簡介。受試者分別代表經過一年，兩年及三年中文訓練的大學院校學生。受試者首先閱讀測試文章並在閱讀後將內容根據記憶詳細地用英語書寫下來，最後再依據閱讀文章時的經歷填寫一份

---

[1] This project was funded by two research grants of Williams College: The Oakley Center for the Humanities and Social Sciences Fellowship and the Faculty World Fellowship.

閱讀策略調查問卷。數據分析首先調查跨年級閱讀策略與閱讀理解之間的相關性以及跨年級閱讀策略的使用情形以期發現閱讀策略在三個水平之間是否存在任何發展形態。除此之外，各年級受試者又依閱讀理解成績被劃分為高、低能力讀者，進一步對其策略使用情況進行比較。

調查結果首先顯示閱讀策略與閱讀理解之間的相關性調查無法呈現明顯的閱讀策略發展形態。由於讀者本身所具備的學習動機，語言水平，及焦慮感等個人因素各有不同，此項結果非屬意外。其次，跨年級的閱讀策略使用情況調查透露語言水平越高，宏觀性策略的使用越為頻繁。例如高年級讀者在預期下文，對內容的融會貫通，及對文章結構的敏感度上都比低年級讀者勝出一籌。此外，單一水平上高、低能力讀者的策略比較更明確指出無論是哪個年級宏觀性策略的使用與否是閱讀能力高低的一個指標，顯示宏觀性策略的優越性。更重要的是各年級高能力讀者使用的宏觀性策略在本質上大有區別。具體來說，二年級高能力讀者善於借用上下文及自身經驗來猜測字義，彌補語言能力的不足，屬於一種彌補性策略。三年級高能力讀者注重建立宏觀理解，因此在策略的使用上反映出對文本整體結構的分析，屬於一種以文本為主的認知性能力。比較之下，四年級的高能力讀者不但能對文本進行分析，區別主題與細節，更對如何進行高效率閱讀有清楚的認識。呈現一種認知性能力 (declarative) 與程序性能力 (procedural) 雙向發展的趨勢。

根據以上研究結果，本文主張教師及教材編纂者應該有系統地將宏觀性閱讀策略的教授反映在教學及教材設計上，以矯正時下閱讀教學多以字詞為主而置閱讀策略於不顧的偏失現象。其次，本文指出，語言水平與學習策略的使用有一定的關係，因此各年級在教授宏觀性閱讀策略時亦或需有所側重，以達到最佳教學成果。最後，本文呼籲在教授閱讀策略的同時，教師們絕對不能矯枉過正而忽略對學生字詞知識的培養。

對日後研究方向，本文提出以下兩點。一). 為了有效提倡閱讀策略的教學，學界對策略教學的成效應進行系統的研究。二). 如想更精確地了解學生閱讀能力的發展，我們需要長期地對固定學生進行調查。

The ultimate goal of any study on learners' strategies is to identify and promote effective strategies to optimize learners' proficiency. The first step in this process is to discover what the learners already know and do and what strategies differentiate highly proficient learners from those who are less proficient.

The primary focus of most research in both Chinese first-language (L1) and second-language (L2) reading has been on the character or word level, including studies with specific emphasis on the effects of Chinese orthography on character or word acquisition (Everson, 1998; Han, 1994; Hayes, 1987, 1988, 1990; Ke, 1998a; Peng, Li, & Yang, 1997; Shen, 2005; Xiao, 2002; Yang, 2000; Yu, Feng, Cao, & Li 1990; Zhu & Taft, 1994) and studies on character-learning strategies (Ke, 1998b; Yin, 2003). Similarly, cross-linguistic studies on Chinese and other languages have focused on the effects of L1 orthography on L2 processing at the word level (Koda, 2000; Taylor & Park, 1995). While a few researchers have turned their attention to global processing by readers of Chinese as a foreign language (CFL; Everson & Ke, 1997), the proficiency levels investigated were limited to more advanced levels (i.e., after at least 2.5 years of Chinese study). What remains lacking is a systematic investigation into the processing of Chinese texts at the *discourse* level. Furthermore, information on how CFL readers read *across* a wider range of proficiency levels is greatly needed because comprehensive knowledge about the strategies students use at different stages of language acquisition is a requisite first step to developing sound reading pedagogy with coherent articulation.

This study investigated the reading strategies of college CFL readers of three proficiency levels—2 (after 1 year of studying Chinese), 3 (after 2 years of study), and 4 (after 3 years of study)—and the relationship between their strategy uses and comprehension performance.

Why reading strategies?

Approaches to the study of L1 and L2 reading have dramatically changed in the last 20 years, from viewing reading as a serial (or bottom-up) process to an interactive process (Bernhardt, 1991; Just & Carpenter, 1992; Kintsch & van Dijk, 1978; McClelland & Rumelhart, 1981; Stanovich, 1980). A bottom-up view of the reading process, as its name suggests, posits that the reader begins reading by constructing meaning from the written text (the bottom). In other words, the reader begins with letters, and goes on to words, phrases, sentences, and so on, thus processing the text in a linear fashion through a series of discrete stages. In this view, comprehension is assumed to take place automatically as long as the reader successfully goes through all of the necessary stages in the reading process. In contrast, the contemporary interactive view of the reading process looks at readers as active and contributing members who dynamically use a wide variety of resources and strategies to construct a representation of the information that they read during the process. The explosion of research in L2 reading since the 1980s has thus focused a great deal of energy on readers' strategies. Reading strategies are the mental operations involved when readers effectively approach a text to make sense of what they read (Barnett, 1988). Reading strategies are of interest for what they reveal about readers' orchestration of the cognitive resources available to them in the interaction with the written text and how these strategies are related to comprehension performance.

Research in L2 reading has identified a gamut of strategies including skimming and scanning, contextual guessing or skipping unknown words, tolerating ambiguity, reading for meaning, making inferences, activating background knowledge, and recognizing text structure. The actual use of these strategies by L2 learners and the relationship between strategy use and text comprehension have also been investigated in empirical studies (N. J. Anderson, 1991; Barnett, 1988; Block, 1986, 1992; Hosenfeld, 1977). Findings from these studies showed that proficient readers tend to keep the meaning of a passage in mind. They read in broad phrases, skip unimportant and unknown words, and treat looking up words as a last resort. They routinely integrate information in the text and have positive self-images as readers. Conversely, less proficient readers often act in the opposite way. Furthermore, proficient readers were found to deal directly with the message conveyed by the author and focus more on understanding the author's ideas. Less proficient readers often affectively relate to the text and direct attention away from the text and toward themselves—they focus on their own thoughts and feelings, rather than the information stated in the text. These findings on the strategies that proficient readers use for comprehension provide indispensable information for foreign-language educators in designing reading instruction that could better facilitate the development of skills in L2 reading.

Reading strategies and proficiency level

Reading is a process in which comprehension activities take place at multiple levels. Local processing includes cognitive activities that involve gaining access to lexical/semantic and syntactic elements in a text, whereas global processing refers to cognitive activities that contribute to constructing a coherent mental representation of the text, such as generating inferences to integrate text propositions and to assimilate new information into readers' preexisting knowledge, noticing text organization, differentiating between main points and supporting details, and activating background knowledge (Kintsch & van Dijk, 1978).

The strategies used to ensure the success of these cognitive activities denote the reader's knowledge about *what* to do and are thus considered declarative (J. Anderson, 1980; Ellis, 1990).

In addition to the ability to engage in cognitive activities, successful reading also entails metacognitive awareness, both in terms of evaluation and procedural knowledge of strategy use. More specifically, metacognitive awareness refers to a person's knowledge of cognitive processes and states, including memory, attention, knowledge, conjecture, and illusion (Flavell, 1976; Wellman, 1985). Metacognition in reading, then, includes the reader's conceptualization of the reading process (how the reader conceptualizes what he or she is doing in reading), the reader's knowledge about the reading task (whether it is for enjoyment or to get information), the reading text (how hard the syntax is, how familiar the text structure is, etc.), reading strategies (what kind of strategies would be most effective given the task and text), and his or her own learning style (Baker & Brown, 1984). As such, metacognitive strategies are procedural (J. Anderson, 1980; Ellis, 1990).

Metacognition in reading is evidently central to effective reading, for if a reader does not know what is required to read effectively, then he or she will have difficulty taking the steps necessary to meet the challenges of a reading situation or regulating reading strategies in response to comprehension problems. Research on metacognition in L1 reading has shown that readers' control over their own processing develops over time and can affect their ability to understand and to learn from text (Baker & Brown, 1984; Garner, 1987). Compared to L1 reading, metacognition in L2 reading is presumably even more important because the nonnative readers' linguistic processes are underdeveloped and may face greater challenges wrought by the unfamiliar content, a characteristic often associated with foreign-language reading. However, the focus of studies on L2 reading strategies has often been limited to cognitive strategy use. Awareness of the use of strategies, on the other hand, has not received much attention among researchers, let alone been investigated systematically.

Another limitation found in most of the L2 reading-strategy studies is that the studies often look at the strategy use by learners at one particular proficiency level alone, hence providing little insight into the development of cognitive and metacognitive abilities across levels of proficiency. While research has shown that learners can be instructed to use appropriate reading strategies to help them solve comprehension problems and improve their abilities in reading (Carrell, Pharis, & Liberto, 1989; Kern, 1989; Mulling, 1994), ample evidence has shown that the use of strategies for general language learning is related to language proficiency. Specifically, language proficiency level has been found to predict strategy use in terms of types (Rost, 1991), flexibility and appropriateness (Abraham & Vann, 1987; Vann & Abraham, 1990), frequency (Sheorey, 1999; Watanabe, 1990), and variety (Green & Oxford, 1995; Wharton, 2000). L2 readers' strategy use, then, may plausibly be affected by their language proficiency, and they may be prone to use certain types of reading strategies more than others at different stages in their reading development. Without a comprehensive understanding of the strategy use (or lack thereof) by CFL readers across proficiency levels, however, such insight is impossible to attain, textbook writers have little basis for improving a reading curriculum, and language instructors are equally at sea in designing effective reading instruction for different proficiency levels.

To fill this gap, this study is designed to investigate both the use of reading strategies and the awareness of strategy use by learners of CFL at varying stages of acquisition. Furthermore, these cognitive and metacognitive activities were connected to comprehension performance to distinguish between activities engaged in by more and less proficient CFL readers. Finally, a comparison was made to gain a better understanding of the development of these abilities among CFL learners. The research questions were formulated as follows:

1. What is the relationship between CFL learners' cognitive and metacognitive activities during reading and their reading comprehension?
2. How do the cognitive and metacognitive activities differ among learners of varying language proficiencies and between more and less proficient readers?

Method

Participants

To ensure the homogeneity of students' literacy backgrounds, this study only solicited CFL learners who had little or no prior knowledge of the Chinese writing system before they began formal study of the Chinese language. Consequently, Chinese heritage students and Japanese and Korean students who showed prior knowledge of the Chinese writing system were excluded from this study. A letter soliciting participation was sent to Chinese programs at several American universities and colleges and four summer language schools.[2] A total of 96 CFL learners who had recently finished their 1st-, 2nd-, and 3rd-year courses responded to the letter. Test materials and instructions for completing the study were subsequently sent via e-mail to them. The materials were returned as e-mail attachments by 75 students after they completed the study. The study took measures to ensure that no participants found the reading topic or the language of the text to be either extremely difficult or extremely easy to better control the possible effects of atypical familiarity with the topic or difficulty with the text language on the ways that readers read (Carrell, 1983; Clarke, 1988; Cziko, 1980). Specifically, after reading the test passage, the readers were asked to rate on a Likert scale of 1–5 (1=strongly disagree, 5=strongly agree) the degree to which they agreed with the statements that they considered the reading topic familiar and language difficult (see Appendix B for the questionnaire). Those who rated Question A as 1 or 5 were removed from the participant pool, and their data were excluded from further statistical analyses. In other words, only those readers who rated Question A as 2, 3, or 4 constituted the participant pool. The study ultimately had 66 participants, with 20 participants at Level 2 (average age of 19.8), 25 participants at Level 3 (average age of 22.2), and 21 participants at Level 4 (average age of 23). All 75 participants who sent back the test materials were offered nominal compensation.

Instrumentation

Reading test materials

The test passages are based on one of the many sets of reading materials used for progressive reading in the Chinese language program at the University of Southern California (Li, 1998). Each set of the reading materials consists of two to three passages. All of the passages in each set are about the same topic but with increasing linguistic complexity developed for reading at higher proficiency levels. The topic of the set of materials chosen for this study is the development of Chinese characters and has three passages that are developed for reading at the 2nd-, 3rd-, and 4th-year levels.

---

[2] These school programs included the International Chinese Language Program in Taipei, Princeton-in-Beijing, Middlebury Chinese Summer School, Duke-in-China, Duke University, Brown University, Williams College, Washington University, University of Pennsylvania, University of Virginia, Mt. Holyoke College, University of Wisconsin at Milwaukee, Harvard University, Princeton University, Hamilton College, University of Chicago, Wesleyan University, Yale University, Oberlin College, and Emory University.

Because the original passages were deemed too long for the purposes of this study, a few modifications were made to ensure comparability among the three passages in terms of text organization. First, one paragraph was eliminated from the original passages, reducing the number of paragraphs from four to three in each of the passages. Second, to ensure consistency in text organization in all three passages, one paragraph that appeared in both the 3rd- and 4th-year passages but not in the 2nd-year passage was used to replace the one paragraph in the original 2nd-year passage that was not in the 3rd- and 4th-year passages. The resulting text structure of all three passages is summarized as follows. In each passage, the first paragraph illustrates the integral role that Chinese characters play in the daily lives of the Chinese people, followed by a brief account of the development of Chinese characters, and ends with a description of the artistic values in character writing, or calligraphy. The passages vary in length: 216, 252, and 316 characters for Levels 2, 3, and 4. Consequently, the number of propositions (basis for scoring comprehension performance) included in each passage increased according to the levels: 63 for Level 2, 74 for Level 3, and 90 for Level 4 (see Appendix A).

Reading strategy questionnaire
To probe the cognitive and metacognitive strategies that the readers used during the reading process, a questionnaire was developed. The questionnaire was based on the one used by Carrell (1989), with some revisions to reflect characteristics of reading in Chinese, such as using radical knowledge to discern meanings of characters and recognizing word boundaries in Chinese sentences. In addition, a new category, metacognitive effort, was created to contrast with the category of cognitive ability (see Appendix B). The purpose of adding the new category was to differentiate what the students did and what they consciously tried to do (i.e., declarative vs. procedural knowledge). This distinction proved to be useful in the analyses, as can be seen in the discussion. Using a 5-point Likert scale (1=strongly disagree, 5=strongly agree), the resulting 49-item questionnaire was devised to reflect the readers' reading behaviors in six areas: (a) cognitive ability (Items 1–7), (b) metacognitive effort (Items 8–14), (c) repair strategies (Items 15–18), (d) effectiveness of strategy use (Items 19–32), (e) difficulty with various aspects of text processing (Items 33–41), and (f) conceptualization of an effective reader at their current proficiency level (Items 42–49; see Appendix B for the questionnaire). Categories a, c, and e indicate what the students were able or unable to do during the reading process and thus are considered cognitive or declarative in nature, whereas categories b, d, and f reflect their conceptualization of their strategy use and thus are considered metacognitive or procedural in nature (see Appendix B).

Procedures

Each participant was instructed to silently read the test passage designated for his or her proficiency level. They were asked to put away the reading passage after reading it and write down in English (the native language of most of the participants) what they remembered (recalled) about the content of the passage. The reason for writing the recall in English instead of Chinese was to avoid any complications in reporting due to underdeveloped language competence in the L2.

After the recall, the participants also filled out the questionnaire designed to probe both their cognitive strategy use and metacognitive conceptualizations about silent reading strategies in the L2.

Data analysis

Recall

The recall protocols were scored based on a propositional analysis system originally put forth by Meyer (1985) and used in Everson and Ke (1997). In this system, text structure is analyzed by using a tree diagram similar to a linguistic analysis. First, relationships among ideas in the paragraphs (macropropositions) are identified, then sentences are analyzed according to the way the ideas are organized into sentences and how the sentences relate to each other within the text (micropropositions). Points are given for the presence of recalled idea units both in terms of lexical predicates and relationships.

Based on this system, five basic groups of relations can be identified in any expository text at the macropropositional level—*collection, causation, response, comparison,* and *description*—and these basic relations can appear in combination to display the underlying logic of the text organization.

When analyzing the text at the micropropositional level, Meyer (1985) focused on identifying the roles of lexical predicates. For instance, the *agent* is the instigator of an action; the *patient*, on the other hand, is the thing that is affected by the action of the agent. The *instrument* is something used inanimately by the agent to perform an action, while the *force*, though the cause of a process, is devoid of responsibility for it. The *vehicle* is something that conveys a patient or moves along with it. The *former* is where the motion begins or the source, in contrast to the *latter*, which represents where a motion ends or the goal. Finally, *range* limits the extent of a verb, representing the path or area covered or the static location of an object. The following examples illustrate these roles:

- The ball (patient) was thrown by the boy (agent).
- The woman (patient) died of cancer (force).
- The chef (agent) cut the meat (patient) with a knife (instrument).
- The peasant girl (agent) carried the water (patient) on her head (vehicle) with a jar (instrument).
- The apple (patient) fell from her hand (former) to the floor (latter).
- Taipei (range) is hot.
- They (agent) talked about social issues (range).

In preparation, the author and a research assistant familiarized themselves with the derived text structure to gain quick access to the location of the information in the structure. They then read each protocol completely before the actual scoring. The interrater reliability after scoring 5% of the protocols was 88%. Discrepancies between the scoring results were resolved in discussion, and the raters then coded another 10% of the protocols, with the agreement reaching 96%. After resolving the disagreements, the assistant scored the rest of the protocols.

Questionnaire

To find out the specific cognitive and metacognitive activities related to recall, correlations were run for each of the three groups as whole groups between each questionnaire item and the mean proportions of recall. Next, based on the proportions of the idea units recalled, the readers in each group were divided into proficient readers (those who recalled 50% or more of the text content) and less proficient readers (those who recalled less than 50% of the text content; see Table 1). To assess whether the cognitive and metacognitive strategies used differed among the proficiency levels and between more and less proficient readers of each proficiency level, the author cross-tabulated the three proficiency levels with the five response levels of the survey questions. Significance was tested by using asymmetric Somers' D, with questionnaire items as dependent and proficiency levels as independent variables. An alpha level of .05 was chosen as the significance level.

Table 1. Case summary of mean recall proportions of proficient and nonproficient readers according to groups

	n	range	mean	SD
level 2 (N=20)				
proficient	7	0.51–0.9	0.66	0.127
nonproficient	13	0.22–0.49	0.35	0.107
level 3 (N=25)				
proficient	9	0.51–0.76	0.61	0.1
nonproficient	16	0.12–0.49	0.33	0.144
level 4 (N=21)				
proficient	9	0.5–0.73	0.61	0.085
nonproficient	12	0.2–0.47	0.38	0.084

Results

Proficiency groups as whole groups

Relationship between survey questions and recall performance
The results of the correlations with proficiency groups as whole groups did not show a strong relationship between the survey questions and recall performance (the highest correlation obtained was .042), suggesting no clearly discernible pattern in the development of the abilities across the three proficiency levels.

Differences among proficiency levels on survey questions
The results of the cross tabulations showed that the three groups differed on six questionnaire items, namely, Questions 1 (ability to anticipate incoming information), 30 (effectiveness of focusing on text details), 38 (difficulty in assimilating text information with one's own knowledge), 40 (difficulty in recognizing text organization), 41 (difficulty in remembering what one has read), and 44 (belief in ability to guess at unknown words; see Table 2). Specifically, as general proficiency improved, there was an increasing trend in reader ability to anticipate incoming information and greater difficulty in remembering text content (presumably due to the increasing lengths of texts for higher proficiency levels). In contrast, there was a decreasing trend in considering focusing on text details as an effective strategy for reading the test passage, in difficulty with assimilating text information into existing knowledge and with recognizing text organization, and in considering guessing the meanings of unknown words a good reader strategy for their current proficiency levels.

Table 2. Questionnaire items that differed among proficiency levels

question		Somers' D	asymmetric significance
1	ability to anticipate incoming information	.233	.036
30	effectiveness of focusing on text details	−.219	.044
38	difficulty with assimilating text information with one's own knowledge	−.201	.046
40	difficulty with recognizing text organization	−.225	.029
41	difficulty with remembering what has been read	.26	.024
44	value of ability to guess at unknown words	−.202	.037

note: Positive values show an ascending trend as proficiency level increases. Negative values show a descending trend as proficiency level increases. *p*<.05.

Proficiency groups with subgroups of more and less proficient readers

The results from the cross tabulations on the questionnaire items that differentiated more and less proficient readers at each proficiency level are reported in Table 3 and are summarized in the following sections.

Table 3. Questionnaire items that differentiate less and more proficient readers according to proficiency levels

level	question		Somers' D	asymmetric significance
2	5	ability to use prior knowledge	.495	.014
	23	focusing on meanings of words	.516	.006
	25	using context to guess at unknown words	.462	.003
	33	difficulty with unclear pronunciations of characters/words	−.473	.029
3	2	ability to distinguish main points from supporting details	.382	.048
	33	difficulty with unclear pronunciations of characters/words	−.431	.036
	39	difficulty with text meaning	−.618	.005
	40	difficulty with text organization	−.535	.013
	41	difficulty with remembering what has been read	−.479	.021
4	1	ability to anticipate incoming information	−.444	.04
	13	effort in monitoring comprehension	.574	.002
	14	effort in identifying problems	.574	.013
	17	reread from sentence prior to problematic part for repair	−.407	.049
	29	distinguishing important from unimportant parts	−.426	.039
	48	value ability to remember details	.63	0

note: Positive values show an ascending trend as proficiency level increases. Negative values show a descending trend as proficiency level increases. *p*<.05

At Level 2, proficient readers

- were better able to bring their prior knowledge of the reading topic to the reading than less proficient readers (Question 5),
- focused more on knowing the meaning of each word as they read (Question 23),
- used context more actively to guess at the meanings of unknown words (Question 25), and
- had stronger tolerance for not knowing the pronunciations of characters and words (Question 33).

At Level 3, proficient readers

- had better ability than less proficient readers to distinguish main points from supporting details (Question 2),
- had stronger tolerance for not knowing the pronunciations of characters and words (Question 33),
- had better abilities to understand the overall text meaning (Question 39),
- could better recognize the organization of the text (Question 40), and
- could better remember what they had read (Question 41).

At level 4, proficient readers

- indicated stronger abilities than less proficient readers to anticipate incoming information (Question 1),
- showed greater effort in monitoring their comprehension (Question 13) and in identifying sources of comprehension problems (Question 14),
- reread from the sentence prior to the problematic part for repair more than less proficient readers did (Question 17),
- did not merely focus attention on important parts of the text when they read (Question 29), and
- regarded the ability to remember text details as desirable more than less proficient readers did (Question 48).

Discussion

This study aimed to gain a better understanding of the cognitive and metacognitive abilities of college CFL readers of three proficiency levels: after 1 (Level 2), 2 (Level 3), and 3 years (Level 4) of Chinese study. The participants of each proficiency level read one test passage appropriate for their current linguistic abilities and recalled what they read in writing in English. They also filled out a questionnaire designed to probe their cognitive and metacognitive abilities when processing a Chinese text. Statistical analyses were done for each proficiency level not only as a whole group, but also as subgroups of more and less proficient readers.

The results of the correlations of proficiency groups as whole groups showed that the students at each level varied widely in the types of cognitive and metacognitive activities they used, and no clearly discernible pattern appeared in the development of abilities across the three proficiency levels. This finding was not surprising given the numerous factors associated with learner variables that have been demonstrated to account for the differences in the development of proficiency in a second language. These factors range from individual variables, such as motivation and attitudes (e.g., Ely, 1986; Gardner & Lambert, 1972; McGinnis, 1999; Wen, 1999), disposition (Bacon & Finnemann, 1990; Beebe, 1987), and anxiety (e.g., Gregerson, 2002; Onwuegbuzie, 2002), to social and cultural (Bacon, 1987; Wong Fillmore, 1976) variables. These learner factors, along with factors associated with the linguistic aspects of reading—orthography, genre, and structure (Allen, Bernhardt, Berry, & Demel, 1988; Koda, 2000)—make interpretation and prediction of the development of L2 reading proficiency difficult.

A closer examination of the survey items correlated with recall performance at the three proficiency levels, however, did reveal a trend of moving from local processing activities at Level 2 (knowing the meanings of words) toward global processing activities at Level 3 (ability to connect incoming information with information already read; less difficulty in understanding the gist of the text and in recognizing text organization) and at Level 4 (not only able to, but also consciously trying to question the truthfulness of what the author has written; less difficulty in assimilating text information with one's preexisting knowledge). The results of cross tabulations further showed that readers at the three proficiency levels differed on many items that reflected global processing. For instance, readers at higher proficiency levels were better able to anticipate incoming information, they did not only focus on text details when they read, and they had less difficulty in assimilating text information into their existing knowledge and in recognizing text organization.

Based on these results, a sketch of the cognitive and metacognitive abilities of the CFL readers at the three proficiency levels can be offered below. As whole groups, CFL readers at each of the three proficiency levels in general still varied widely in the use of cognitive and metacognitive strategies in reading. This was particularly true at Level 2. After only 1 year of Chinese study, readers at Level 2 still seemed to be searching for and developing their own sense of how to effectively comprehend a Chinese text. As a result, the strategies used by these CFL readers and their various metacognitive conceptualizations of effective reading, including ideas of a good reader at their current proficiency level, were still vastly diverse.

While uniformity is still lacking for readers at Level 3 in effective reading abilities, there is evidence of the positive effects of enhanced linguistic ability on successful reading, as manifested in the correlation between less difficulty with sentence parsing, grammar, text gist, and text organization on the one hand and better recall on the other. Also, with these improved linguistic abilities, readers who were more able to connect incoming information with previously read text propositions recalled the text content better than those who were less able to do so. Together, these findings seem to suggest that CFL readers at Level 3 were moving toward using more text-driven global-level processing strategies when they read. At the same time, they exhibited strong perseverance in making repairs on comprehension problems, except that their approaches to repair were still quite inconsistent between rereading the problematic part and rereading from a prior sentence before the problematic part, and only their reluctance to ignore and to give up on a detected problem was found to be correlated with recall performance.

The trend of moving from local to global processing strategies found at Level 3 is also evident at Level 4. There are indications that readers at this level started to use both text- and knowledge-driven strategies to aid their comprehension. Specifically, those readers who went back to a prior sentence before a problematic area and reread from there to repair a comprehension problem were found to have better recall. Also, the more they agreed that a good reader at Level 4 should remember text details, the better their recall. These are clear indications that readers at Level 4 not only engaged in but also valued strategies that were text driven. The aptitude that Level-4 readers showed for remembering text detail in turn can be viewed as a reflection of their increased procedural knowledge of how to better accomplish a reading task—in the current study, recalling everything in written English. On the other hand, in contrast to Levels 2 and 3, where only the ability to question the truthfulness of what the author had written was positively correlated with recall, both the ability and the conscious effort to do so were positively correlated with recall performance for readers at Level 4. These findings once again suggest that, in addition to ability of strategy use, Level-4 readers were developing an awareness of strategy use (procedural knowledge). This is further revealed by the fact that Level-4 readers did not value the ability to guess at unknown words as much as readers at Levels 2 and 3 (see Table 3, Question 44). Because vocabulary knowledge has been demonstrated to be strongly related to reading comprehension (Beck, Perfetti, & McKeown, 1982; Stahl, 1983) and the word variable is more highly predictive of comprehension than the ability to make inferences or to grasp main ideas (R. C. Anderson & Freebody, 1981), as their reading experience increased, Level-4 readers seem to have become better informed as to how to go about the process of reading Chinese more efficiently, purposefully, and with greater success. Finally, the fact that recall performance was negatively correlated with the degree to which these readers had difficulty in assimilating text information into their preexisting knowledge about the topic lends additional evidence that Level-4 readers strove to use knowledge-based information to aid their comprehension.

Aside from the analyses of the proficiency levels as whole groups, the comparisons between the strategies that differentiated more and less proficient readers at each level may be even more illuminating for our understanding of the cognitive and metacognitive abilities across the three proficiency levels. The results reported in Table 3 reveal that global processing characterized the reading strategies used by more proficient readers at each of the three proficiency levels. Furthermore, the nature of the global processing strategies appears to be distinctive across the proficiency levels. Specifically, three of the four global strategies used by the proficient readers at Level 2 had to do with reactions to various aspects of lexicon problems. On the one hand, proficient Level-2 readers appeared to pay close attention to the meaning of each word when they read it; on the other hand, they appeared less concerned if they did not know the pronunciations of the characters that constituted the words, and they used context to discern the meanings of unknown words during the reading process. They were also able to tap into their prior knowledge or experience to help them understand the content of the text. In other words, while these readers understood the importance of knowing the meanings of the words, they were not bogged down by unknown words; instead, they strategically used various resources to compensate for this deficiency. Consequently, the global strategies used by proficient readers at Level 2 can be understood as what Oxford (1990) called *compensation strategies*; that is, the more students were able to compensate for their inefficient word knowledge, the better they read.

In contrast, what separated more and less proficient readers at Level 3 seems to be global strategies that were facilitated by enhanced general linguistic ability. The global processing strategies used by proficient readers at this level were largely aimed at constructing a coherent text-based representation. Particularly, compared to less proficient readers, proficient readers were better able to distinguish main points from supporting details in the text, they had less difficulty in understanding the overall meaning of the text, and they had less difficulty with the text organization. Their improved linguistic ability also enabled the proficient readers to better remember what they had read than the less proficient readers. At the same time, as with proficient readers at Level 2, not knowing the pronunciations of characters or words did not hinder the processing of the text information for proficient readers at Level 3.

Thus, the global strategies that distinguished more and less proficient readers at Level 3 seemed to reflect their enhanced general linguistic ability in constructing a coherent textbase. Consequently, these strategies can be understood as text-driven, declarative processing strategies.

Compared to those at Level 3, proficient readers at Level 4 exhibited both declarative and procedural abilities. In addition to being better able to anticipate incoming information, the strategy used by proficient readers at Level 4 to repair a detected problem was to reread from a sentence prior to the problematic area, rather than simply focusing on the problematic area. While these two global processing strategies are still declarative, the others are distinctively procedural. Specifically, Level-4 proficient readers strove to monitor their comprehension and to identify comprehension problems more than less proficient readers. Such readers also indicated a strong conviction in their abilities to distinguish important and unimportant text propositions. Furthermore, the fact that Level-4 proficient readers considered remembering text details a desirable ability could be an indication that they were sensitive to the types of strategies used in response to the specific reading task at hand—recalling everything in writing.

While most of these strategies are text-driven, the ability to anticipate incoming information is clearly knowledge-driven. As such, the global strategies used by the proficient Level-4 readers are characterized by their bidirectional (both declarative and procedural) nature, as well as by the emergence of knowledge-driven strategies.

To sum up, the global-processing activities used by more proficient readers at each of the three proficiency levels differed not only in scope but also in their specific applications. The development moved from coping with local issues at the lower levels to engaging in global processing at the higher levels. Such development certainly takes place over a long period of time and further attests to the challenges when learning to read in the Chinese orthography.

Pedagogical implications

Advocacy of improving CFL reading pedagogy with explicit instruction on reading strategies is certainly not new (Liu, 1999; Spring, 1999; Wen, 1998). The current study contributes to this endeavor by providing a specific focus for classroom practitioners and textbook writers to consider when they design coherent strategy training curricula for students at varying proficiency levels—as well as across them—to read at the discourse level. First and foremost, findings regarding the strategy use that separated more and less proficient readers at each of the three proficiency levels showed that, regardless of the level of linguistic proficiency, what makes a reader more proficient than his or her peers is the ability to use global processing. Thus, to help students become more proficient in discourse-level reading, classroom practitioners and textbook writers must develop and integrate systematic instruction on strategy use into the reading pedagogy that aims at developing the ability to engage in global processing.

Second, the distinctive nature of the global processing strategies used by the proficient readers at each level suggests that less proficient readers at different proficiency levels may benefit from training in using specific types of strategies. For example, findings from this study suggest that less proficient readers at Level 2 may benefit the most from training on how to be more tolerant of ambiguity, particularly when it is associated with pronunciations and meanings of lexical items. Likewise, global compensation strategies such as using context to approximate the meanings of unknown words and actively applying prior knowledge to aid comprehension may be more useful for students at this level than those at a higher proficiency level. In support of this theory, Hudson's 1982 study showed that explicitly introducing schemata prior to reading to facilitate the comprehension process was more effective for readers at beginning and intermediate levels than for readers at advanced levels.

In contrast to the proficient readers at Level 2, the proficient readers at Level 3 demonstrated stronger sensitivities to properties of text structure. For instance, compared to less proficient readers at the same level, the Level 3 proficient readers were not only better able to distinguish main points from supporting details, but they also had less difficulty in recognizing text organization, in getting the overall meaning of the text, and in remembering what they read. Together, these findings suggest that developing readers' sensitivities to various aspects of text structure should be an essential component of strategy instruction at this stage.

On the other hand, Level 4 proficient readers' strategy use demonstrated an emergence of procedural abilities. This is evidenced by their awareness of the importance of, and hence, effort in, monitoring their comprehension and identifying the sources of comprehension problems and their ideas of effective reading in response to specific reading tasks. Accordingly, reading pedagogy for this stage should reflect a stronger emphasis on instruction that will help develop a keener metacognitive awareness in students of their conceptualization of the reading process (e.g., the types of activities they are doing at any particular moment), the reading task (e.g., searching for information or test taking), the reading text (e.g., the underlying organizations of narrative vs. expository texts), and reading strategies (e.g., effective orchestration of local and global strategies in response to specific reading objectives).

The respective emphasis of strategy instruction recommended for the three proficiency levels does not mean that they are to be taught exclusive of other strategies. On the contrary, all effective strategies should be taught concurrently from the early stages of the study of Chinese (Spring, 1999). Findings from this study provide some clues about the specific strategies that readers can be expected to use at each of the three proficiency levels. Consequently, the recommendations made above signify only the promising focus of strategy instruction at each of the proficiency levels because researchers have argued that strategies are the causes and the outcomes of improved language proficiency (MacIntyre, 1994; Phillips, 1991; Rost, 1991) and that "only by reaching a certain level will a student be likely to use a given strategy" (Bremner, 1999, p. 495).

Finally, in addition to the progression toward global processing strategies as language proficiency improves, the higher-level readers also showed keener awareness of the importance of word knowledge than the lower-level readers. This finding is particularly illuminating because it is consistent with what vocabulary research has demonstrated, that is, that readers need to know a large number of words in a text before anything resembling a comfortable reading level can be achieved. Perhaps as their experience in language learning increases, readers realize that guessing at unknown words is a strategy simply not to be trusted and that even in cases where strategies can be used, texts remain unclear without sufficient knowledge of the vocabulary in the texts. Consequently, CFL educators must bear in mind as vitally important that reading strategies should not be taught at the expense of developing vocabulary knowledge. Laufer (1997) put it well: "Reading may well be a psycholinguistic guessing game. But words are the toys you need to play it right" (p. 32).

As Allen, Bernhardt, Berry, and Demel (1988) pointed out, "textbooks and method which teachers employ to teach (reading) also reflect a set of assumptions about the text-based nature of the process of reading in a second language" (p. 164). Therefore, CFL textbook writers must keep abreast of the ever-increasing body of knowledge about second-language reading generated from work on genre theory, discourse analysis, and background and cultural knowledge in enriching reading curricula and in transforming the ways in which reading has been conceptualized and approached by classroom practitioners in the field of CFL. Compared to most of the previous studies of CFL reading strategies, which focused primarily on the *character* level, the current study of CFL reading at the *discourse* level is a first attempt in many regards. Findings from the study, while preliminary, provide textbook writers and classroom practitioners with specific direction for improving CFL reading curricula.

Limitations and future research

While findings of the current study shed some light on the differences between levels of CFL reading proficiency, bear in mind that this study is of an exploratory nature and has a few limitations. First, the survey questions do not reflect all of the reading strategies that may have been used by the readers, and they do not distinguish strategies used in specific reading tasks. In addition, many statistical analyses in this study dealt with comparisons of unequal sizes, which may make the comparisons unreliable.

In regard to the pattern of development of the cognitive and metacognitive abilities across the three proficiency levels, this study yielded data that was difficult to interpret. This may be largely due to effects attributable to individual differences as manifested in learner motivation, attitudes, dispositions, and so on, especially because the participants came from different programs.[3] The relatively small number of participants at each proficiency level (after elimination of outliers), on the other hand, may have also contributed to this outcome. Accordingly, future studies with large numbers of participants and variables that are clearly defined are needed to further enrich our understanding of the development of CFL readers.

In the meantime, the lack of uniformity in reading strategies may be indicative of a transitional phase that the field of CFL is going through in terms of approaches to teaching reading. As Ning (2003) pointed out in a survey of the CFL textbooks in the United States, one of the characteristics of the textbooks that are influenced by the more traditional audiolingual approach to language teaching is that reading is viewed as a bottom-up process; as long as students understand the meaning of every word in the text, they can understand the meaning of the entire text. Within this approach, a comprehensive vocabulary list with Chinese pronunciations, English correspondents, and occasional explanations on word usage are deemed to be the principal means of helping students learn to read a Chinese text. Michael Everson (personal communication, July 10, 2006) has stated that this "three-section approach"—texts, glosses, and grammar notes—has dominated the ways that CFL reading is taught and has led students and untrained teachers to believe that these are the only things that one needs to know about reading.

Recently, however, recognition of reading as an interactive process has prompted textbook writers to develop materials that promote cognitive learning not only at the character and

---

[3] Students were included from different programs to increase the sample size because locating a sufficient number of qualifying participants from one or two programs is difficult, especially at the more advanced levels. The consequence of such a decision, however, is the increase in individual variables. To account for this, the investigator decided to eliminate the data of the outliers at each proficiency level to isolate and focus on typical reading performances for each of these groups.

word levels (Mickel, 1995; Yan & Liu, 1997) but also with increasing attention to processing strategies at the discourse level (Tang & Chen, 2005). Influenced by the constructive nature of reading, scholars have considered the acquisition processes of CFL learners at the character and word levels (see the introduction of this chapter). Findings from these studies are unquestionably valuable to Chinese educators in terms of refining pedagogy for character and vocabulary learning. At the same time, teaching and raising student awareness of text structure has been focused on as a means of leading students away from a processing method that solely reflects the bottom-up approach (Bai, 1997).

Judging from the inconsistent strategy use among readers at all levels from different programs in the current study, however, the impact of these new trends in materials development, research, and classroom practices still is not apparent. Spring (1999) noted that while the importance of viewing reading as an interactive process and reading strategies as skills that must be actively taught has gained some prominence in studies on reading in Chinese, "implementation and assessment of such reading programs are still controversial" (p. 52). The lack of uniformity in strategy use is plausibly a result of a lack of common practice in terms of instruction on reading strategies, either taught overtly in class or suggested in textbooks, and that students are left to their own devices to read effectively. Without a current fundamental consensus on approaches to and specific implementations of how to teach CFL reading, the impact of these new approaches to reading instruction on the Chinese teaching field as a whole may not be systematically assessable for a long time. However, to come to a consensus on approaches to teaching reading, no matter how long the process might be, what is urgently needed is data about the effects of the different approaches on reading ability. Thus, at the same time that new ideas for the instruction of reading strategies are being developed, studies that test for the effects of these new approaches must also be advanced.

Finally, when comparing the results for the readers at different proficiency levels, note that the distribution of abilities may differ across the proficiency levels due to attrition (i.e., the less successful readers in lower levels may be less likely to move on to the next level), so the pools of higher-level readers may look different than the pools of lower-level readers, beyond the extra year of instruction. Accordingly, longitudinal studies are needed that look at the reading strategies of the same participants as their general linguistic proficiency advances to gain greater insights into the development of reading ability.

References

Abraham, R. G., & Vann, R. J. (1987). Strategies of two language learners: A case study. In A. Wenden & J. Rubin (Eds.), *Learner strategies in language learning* (pp. 85–102). Englewood Cliffs, NJ: Prentice Hall.

Allen, E., Bernhardt, E., Berry, M., & Demel, M. (1988). Comprehension and text genre: An analysis of the secondary school foreign language readers. *Modern Language Journal, 72*, 163–172.

Anderson, J. (1980). *Cognitive psychology and its implications*. San Francisco: Freeman.

Anderson, N. J. (1991). Individual differences in strategy use in second language reading and testing. Modern Language Journal, 75(4), 460–472.

Anderson, R. C., & Freebody, P. (1981). Vocabulary knowledge. In J. T. Gutrie (Ed.), *Comprehension and teaching: Research review* (pp. 77–117). Newark, DE: International Reading Association.

Bacon, S. (1987). Mediating cultural bias with authentic target-language texts for beginning students of Spanish. *Foreign Language Annals, 20,* 557–563.

Bacon, S., & Finnemann, M. (1990). A study of the attitudes, motives, and strategies of university foreign language students and their disposition to authentic oral and written input. *Modern Language Journal, 74,* 459–473.

Bai, J. (1997). Teaching text structure: Why and how? *Journal of the Chinese Language Teachers Association, 32*(3), 31–40.

Baker, L., & Brown, A. L. (1984). Metacognitive skills and reading. In P. D. Pearson, R. Barr, & M. L. Kamil (Eds.), *Handbook of reading research* (pp. 353–394). New York: Longman.

Barnett, M. A. (1988). Reading through context: How real and perceived strategy use affects L2 comprehension. *Modern Language Journal, 72*(2), 150–162.

Barnett, M. A. (1989). *More than meets the eye: Foreign language learner reading: Theory and practice.* Englewood Cliffs, NJ: Prentice Hall Regents.

Beck, I. L., Perfetti, C. A., & McKeown, M. G. (1982). Effects of text construction and instructional procedures for teaching word meanings on comprehension and recall. *Journal of Education Psychology, 74,* 506–521.

Bernhardt, E. B. (1991). *Reading development in a second language: Theoretical, empirical, and classroom perspectives.* Norwood, NJ: Ablex Publishing Corporation.

Block, E. (1986). The comprehension strategies of second language readers. *TESOL Quarterly, 20*(3), 463–494.

Block, E. (1992). See how they read: Comprehension monitoring of L1 and L2 readers. *TESOL Quarterly, 26*(2), 319–343.

Bremner, S. (1999). Language learning strategies and language proficiency: Investigating the relationship in Hong Kong. *Canadian Modern Language Review, 55*(4), 490–514.

Carrell, P. L. (1983). Three components of background knowledge in reading comprehension. *Language Learning: A Journal of Applied Linguistics, 3*(2), 183–207.

Carrell, P. L. (1989). Metacognitive awareness and second language reading. *Modern Language Journal, 73*(2), 121–134.

Carrell, P. L., Pharis, B. G., & Liberto, J. C. (1989). Metacognitive strategy training for ESL reading. *TESOL Quarterly, 23*(4), 647–678.

Clarke, M. A. (1988). The short circuit hypothesis of ESL reading—or when language competence interferes with reading performance. In P. L. Carrell, J. Devine, & D. E. Eskey (Eds.), *Interactive approaches to second language reading* (pp. 114–124). Cambridge, England: Cambridge University Press.

Cziko, G. A. (1980). Language competence and reading strategies: A comparison of first- and second-language oral reading errors. *Language Learning: A Journal of Applied Linguistics, 30,* 101–116.

Dufour, R., & Kroll, J. F. (1995). Matching words to concepts in two languages: A test of the concept mediation model of bilingual representation. *Memory & Cognition, 23,* 166–180.

Ellis, R. (1990). *Instructed second language acquisition.* Oxford, England: Basil Blackwell.

Ely, C. (1986). Language learning motivation: A descriptive and causal analysis. *Modern Language Journal, 70,* 28–35.

Everson, M. E. (1998). Word recognition among learners of Chinese as a foreign language: Investigating the relationship between naming and knowing. *Modern Language Journal, 82,* 194–204.

Everson, M. E., & Ke, C. (1997). An inquiry into the reading strategies of intermediate and advanced learners of Chinese as a foreign language. *Journal of the Chinese Language Teachers Association, 32*(1), 1–20.

Flavell, J. H. (1976). Metacognitive aspects of problem solving. In L. B. Resnick (Ed.), *The nature of intelligence* (pp. 231–235). Hillsdale, NJ: Erlbaum.

Garner, R. (1987). *Metacognition and reading comprehension.* Norwood, NJ: Ablex.

Gardner, R., & Lambert, W. E. (1972). *Attitudes and motivation in second language learning.* Rowley, MA: Newbury House.

Green, J. M., & Oxford, R. L. (1995). A closer look at learning strategies, L2 proficiency, and gender. *TESOL Quarterly, 29,* 261–297.

Gregersen, T. (2002). Language learning and perfectionism: Anxious and non-anxious language learners' reaction to their own oral performance. *Modern Language Journal, 86,* 562–570.

Han, B. X. (1994). Frequency effect of constituent in Chinese character recognition. In Q. C. Jing, H. C. Zhang, & D. L. Peng (Eds.), *Information processing of Chinese language* (pp. 87–98). Beijing, China: Beijing Normal University Publishing Co.

Hayes, E. (1987). The relationship between Chinese character complexity and character recognition. *Journal of the Chinese Language Teachers Association, 22*(2), 45–57.

Hayes, E. (1988). Encoding strategies used by native and non-native readers of Chinese Mandarin. *Modern Language Journal, 72,* 188–195.

Hayes, E. (1990). The relationship between 'word length' and memorability among L2 readers of Chinese Mandarin. *Journal of the Chinese Language Teachers Association, 25*(3), 31–41.

Hosenfeld, C. (1977). A preliminary investigation of the reading strategies of successful and non-successful second language learners. *System, 5,* 110–123.

Hudson, T. (1982). The effects of induced schemata on the 'short circuit' in L2 reading: Non-decoding factors in L2 reading performance. *Language Learning, 32*(1), 1–31.

Just, M. A., & Carpenter, P. A. (1992). A capacity theory of comprehension: Individual differences in working memory. *Psychological Review, 99*(1), 122–149.

Ke, C. (1998a). Effects of language background on the learning of Chinese characters among foreign language students. *Foreign Language Annals, 31*(1), 91–100.

Ke, C. (1998b). Effects of strategies on the learning of Chinese characters among foreign language students. *Journal of the Chinese Language Teachers Association, 33*(2), 93–112.

Kern, R. (1989). Second language reading strategy instruction: Its effects on comprehension and word inference ability. *Modern Language Journal, 73*(2), 135–149.

Kintsch, W., & van Dijk, T. A. (1978). Toward a model of text comprehension and production. *Psychological Review, 85*(5), 363–394.

Koda, K. (2000). Crosslinguistic interactions in the development of L2 intraword awareness: Effects of logographic processing experience. *Psychologia: An International Journal of Psychology in the Orient, 43*(1), 27–46.

Laufer, B. (1997). The lexical plight in second language reading. In J. Coady & T. Huckin (Eds.), *Second language vocabulary acquisition* (pp. 20–34). Cambridge, England: Cambridge University Press.

Li, Y. H. (1998). Steps toward reading proficiency: Progressive readings. *Journal of the Chinese Language Teachers Association, 33*(4), 79–95.

Liu, H., Bates, E., & Li, P. (1992). Sentence interpretation in bilingual speakers of English and Chinese. *Applied Psycholinguistics, 13*(4), 451–484.

MacIntyre, P. D. (1994). Toward a social psychological model of strategy use. *Foreign Language Annals, 27*(2), 185–195.

McClelland, J., & Rumelhart, D. (1981). An interactive activation model of the effect of context in perception. *Psychological Review, 88*, 375–407.

McGinnis, S. (1999). Student goals and approaches. In M. Chu (Ed.), *Mapping the course of the Chinese language field. Chinese Language Teachers Association monograph series, Vol. III* (pp. 151–188). Kalamazoo, MI: Chinese Language Teachers Association, Inc.

Meyer, B. (1985). Prose analysis: Purposes, procedures, and problems. In B. K. Britton & J. B. Black (Eds.), *Understanding expository text: A theoretical and practical handbook for analyzing explanatory text* (pp. 10–64). Hillsdale, NJ: Erlbaum Publishers.

Mickel, S. (1995). *Reading Chinese newspapers: Tactics and skills.* New Haven, CT: Yale University Press.

Mulling, S. (1994). A study of directed comprehension monitoring. *College ESL, 4*, 59–66.

Ning, C. (2003). 美国国内的汉语教材 [A survey of the Chinese textbooks in the United States] *International Chinese Language Teaching and Learning, 3*, 32–39.

Onwuegbuzie, A. (2002). The role of foreign language anxiety and students' expectations in foreign language learning. *Research in the Schools, 9*, 33–50.

Oxford, R. L. (1990). *Language learning strategies: What every teacher should know.* Boston: Heinle & Heinle Publishers.

Peng, D. L., Li, Y. P., & Yang, H. (1997). Orthographic processing in the identification of Chinese characters. In H. C. Chen (Ed.), *Cognitive processing of Chinese and related Asian languages* (pp. 85–108). Hong Kong: The Chinese University Press.

Phillips, V. (1991). A look at learner strategy use and ESL proficiency. *CATESOL Journal, 4*, 57–67.

Rost, M. (1991). Learner use of strategies in interaction: Typology and teachability. *Language Learning, 41*, 235–273.

Shen, H. (2005). An investigation of Chinese character learning strategies among non-native speakers of Chinese. *System, 33*(1), 49–68.

Sheorey, R. (1999). An examination of language learning strategy use in the setting of an indigenized variety of English. *System, 27*, 173–190.

Spring, M. K. (1999). Improving reading instruction in upper-level Chinese courses: Challenges and possibilities. In M. Chu (Ed.), *Mapping the course of the Chinese language field. Chinese Language Teachers Association monograph series, Vol. III* (pp. 51–70). Kalamazoo, MI: Chinese Language Teachers Association, Inc.

Stahl, S. (1983). Differential word knowledge and reading comprehension. *Journal of Reading Behaviour, 15*, 33–50.

Stanovich, K. E. (1980). Toward an interactive compensatory model of individual differences in the development of reading fluency. *Reading Research Quarterly, 16*, 32–71.

Tang, Y., & Chen, Q. (2005). *Advanced Chinese: Intention, strategy, & communication.* New Haven, CT: Yale University Press.

Taylor, I., & Park, K. (1995). Differential processing of content words and function words: Chinese characters vs. phonetic scripts. In I. Taylor & D. R. Olson (Eds.), *Scripts and literacy* (pp. 185–194). Dordrecht, the Netherlands: Kluwer Academic.

Vann, R. J., & Abraham, R. G. (1990). Strategies of unsuccessful learners. *TESOL Quarterly, 24,* 177–198.

Watanabe, Y. (1990). *External variables affecting language learning strategies of Japanese EFL learners: Effects of entrance examination, years spent at college/university, and staying overseas.* Unpublished master's thesis, Lancaster University, Lancaster, England.

Wellman, H. M. (1985). The origins of metacognition. In D. L. Forrest-Pressley, G. E. MacKinnon, & T. G. Waller (Eds.), *Metacognition, cognition, and human performance, I: Theoretical perspectives; II: Instructional practices* (pp. 4–31). Orlando, FL: Harcourt Brace Jovanovich.

Wen, X. H. (1998, November). *Improving reading strategies through an understanding of culture and language.* Paper presented at the annual meeting of the American Council on the Teaching of Foreign Languages, Chicago.

Wen, X. H. (1999). Chinese language learning motivation: A comparative study of different ethnic groups. In M. Chu (Ed.), *Mapping the course of the Chinese language field. Chinese Language Teachers Association monograph series, Vol. III* (pp. 121–150). Kalamazoo, MI: Chinese Language Teachers Association, Inc.

Wharton, G. (2000). Language learning strategy use of bilingual foreign language learners in Singapore. *Language Learning, 50*(2), 203–243.

Wong Fillmore, L. (1976). *The second time around: Cognitive and social strategies in second language acquisition.* Unpublished doctoral dissertation, Stanford University.

Xiao, Y. (2002). The effect of character density on learning Chinese as a foreign language. *Journal of the Chinese Language Teachers Association, 37*(3), 71–84.

Yan, M., & Liu, L. C. (1997). *Interactions: A cognitive approach to beginning Chinese.* Bloomington: Indiana University Press.

Yang, J. (2000). Orthographic effect on word recognition by learners of Chinese as a foreign language. *Journal of the Chinese Language Teachers Association, 32*(2), 1–18.

Yin, Y. (2003). 美国大学生记忆汉字时使用的方法—问卷调查报告 [Translated title]. *Journal of the Chinese Language Teachers Association, 38*(3), 69–90.

Yu, B., Feng, L., Cao, H., & Li, W. (1990). Visual perception of Chinese characters effect of perceptual task and Chinese character attributes. *Acta Psychologica Sinica, 22*(2), 141–1

Zhu, X. P., & Taft, M. (1994). The influence of perceptual experience on Chinese character processing. In H. W. Cheng, J. T. Huang, C. W. Hue, & O. J. L. Tzeng (Eds.), *Advances in the study of Chinese language processing* (pp. 85–99). Taipei: Department of Psychology, National Taiwan University.

Appendix A: Test passages used for each proficiency level

While only the simplified versions of the test passages are given here, both the traditional and simplified versions were presented to the readers in the study.

【汉字】

Level 2 (216 characters)

汉字在中国人的生活中很有用。去商店买东西, 或者出去玩儿, 在很多地方都可以看到汉字。在中国旅游, 这是一个重要的文化内容。

汉字有非常长的历史。人类历史上有四大文明古国: 巴比伦、古埃及、古印度 和中国。这四大文明古国的古代居民都发明了自己的文字, 但是, 今天还在使用的只有汉字。其他几种文字都已经变成了博物馆里的东西。

汉字的样子非常特别, 有的字有很多笔画, 有的字笔画很少。写一个字, 常常跟画画儿差不多, 上下、左右、大小, 等等, 都要想到。写好汉字, 是很不容易的事。汉字书法是一种特别的艺术。

Level 3 (252 characters)

汉字和中国人的生活有很密切的关系, 平时常常要用到它, 走到哪儿都能看到它。上街, 会见到商店的各种各样的门牌字号。出门旅游, 每到一个有名的地方, 往往就能看到古今人物的题词留字。在中国旅游, 这是一个重要的文化内容。

汉字有非常长的历史。人类历史上有四大文明古国: 巴比伦、古埃及、古印度和中国。这四大文明古国的古代居民都发明了自己的文字, 但是, 今天仍然在使用的只有汉字。其他几种文字都已经变成了博物馆里的东西。

汉字的样子非常独特, 笔画丰富多样。写一个字, 往往和画一幅画差不多, 上下左右, 粗细大小, 等等, 都要想到。写好汉字, 是很不容易的事。所以书法成为一种特别的艺术。

Level 4 (316 characters)

汉字和中国人的生活密切相关, 平时常常要用到它, 走到哪儿都能看到它。上街, 会见到各种各样的门牌字号。出门游历山川, 每到一处名胜之地, 往往就能看到古今人物的题词留字。这些 匾、联、题字有时起着画龙点睛的作用。在中国旅游, 这是一个重要的文化游览的内容。

汉字有悠久的历史。人类历史上有四大文明古国: 巴比伦、古埃及、古印度和中国。这四大文明古国的古代居民都发明了自己的文字, 但是, 传到今天并且仍然在使用的只有汉字。其他几种文字都已变成了博物馆里的古董。

汉字具有美的价值。它的造形非常独特, 笔画形态丰富多样。写一个字, 往往和 画一幅画差不多, 上下左右, 粗细大小, 比例虚 实, 呼应协调, 处处要顾及到。写好汉字, 是很不容易的事。所以书法成为一门特殊的艺术, 它可以让人表现出自己的情感与个性, 体现一种独特而高雅的创造精神。

Appendix B: See how they read

Questionnaire

The following statements are about your reading behaviors in reading the Chinese passage earlier. Based on reflection on what you did when reading the passage, please indicate the level of your agreement or disagreement with each statement by underlining the appropriate number: 5 indicates strong agreement, 1 indicates strong disagreement.

		strongly agree				strongly disagree
A.	I find the content of the passage familiar.	5	4	3	2	1
B.	I find the language of the passage difficult.	5	4	3	2	1

When reading the test passage silently,

1.	I was <u>able to</u> anticipate what would come next in the text.	5	4	3	2	1
2.	I was <u>able to</u> recognize the difference between main points and supporting details.	5	4	3	2	1
3.	I was <u>able to</u> relate information that came next in the text to previous information in the text.	5	4	3	2	1
4.	I was <u>able to</u> question the significance or truthfulness of what the author said.	5	4	3	2	1
5.	I was <u>able to</u> use my prior knowledge and experience to understand the content of the text I was reading.	5	4	3	2	1
6.	I had a good sense of when I understood something and when I did not.	5	4	3	2	1
7.	I was <u>able to</u> identify the source of comprehension difficulty.	5	4	3	2	1
8.	<u>I consciously tried</u> to anticipate what would come next in the text.	5	4	3	2	1

When reading the test passage silently,

9.	I consciously tried to recognize the difference between main points and supporting details.	5	4	3	2	1
10.	I consciously tried to relate information that came next in the text to previous information in the text.	5	4	3	2	1
11.	I consciously tried to question the significance or truthfulness of what the author said.	5	4	3	2	1
12.	I consciously tried to use my prior knowledge and experience to understand the content of the text I was reading.	5	4	3	2	1
13.	I consciously tried to monitor when I understood something and when I did not.	5	4	3	2	1
14.	I consciously tried to identify the source of comprehension difficulty.	5	4	3	2	1

When reading the test passage silently, if I didn't understand something,

15.	I ignored the problem and kept on reading, hoping for clarification further on.	5	4	3	2	1
16.	I reread the problematic part.	5	4	3	2	1
17.	I went back to the sentence before the problematic part and reread from there.	5	4	3	2	1
18.	I gave up and stopped reading.	5	4	3	2	1

When reading the test passage silently, the things I did to read effectively were to focus on

19.	mentally sounding out parts of the words.	5	4	3	2	1
20.	recognizing each character.	5	4	3	2	1
21.	recognizing each word.	5	4	3	2	1
22.	understanding the meaning of each character.	5	4	3	2	1
23.	understanding the meaning of each word.	5	4	3	2	1
24.	using radicals to guess at the meanings of unknown characters.	5	4	3	2	1
25.	using context to guess at the meanings of unknown words.	5	4	3	2	1
26.	getting the overall meaning of the text.	5	4	3	2	1
27.	the grammatical structures.	5	4	3	2	1
28.	relating the text to what I already know about the topic.	5	4	3	2	1
29.	distinguishing important parts from unimportant parts.	5	4	3	2	1
30.	the details of the content.	5	4	3	2	1
31.	the organization of the text.	5	4	3	2	1
32.	making inferences to connect information in the text.	5	4	3	2	1

When reading the test passage silently, things that made the reading difficult were

33.	not knowing the pronunciations of characters.	5	4	3	2	1
34.	not knowing the meanings of characters/words.	5	4	3	2	1
35.	recognizing word boundary (i.e., whether a character should go with the character(s) that precede(s) or follow(s) it to form a word).	5	4	3	2	1
36.	parsing a sentence into meaningful units.	5	4	3	2	1
37.	the grammatical structures.	5	4	3	2	1
38.	relating the text to what I already know about the topic.	5	4	3	2	1
39.	getting the overall meaning of the text.	5	4	3	2	1
40.	the organization of the text.	5	4	3	2	1
41.	remembering what I have read	5	4	3	2	1

In my opinion, in order to read effectively, a good reader in Chinese <u>at my current proficiency level</u> should:

42.	recognize every word (character) in a text.	5	4	3	2	1
43.	understand the overall meaning of a text.	5	4	3	2	1
44.	guess at word meanings.	5	4	3	2	1
45.	look up every unknown character or word in a dictionary.	5	4	3	2	1
46.	know when to skip unimportant information.	5	4	3	2	1
47.	integrate the information in the text with what he/she already knows.	5	4	3	2	1
48.	remember the details of the content.	5	4	3	2	1
49.	grasp the organization of the text.	5	4	3	2	1

对日本汉语学习者的自由复述过程的分析

Free Recall from Japanese Learners of Chinese

Aiqun Liu
Ritsumeikan University Language Education Center, Kyoto, Japan

本调查旨在考察日本汉语初学者对汉语语篇信息加工及提取的心理现象,采用即时自由复述方式,请学习者就听到的短文尽可能多地写出所能记住的东西。复述结果的记录材料分别有日语和目的语汉语两种。初步结果表明:学习者在复述时有偏重内容意义的倾向。具体表现为:各个语义内容成分其复述结果会受语篇中所处位置的影响;在复述时学习者会采用一些处理策略,像细节省略、内容添加,顺序改变等。学习者在复述时很可能在某种程度上受到了认知图示的影响。此外,语言项目的规则特点、母语、以及其他外语学习经验等因素对复述的结果也有一定影响。

Two important topics in second-language acquisition (SLA) research are the extent and cause of limitations on the content that filters through to learners (S. M. Gass, 1997). Those limitations, which apply during cognitive processes of second-language learning, are related to the process of accessing input, the process of making output, or an intermediate process (R. Ellis, 1994, 1997; Gass; B. Van Patten, 1996, 2004). According to Van Patten (1996, 2004), Gass, and others (S. Gui, 2000; Z. Xu, 2000, 2003), second-language learners have limited attentional resources. They have difficulty processing all input properly in real time; that is, completely or properly establishing all form-meaning relationships (performing all processes) is difficult for them when they handle target language input in real time.

This chapter discusses the process of immediate free recall by 32 Japanese learners of Chinese and specifically describes some limits that learners might confront during the processes described above. The limits include mechanisms of working memory and attention, processing strategies (Van Patten, 1996, 2004), semantic components in different locations in a passage, knowledge schema, learners' experiences of learning other second languages, and interference from the learners' native language.

Liu, A. (2010). Free recall from Japanese learners of Chinese. In M. E. Everson & H. H. Shen (Eds.), *Research among learners of Chinese as a foreign language* (Chinese Language Teachers Association Monograph Series: Vol. 4). (pp. 117–132). Honolulu: University of Hawai'i, National Foreign Language Resource Center.

Immediate written recall was used to measure listening comprehension: The learners were asked to report in Japanese and in the target language, Chinese, on everything they remembered about the passage they had just heard. The results revealed that the learners tended to weight the content meanings more heavily than the linguistic forms. The recall of semantic components in the passage seemed to be influenced by their locations in the passage. Some strategies were apparent: Details tended to be abbreviated, something new was added, and the sequence of semantic components was changed slightly. The use of knowledge schema was also investigated. Characteristics of linguistic forms, the learners' native language, and their experiences of learning other foreign languages apparently influenced their free-recall results.

引言

日本大学初级阶段的汉语课堂教学多以句子为中心，但学习者在用汉语交际过程中并非只限于听一句话或只看一个句子，还会接触比句子长的语言单位，需要理解语段篇章。因此，课堂教学在初级阶段也加入一些语篇内容，比如让学习者阅读或听短文、会话，并请学习者回答问题。内容的理解的练习类型多为判断正误、问答或多项选择等等。这些练习只是教学手段，也许不能帮助我们从认知角度很好地把握学习者对语篇的理解与记忆的过程和特点。

本文把由几个或多个有内在意义连贯性的句子所构成的段落单位称为语篇（有的研究称为语段）。语篇既有口头的也有书面的。探讨比句子长的语言单位的理解记忆过程，既要借助语篇的研究分析方法又要参考句子理解的研究方法。语篇理论与语篇分析已是当前应用语言学界热点之一。在第二语言（下称二语）习得领域，也有对语篇记忆的研究，但多涉及英语等欧美语言，并集中在阅读领域。举例来说，李慧、李杨、刘军平（2002）围绕语篇阅读对影响中国大学生对英语语篇记忆的若干因素进行了观察和分析。研究涉及了命题、图式和阅读方式。文章把命题分为三个层次：核心命题（文章主题）、重要命题（段落主题或主要情节）和边缘命题（细节）。作者提出：命题根据重要性被有选择地记忆，大命题的记忆优先于小命题的记忆。文中还提到图式在语篇处理中的作用。作者用说明文、议论文和叙述文三种类型的文章作为测量内容，并设定了有图式提示和无图式提示的两种阅读条件，分别从定性、定量两方面作了分析。结果表明：语篇阅读中命题分级存储于命题网结构中，记忆程度逐级变弱，并易受阅读方式、语篇体裁和语言水平等诸因素影响。

刘桂玲（2005）对近三十年来欧美心理学家和语言学家对于阅读后篇章记忆的研究进行了评述，文章考察了句子间的因果关系、语篇中名词或代词的照应指代关系、阅读时所作的推论等影响语篇记忆的多种因素，并提出：从记忆中提取语篇信息的过程是一个系统且有规律的过程。在教学中教师应适当增强篇章中语句间因果关系的分析，要帮助学生注意词语的照应关系，另外也应鼓励学生多用推理手段来加深对文章的理解和记忆。

对外汉语教学的语篇研究多集中在实践领域，重点放在"如何教"。朱其智（2001）彭小川（2004）等都探讨过如何在汉语课堂教学中应用语篇理论和语篇分析。比如，朱其智（2001）从语篇中词语的复现和同现、指称替代和省略、语篇衔接成分以及语篇宏观结构来介绍在精读课中如何应用语篇分析技巧。文章指出，应用自上而下的方法，帮助学生注意词语的复现率来抓文章的主题；弄清指称替代和省略关系来掌握语篇的发展脉络、提醒学生寻找语篇衔接成分来分析段落层次；也可通过画图表来显现语篇的宏观结构。彭小川（2004）则指出语篇教学中存在的问题。比如：教师的语篇教学意识还有待加深、语篇教学的研究成果不多、教材中缺少语篇训练内容。这些问题的根源在于语篇教学的范围和内容还未明确。作者提出把教学重点放在由句子组成语段、由语段组成语篇的衔接成分与衔接方式上。对语篇教学框架的整体设计，文章主张从纵横两方面考虑：所谓"纵"是指语篇训练的导入时期，在经过初级阶段的单句教学后，应在对字词句教学的同时开始语篇的基础训练。所谓"横"是指语篇训练并非只是精读课的"专利"，阅读、听力、口语、写作、语法等课程也都该纳入语篇教学的内容。

在"如何学"方面主要集中在对语篇中的各个句子的理解,比如,刘威(1996)从语篇阅读中的句子认知入手,在短时记忆中考察学习者对句子的理解。刘的调查显示:在认知过程中受到母语迁移的影响;中级阶段的学习者在阅读理解汉语句子时表现出更关注句子的核心意义的倾向;同时也有把多动词句转换为以某个动词为中心的动词谓语句的倾向。

从以上介绍可以看出,朱其智(2001)彭小川(2004)等提示我们在汉语课堂教学中不能只限于字词句的教学,要融入语篇教学的内容。这些研究提供了教学的具体构思和技巧,但这些构思和技巧的理论基础是什么?有何二语习得方面的理论依据?这些问题还有待探讨。此外,刘威(1996)、李慧、李杨、刘军平(2002)的研究所用的参试者多处在中高级阶段,研究材料以书面语为主,且均以阅读方式进行,而对初级阶段的学习者对声音符号系列的理解记忆都未涉及。虽然如此,这些研究从认知心理学角度出发,涉及了命题、图式(李慧、李杨、刘军平2002)、从记忆中提取语篇信息的有规律性(刘桂玲2005)、受母语迁移的影响、关注句子的核心意义的倾向(刘威1996)等因素,对本研究的实施很有启示。在前人研究的基础上,本研究将结合二语习得心理机制,从听解角度观察处在初级阶段的日本汉语学习者对语篇的信息加工及提取的情况。

理论框架

一般来说,语篇记忆主要考察学习者是怎么把句子组合到一起,比考察单句复杂。桂诗春(2000)介绍说语篇记忆涉及认知心理策略,又涉及目的语的语言规则特点以及学习者的中介语规则结构,同时也与学习者对世界的一般知识有关。这些要素在二语习得过程中都发挥着重要作用,因此考察语篇记忆需要在二语习得研究的框架下结合认知心理学的基本原理来进行。

二语习得过程在相当大的程度上与记忆这个心理机制密不可分。实际上很多二语习得模式也都离不开记忆(Ellis, 1994; Gass, 1997; VanPatten, 1996)。Ellis曾考察其它二语习得理论并总结出认知主义的二语习得流程模式(图1)。该流程描述了二语输入(L2 input)是如何被知觉(noticed)、理解(comprehended)、内化(intake)、如何进入学习者的中介语系统(interlanguage [IL] system),后来又如何被提取成为二语输出(L2 output)的过程。

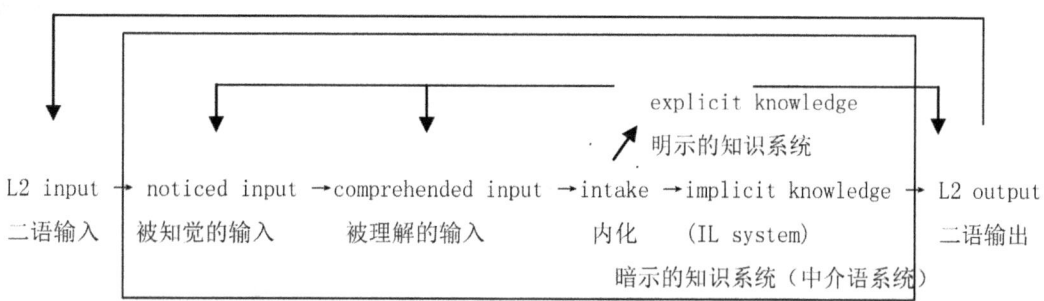

图1. 第二语言习得过程 (根据Ellis, 1994, p. 349 整理)

认知心理学把人的记忆分为感觉记忆、短时记忆和长时记忆等几种(桂诗春2000,徐子亮2000)。结合二语习得过程看,图1中的知觉是指浅层的未发生"形式-意义"联系的过程,比如对声音或文字的感知;理解是指赋予一定意义的过程;内在化指的是语言形式与意义之间建立"形式-意义"联系并进入短时记忆的过程。如图1所示:二语输入的一部分并非全部经内化进入到二语知识系统即中介语言系统(指长时记忆),也就是说并非所有的输入都能进入到短时记忆并由短时记忆再进入到长时记忆。认知心理学指出短时记忆空间既要存放材料又要对其加工,所以又称工作记忆(working memory)。因为短时记忆容量小,所加工的信息量有限,所以会牺牲或丢弃一些线索(徐子亮2000, p. 28)。在加工过程中,"注意"起着重要的作用。"注意"是一种心理过程,有选择性、专注性和分配

性 (徐子亮2003, p. 301) 的特点。徐子亮指出 (2003, p. 305)：在语言信息处理过程中，记忆单位通常表现为单词、短语或子句。这些语言信息在短时记忆中，通过句法规则构成一定的意义单位，被理解提取之后，语言形式便消失或被清除，以便接纳新的输入。由于二语学习者对目的语的处理能力弱尤其是短时记忆容量很小，并且受"注意"的制约，很难同时处理 (指建立"形式-意义"联系) 所有输入的信息，但是他们的"处理"是有规律可循的 (VanPatten, 1996)。

虽然学习者的记忆在"黑匣子"(图1的方框内) 内进行，看不见摸不着，但其记忆"产品"却能提供很多信息。桂诗春 (2000) 介绍说，语篇记忆研究多利用自由复述 (recall，也说回述) 来考察。一般来说，学习者在复述时有时会采取回避、借用母语、迂回表达、多用常见词语少用复杂词语等策略，他们的复述往往会受到"图式 (schema)"的影响。所谓图式是指人们理解眼前的事物、现象时所利用的某种认知性知识结构 (Shirahada, Tomita, Murano, & Wakabayashi, 1999, pp. 266–267)。李慧、李杨、刘军平 (2002) 把图式定义为语义记忆中对信息的预理解结构，并指出图式对记忆有很强的指导作用，比如与图式关系紧密的命题记忆深刻，不紧密的则容易丢失。图式有不同种类 (Cravotta, 2001)，可以是背景知识或关于世界的一般知识，也可与篇章结构、句法和修辞等相关，是一种自上而下的处理过程。对输入的语篇信息的处理过程，Abe, J., Momouchi, Y., Kaneko, Y., & Yi.K. (1994) 谈到，这是一个能动的过程，其理解进程会受到自身既有知识、对状况(situation)的把握程度、认知机制等多种因素的影响。既有知识至少有三类：语言、世界、对推理演绎规则的了解程度。状况主要指语境等背景内容。认知机制则包括感觉、知觉、记忆、思考、学习等复杂过程。在对输入的语篇信息处理过程中，人们在利用上述资源的同时也受到了这些资源的制约，人们会进行一些操作，比如回忆、推理、概括等。

VanPatten (1996, 2004) 从语言规则的特点与认知策略的交互作用的角度提出"输入处理策略 (input processing strategies)"理论，该理论主要描述学习者在线处理过程中如何使输入的语言形式赋予意义的过程，这一过程与"注意"的分配有关。输入处理策略据说是由输入进入到内化的过程中 (图1) 被学习者所使用，并与短时记忆有关，主要含三类：(1) 偏重内容意义 (content preference) (2) 句首名词或代词策略 (first noun strategy)，以及 (3) 句子位置影响 (sentencelocation)。其中第一种最具代表性。它指明学习者在"处理"输入时 (=建立"形式-意义"联系) 他们的"注意"主要集中在理解内容意思上，有些语法项目、语序、表示语法功能的虚词等往往未能得到充分"注意" (VanPatten, 1996)。

以上提及的理论框架，多以欧美语言的二语习得为背景，在汉语作为二语习得领域，以认知心理学记忆理论的框架为基础，结合二语习得理论考察语篇记忆机制，就目前来说仍是一个涉足不深的前沿课题。从理论方面说，以上提到的输入处理策略主要针对句子处理而言，在语篇理解方面是否能在某种程度上得到验证？汉语学习者对语篇输入中的信息又是怎么加工提取的呢？从实践方面说，教材教法的选用，除了教学经验外又该根据何种理论进行呢？这些问题都有待探讨。

在日本的很多大学，学生多把汉语作为第二公共外语来学习。日语中有常用汉字1900多字，日本学习者的汉字知识对阅读理解记忆的影响不能忽略不谈。在教学中常会发现日本学习者对声音符号系列的处理能力与对文字 (汉字) 符号系列的处理能力差距很大。为尽量避免汉字的影响，本文采用听后自由复述的方式采集数据。本文将以认知心理学记忆原理为基础，结合二语习得理论来考察日本汉语学习者对汉语语篇的信息加工及提取的心理现象。具体探讨以下几个问题：

1. 语义内容的回忆是否受语篇中所在位置的影响？
2. 日本汉语学习者在对语义内容做复述时使用了什么样的认知加工策略？具体表现如何？
3. 学习者用目的语汉语复述时，其重新编码的语言形式有何特点？

本文的作者希望通过对以上问题的讨论，能进一步了解学习者对汉语作为二语习得的认知机制，同时也希望能帮助教师根据学生的认知规律更好地设计教学用语料、做好有针对性的预备练习。

方法步骤

参与者

参与者为日本某大学二年级上半学期一个自然班共32名学习者。之所以选择二年级是因为一年级需花大量时间练习发音，词汇量有限，二年级的学生通过一段时间的学习对汉语有一定理解能力。参加者所学汉语时间约为90小时，掌握词语500个左右（每周两节，一节90分，一学年26周左右）。所用教材为大学指定，教材按功能项目编排，如自我介绍、购物、问路等。每课围绕一个功能项目，分别有4个会话，每个长度约3-4句。每个会话都配有句型替换练习，会话后有短文阅读、听力练习，内容都与同一功能项目相关；此外，还有相关词汇、语法练习。前文介绍过，日本学生在学习汉语前就有一定汉字基础，因此汉字教学多集中在区分日语汉字与汉语汉字的差异。教学重点在句型操练、发音、会话和听力上，教学方法基本上以教师为中心。另外，日本学习者学习汉语时的一个显著特点就是要把听到或看到的汉语翻译成日语，如果不知道日语的意思学习者常常会觉得不安，因此，课堂教学中课文的日语翻译是不得不做的功课。该班的任课教师从入门阶段起就是汉语为母语的中国教师，课堂教学用语使用学习者的母语日语。

测量工具

为考察语篇记忆，本调查采用听后即时自由笔头复述 (immediate written recall)。调查时先让学习者听一个短文，然后让学习者尽可能回忆并写出听过的内容。采用听的方式，是因为日本学习者阅读能力远比听解能力强，考察对声音符号系列的处理，可避免汉字的影响。同时，为避免题目的类型或问答的内容可能会为学习者提供一些线索，本调查不采用判断正误、问答、或多项选择等做法。

本调查方法的选用也有二语习得研究方法论上的依据。桂诗春 (2000) 介绍说，最简单而最直接评估语篇记忆能力的方法是即时自由复述。Ellis & Barkhuizen (2005) 也谈到评估语篇记忆的方法，比如先让学习者听一些含有一定的语言项目的句子，然后让学习者尽可能回忆并确切地复述出听过的句子。此法的出发点是：如果句子长，学习者也许就会记不住或回忆不出原来的词语，但即时要求他们回忆并复原听过的话，学习者会尽量通过意义内容来组织复述，使句子的意思与原文保持一致。在此过程中学习者需要根据他们自身的语言规则资源 (中介语) 就意义内容重新编码。基于这个原因，本调查选用了即时自由复述。

调查者根据学习者的汉语水平 (词汇、语言项目、课堂教学安排) 设计了以下一段话。该短文根据学习者所用教材内容作了改动，含标点长短共62字，内容为叙事，文中出现的语法项目或词汇，除了"门口"（调查时告诉了学习者该词的发音和意思）这个词语以外，都未超出学习者的水平。

> 我对看电影很有兴趣（"很"重读）。我经常去大通（地名）看电影。我的朋友有两张今天晚上的电影票。我们下午六点在学校门口见面，一起坐地铁去大通看电影。

该短文共有4个完整句子，均为动词谓语句，其中单动词句2个，多动词句2个。带介词短语做状语的2句，带多项定语的1句。短文中出现的副词为"很"、"经常"、"一起"。文中涉及细节的部分为"很"、"经常"、"两张"、"今天晚上"、"下午六点"、"在学校门口"、"一起"和"坐地铁"等。考察学习者的复述内容时可以根据语篇内各个语义信息的排列先后、细节部分的处理情况、语序有否变化、复述内容上有否改变等情况来了解学习者对语篇信息提取加工的过程。

数据收集

调查是在日常课堂教学中进行的。本文作者是任课教师,因此参与了调查和观察。调查者让全体学习者听上述短文,短文中各个句子间没有停顿,一气念完。一共念了3遍。听完后要求学习者尽可能在忠实于原文的基础上马上做笔头自由复述。整个过程约10分钟。本调查在第二学年刚开学不久进行。学习者经过一个假期,对很多词汇、语法项目都有不同程度的遗忘。考虑这个因素,首先让学习者用母语做复述。所收集的数据为文字材料,用笔头方式让学习者写下来,而不是用口头表达,主要是因为书面数据在收集处理时容易操作。此外,学习者也比较习惯汉译日的方式,如果没有母语的媒介,很多学习者用汉语直接写出的内容就会很有限,可供分析的材料就会少一些。32名学习者当中有10名也用汉语作了复述。这10份复述材料也作为分析对象。

测量方法

如何评估学习者的复述情况?应依据什么尺度来分析判断?这些问题涉及到原文语篇信息以及学习者的复述结果的量化方法的选用。刘威 (1996) 曾借用命题的概念将句的语义信息量化,然后考察学习者回忆中的语义信息量的多寡。如果单纯利用命题的概念,有些汉语虚词,像"很"的语义等就会较难处理。因此,本调查采用对内容提问的方式将语义信息量化。下面用"我对看电影很有兴趣"一句作为范例来说明如何通过尽可能多地提问获得语义信息:

表1. "我对看电影很有兴趣"的语义信息量化

1. 谁对看电影有兴趣?	我
2. 你对做什么事情有兴趣?	看电影
3. 你看什么?	电影
4. 你对看电影有没有兴趣?	有兴趣
5. 你对看电影是不是很有兴趣?	很有兴趣

通过以上操作,对"我对看电影很有兴趣"一句共提了5个问题 (表1),该句就有5个语义单位,本调查把该句的语义量化值定为5。经此处理,整个复述短文的语义信息总值为25。计算学习者复述中各个语义信息值的高低可在某种程度上考察其记忆的广度。

整个语篇按自然句的停顿及排列顺序,分为开头、中间和末尾三部分。开头部分为"我对看电影很有兴趣。我经常去大通 (地名) 看电影";中间部分指"我的朋友有两张今天晚上的电影票";末尾部分则为"我们下午六点在学校门口见面,一起坐地铁去大通看电影"。按语篇中位置,考察各语义信息所得的值可看出学习者对语义信息的记忆分布。分别考察各个位置的语义信息复述情况,可探讨语篇中所在位置对复述结果可能会带来的影响。

计分方法

按照学习者复述中出现的语义内容单位来计算得分。评分采用分析法。举例来说,"我对看电影很有兴趣"分为5个语义单位:"我"、"看 (电影)"、"电影"、"有兴趣""很"。每个语义内容单位定为1分,这个句子总分为5分。假设学习者的复述为"我对电影有兴趣",可看出该复述的语义信息中缺少了"看"和"很"的内容,对这两部分就不得分,因此,该复述的语义信息总得分就为3分。每个复述的语义内容分别计算,再以上文的5个语义单位为例,比如我们要看看各部分分别都有百分之多少的人复述出来,这个数字就定为正确率 (%)。正确率高的说明复述出来的人多,相反则少,之后可根据各个正确率的高低来进一步考察语言规则特点以及学习者的认知心理机制对复述的影响。

结果及分析

根据认知心理学关于语言处理的原理,一般来说,短期记忆过程中的东西是语义信息即内容意义的聚合而非句法结构即语言形式的汇集,但这个语义信息的汇总不应是任意的而应是有规律的。这个规律在作为二语的汉语语义的再构筑时表现如何呢？为方便分析描述，按照本文研究的问题对复述结果分成三大项进行分析讨论。第一大项与语篇中语义成分所在位置有关，我们分别统计开头中间和末尾不同位置的语义成分其相关复述的正确率，并进行定量分析。第二项与语义内容有关，涉及学习者复述时对汉语语篇的信息加工及提取时所使用的策略。这一项围绕语义内容比较学习者的复述和原文，并根据复述内容的变化形式作分析，具体分为内容添加、细节省略、顺序改变、内容改变（具体定义见下文）。对这部分我们通过举出复述的例证来做些分析描述。最后一项，以学习者用汉语作的复述为分析对象，就语言规则特点等因素做些介绍。

语篇中语义成分所在位置的影响

32名学习者的复述结果分别用图2和图3表示。图2为复述结果的得分分布。满分为25，平均得分12.6，最高23分，最低5分。18分到23分之间合计5人，8分到17分之间合计23人，5分到7分之间合计4人。

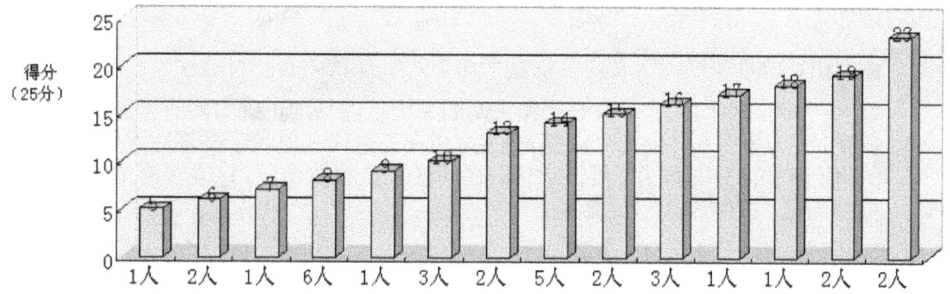

图2. 语义信息复述得分分布（N=32, 满分25分）

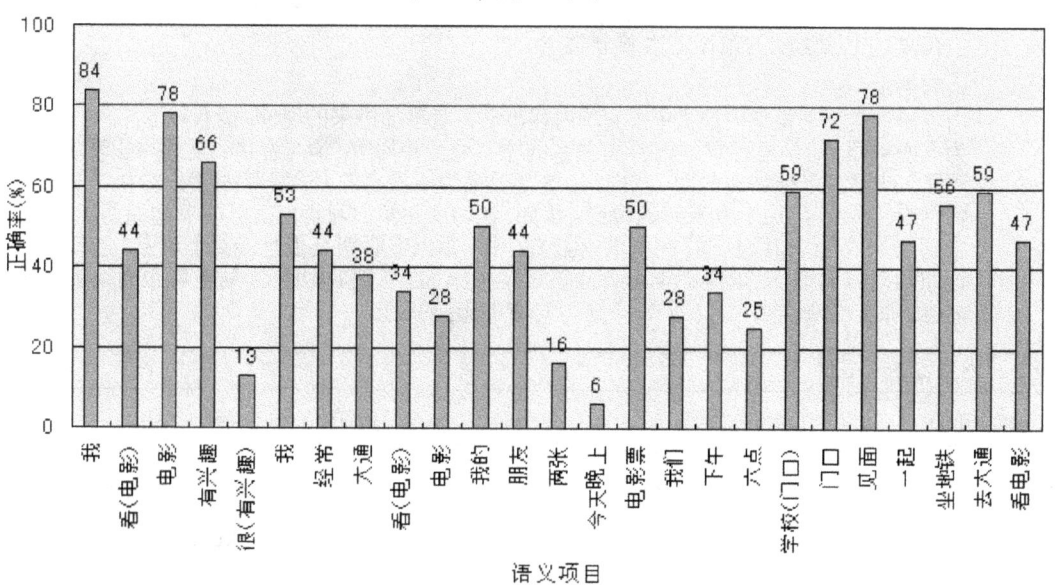

图3. 语义信息分项复述正确率（%, N=32）

图3列出的是语义信息分项复述正确率。按各语义成分在语段中的自然位置，开头中间末尾从左到右依次排列。图中数字为复述平均正确率。整体上，正确率的高低呈现中间低两头高的V字形分布。另外，像"很（13%）"、"两张（16%）"、"今天晚上（6%）"等的复述正

确率都相对很低,而正确率较高的部分分别为最开始的"我 (84%)"、"电影 (78%)"、"有兴趣 (66%)",以及接近末尾的"门口 (72%)"、"见面 (78%)"以及"去大通 (59%)"。

学习者的复述按开头中间和末尾三部分考察,为的是探讨语义成分在语篇中不同位置对学习者的复述有无影响。图4为各部分平均正确率的柱状图。看图可知: 开头的平均正确率53%、末尾52%,两者很接近;中间最低为32%。

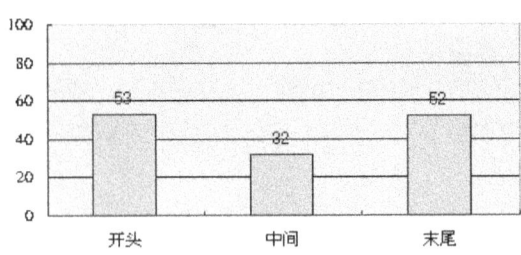

图4. 语篇中不同位置语义内容复述平均正确率柱状图 (%, N=32)

那么,中间的平均正确率与开头和末尾的平均复述平均正确率间有无统计学意义上的差异呢? 经方差分析 (ANOVA) 得F值5.787。查表得知该值大于显著性水平$p<.01$ (两侧) 时的F值 ($F(2, 93) = 4.85$)。可推定它们之间存在显著性差异。这说明语义信息在语篇中的位置对复述的结果有一定影响。

复述中所使用的认知处理策略

对学习者的复述内容进行定性分析后,我们发现,学习者在对汉语语篇的信息加工及提取时,与原文相比复述的语义内容发生了种种变化。这些变化有的是原先没有的内容被添加了进来,有的是原有的细节丢失了,有的是语义内容的排列顺序发生了变化。以下是对学生在复述中所运用的策略的大致分类。

内容添加

内容添加是指在复述时原文中没有的内容被学习者添加进来的现象。请看以下各例 (表2)。为方便对照,与学习者复述内容有关的原文也一并列出。学习者10的复述中出现了"下雨了",以及"坐地铁见的面"的内容,这是原文中所没有的。学习者15的复述中"和朋友常常看"的内容,原文也未明确说过。再如,学习者16和学习者17在复述中增加了在"门口拿到票"、"在门口给我票"的情节,但原文并未指出电影票是否已经给了对方,也未提及把票给对方的地点的内容。学习者22在复述中添加了"她 (指朋友) 对电影很有兴趣"的内容,原文也未说明"她 (朋友)"是否对看电影感兴趣。

表2. "内容添加"举例

学习者	原文	学习者的复述 (汉语译文)
学习者10	…我们下午六点在学校门口见面,一起坐地铁去大通看电影。	Eiga wo mita. Ame ga futta. Chikatetsu ni notte atta ((我) 看电影了。下雨了。坐地铁见的面。)
学习者15	…我经常去大通看电影。…我们下午六点在学校门口见面,一起坐地铁去大通看电影。	Watashi wa fudan eiga wo yoku mimasu. Tomodachi to yoku mimasu. (我常常看电影。和朋友常常看。)
学习者16	…我的朋友有两张今天晚上的电影票。我们下午六点在学校门口见面,一起坐地铁去大通看电影。	Chikatetsu ni notte odori no eigakan ni iki, iriguchi de ken wo moratta. ((我) 坐地铁去大通的电影院, 在门口拿到票。)

学习者17	我对看电影很有兴趣。我经常去大通看电影。我的朋友有两张今天晚上的电影票。我们下午六点在学校门口见面,一起坐地铁去大通看电影。	Watashi wa eiga ni kyoumi ga aru. Odori ni eiga wo mini iku. Watashi no tomodachi ga chiketto wo iriguchi de watashita. Gakkou no ato, chikatetsu de odori ni eiga wo mini itta. (我对电影有兴趣。去大通看电影。我朋友在门口给我票。放学后,坐地铁去大通看电影了。)
学习者22	…我的朋友有两张今天晚上的电影票。我们下午六点在学校门口见面,一起坐地铁去大通看电影。	我朋友,今天晚上的电影票。在学校门口,一起坐地铁去大通看电影。她对电影很有兴趣。

细节省略

所谓细节省略是指对学习者来说语篇中原有的相对不太重要的语义内容(区别于中心语义内容、比如主题或重要情节)在他们的复述中没有出现的现象。细节部分的语义内容其载体多为非中心词语(比如修饰性成分),该类词语语义内容的复述相对中心词语而言正确率较低。

表3. 非中心词语与中心词语语义内容复述情况

非中心词语语义内容		中心词语语义内容	
原文: 我的朋友有两张今天晚上的电影票。 N=32			
两张	16%	朋友	44%
今天晚上	6%	电影票	50%
原文: 我们下午六点在学校门口见面。 N=32			
下午	34%	门口	72%
六点	25%	见面7	8%

比如,位于中部"我的朋友有两张今天晚上的电影票"一句(表3),表示细节的修饰性成分如"两张"和"今天晚上"其正确率分别只有16%和6%。汉语复述中写出了"两张"和"今天晚上"的10名当中也只有2名。"我们下午六点在学校门口见面"一文(表3)的复述也能看到同样的现象。举例来说,表示细节的"下午"正确率为34%、"六点"25%,相比之下较"学校(门口)59%"和"门口(72%)"要低许多。换言之,这些部分正确率之所以低,大多是因为在复述中被丢失所致。这里的"门口"是生词,但复述的正确率很高,多半是因为调查者在调查开始时曾给学习者解释并带读过这个词语的缘故。

顺序改变

顺序改变是指原文中先出现的语义内容在学习者的复述中后出现、或者原文中后出现的语义内容在学习者的复述中提前出现这种前后顺序与原文不一致的现象(表4)。比如,原文的顺序为: 先"在学校门口见面",然后再"一起坐地铁"去"看电影"。学习者11的顺序为: "一起"、"坐地铁"、"看电影",然后才是"在门口见面"。在学习者12的复述中"坐地铁"提前出现,而这是在原文的结尾部分才出现的内容。在学习者16的复述中"电影票"的出现要比原文晚。学习者30的复述内容与原文"我们下午六点在学校门口见面,一起坐地铁去大通看电影"相比较,可发现原文中后出现的"看电影"先出现了,而"在学校门口见面"的内容,却被后置。

表4. "顺序改变"举例

学习者	原文	学习者的复述 (汉语译文)
学习者11	…我们下午六点在学校门口见面,一起坐地铁去大通看电影。	Eiga wo mini iku. Issyo ni chikatetsu ni notte eiga wo mi ni ikimasyou. Gakkou mon de aimasyou. ((我)去看电影。(我们)一起坐地铁去看电影吧。在学校门口见面吧。)
学习者12	我对看电影很有兴趣。我经常去大通看电影。…我们下午六点在学校门口见面,一起坐地铁去大通看电影。	Watashi wa eiga wo miru koto ni kyoumi ga arimasu. Watashi wa itsumo odori no eigakan ni chikatetsu ni notte ikimasu. Kyou gakkou no koumon de machiawasete issyo ni ikimasenka? (我对看电影有兴趣。我常常坐地铁去大通的电影院。今天在学校门口见面,一起去好吗?)
学习者16	我对看电影很有兴趣。…我的朋友有两张今天晚上的电影票。我们下午六点在学校门口见面,一起坐地铁去大通看电影。	Eiga ni kyoumi ga aru. Chikatetsu ni notte odori no eigakan ni iki, iriguchi de ken wo moratta. ((我)对电影有兴趣。坐地铁到大通的电影院,在门口拿到了票。)
学习者30	…我们下午六点在学校门口见面,一起坐地铁去大通看电影。	Eiga wo issyo ni mini ikimasyou. Koumon no tokoro de aimasyou. Odori made issyo ni chikatetsu de ikimasyou. ((我们)一起去看电影吧。在学校门口见面吧。一起坐地铁去大通吧。)

内容改变

除细节省略、顺序改变、内容添加外还有其它有关语义内容发生改变的情况,与以上几种有所不同,这里称为内容改变,是指原有的一些语义内容在学习者的复述中发生了变形。举例来说,在学习者8复述中的"电影票"所属者由原文的"朋友"变为了"我"。同样,学习者26写道"(我) 拿着电影票去门口",也把票的"所有者"改变成"我"。再如学习者17,原文是在"门口见面",而在学习者复述中这个情节被发展为在门口"朋友把票给了我"。再如学习者4提到"我喜欢电影",但原文是"我对看电影很有兴趣",从逻辑上因为"喜欢"所以才能"有兴趣",这样的推理似乎也有道理。此外,学习者30的复述整体是祈使语气。该学习者在用日语复述时使用了表示意愿的形式,而原文是陈述语气,没有表示提案或建议的祈使语气。以上就自由复述中所使用的认知处理策略通过学习者的复述实例作了介绍。这些例子告诉我们: 学习者在对汉语语篇的信息加工及提取时,即使复述这种看似单纯的过程,学习者也会在头脑中生成自己的理解; 也会利用内容添加、细节省略、顺序改变等各种策略,他们复述的内容有的也会发生改变。因此他们的复述不是单纯的重复,而是会发生种种变化,正如理论框架中所介绍的学习者对世界的既有知识与理解进展过程中所采用的策略发生相互作用从而会对理解的结果产生影响。

汉语目的语的重新编码

学习者在回忆复原的过程中也许会记不住或回忆不出原来的词语,他们会通过内容的意义来处理,这时学习者就需要根据其自身的资源 (比如中介语) 就内容意义重新编码。考察学习者用目的语汉语的复述 (10份复述材料) 可以了解一些学习者对目的语重新编码的情况。以下把学习者用汉语所作的复述大致归类,分别从形式改变、语序改变、丢字词等几方面做些介绍。

形式改变

这里的形式改变是指对某个语义内容原文中用形式A表达，而学习者在复述时则用了形式B来表达的现象。比如对"我对看电影很有兴趣"一句的复述，可看到有30%的学习者没有使用原文的"有兴趣"而使用了"感兴趣"。"感兴趣"和"有兴趣"这两种说法，在学习者使用的教材的同一课中出现，学习者也刚刚学过。也许从侧面可以推测，原先的"有兴趣"的语义被理解了，其内容意义再次产出时以"感兴趣"的形式出现。再如学习者10的复述"我坐地铁到大通"与原文"坐地铁去大通"相比，一个是"到"一个是"去"，两者所表达的意义近似。这些现象说明：学习者最初记住的是内容，原文确切的词语或语序等语言形式消失，再次提取时，要根据记住的内容意义进行重新编码，这时有可能以别的语言形式出现，这说明学习者在复述时并不是照相机式地机械重复。

此外，还有一类形式改变，与学习者误听或未能理解内容意义相关联。请看下例 (表5)。

表5. 与误听或未能理解内容意义有关的"形式改变"举例

学习者	学习者的复述
学习者10	我坐地铁到大通。下雨。
学习者25	我们下雨，在学校门口见面。

两名学习者在复述中都提到了"下雨"这个情节。究竟是什么线索会让学习者写出看似与原文内容不相干的字词。原因应在于语音线索"xiawu"的"wu"其发音与日语的"雨 (训读ame、音读u)"的音读很接近。经确认，这两名学习者受母语语音的影响，觉得日语中汉字的"音读"源于汉字的读音，误以为"雨"的发音是"wu"。特别是学习者25写道"我们下雨，在学校门口见面"，句中"下雨"位于主语的后边。这说明学习者在复述时没有足够时间考虑"下雨"在句中的作用、它与全句的内容意义是否相关。

语序改变

语序改变是指学习者的复述中句子内各成分的排列顺序有些与原文不一致的现象 (表6)。

表6. "语序改变"举例

学习者	原文	学习者的复述
学习者12	我经常去大通看电影。	我经常去大通看电影坐地铁。
学习者12	我们下午6点在学校门口见面，一起坐地铁去大通看电影。	今天一起去。在学校门口见面。
学习者20	一起坐地铁去大通看电影。	坐地铁一起去大通看电影。
学习者21	我经常去大通看电影。	经常我去大通看电影。

比如学习者20的复述"坐地铁一起去大通看电影"中的"坐地铁一起去…"的语序不同于原文的"一起坐地铁去…"。再如，学习者21的"经常我去大通看电影"，如只看按语义内容的多寡，该复述与原文一样，但语序上副词"经常"放到了句首，语序也发生了变化。经询问，对学习者21来说，"我星期一去大通看电影"和"星期一我去大通看电影"一样，表示时间的词语"星期一"在句首或主语后都说得通，"经常"与时间有关，也可套用这个规则。另外学习者12的"我经常去大通看电影坐地铁"句中表示方法手段的"坐地铁"被移到了句末。"坐地铁"的内容本是短文末尾部分的内容，却在这里提前出现了。此外，从复述的句子成分的排列看，"坐地铁"被放在最后，其位置不妥，一般不符合汉语习惯。

字词丢失

字词丢失指的是学习者复述中出现的某个表达方式与原文相比缺少了某个字词的现象。学习者的复述中丢字词的现象比较明显。

"看电影"和"电影"

位于开头的"我对看电影很有兴趣"一句,10名中有9名学习者对此部分作了复述。复述中既有"对电影有(感)兴趣"也有"对看电影有(感)兴趣"的说法。其中有两名在复述中没有使用"看"。在用母语所做的复述中两者的正确率相差30%左右,学习者提到"电影"的占78%;而补充了"看"的减少到44%。汉语中像"喜欢吃中国菜"、"喜欢看电影"、"喜欢打棒球"等短语中一般具体点明相关动作行为,而一些日本学习者倾向省去"吃""看""打"之类表示动作行为的词语。对一些学习者来说"看电影"和"电影"似乎没有大的区别。原因可能在于在他们的母语中即使不出现"看"的语义内容,而只说"eiga ni kyoumi ga aru (直译: 对电影有兴趣)"也是完全可以接受的。

"很有兴趣"和"有兴趣"

"我对看电影很有兴趣"一句的后半部"很有兴趣",在调查实施时调查者虽特意重读了"很",但在复述时,很多的学习者没有提到"很"的语义内容,32名用母语复述中含有"很"的语义内容的只有13%(图3)。10名学习者用汉语复述的材料中加了"很"的只有4名。

下面是"我对看电影很有兴趣"的复述情况的几个例子(表7):

表7. "我对看电影很有兴趣"的复述情况

母语日语复述	N=32	目的语汉语复述	N=10
看电影 44%	很有(感)兴趣 13%	看电影 70%	很有(感)兴趣 40%
电影 78%	有(感)兴趣 66%	电影 90%	有(感)兴趣 40%

从整体上,丢字词较多的是对语篇中部"我的朋友张今天晚友有两张今天晚上的电影票"的复述。整个句子丢失的10名中有2名。剩下8名当中,没有一名的复述完全与原文一致。只有3名的复述含主谓宾结构,其他人的复述均为简单的短语或字词。这些复述多由中心词语构成,比如"朋友"(6人)、"电影票"(8人)等中心词语复述出来的较多,相比之下,表示细节的"两张"和"今天晚上"分别只有两人复述出来。这种丢字词,与前边介绍的情况略有不同,这里所丢的字词多为表示细节的词语。

下面是"我的朋友有两张今天晚上的电影票"的复述情况例举(表8):

表8. "我的朋友有两张今天晚上的电影票"复述情况

学习者10	未复述
学习者12	未复述
学习者19	电影票。
学习者20	朋友有两张今天晚上的电影票。
学习者21	朋友有两张电影票。
学习者22	我朋友。今天晚上的电影票。
学习者23	我朋友有电影票。
学习者24	电影票。
学习者25	我朋友。电影票。
学习者32	我朋友。电影票。

"我朋友 (我的朋友)"和"朋友"

对"我的朋友有两张今天晚上的电影票"一句中的主语"我的朋友"的复述,没有交代"谁"的朋友而仅出现"朋友"的有两例 (学习者20和学习者21), 用母语日语复述的材料中,没有明确出现"我的"语义的要占50% (图3)。我们推测,日本学习者在汉语复述中省掉第一人称,很可能是受母语的影响。日语由于语用的要求,很多情况下第一人称作主语 (或作主语的修饰性成分) 时可以不提或不必要点明,第一人称主语省略的现象比较多。也许日本学习者把这个语用规则迁移到汉语上,在有一定上下文的语境中,也会较少使用汉语的第一人称。

这部分的复述还有一个有趣的现象,就是原先的"我的朋友"在4名学习者的复述中变为"我朋友",结构助词"的"没有出现。是否可以考虑,结构助词"的"发音是轻声,没被学习者充分注意到,当然这个问题还有待进一步证实。

讨论及建议

以上分析和介绍了以日语为母语的汉语初学者自由复述情况。调查结果表明: 总体上学习者在对汉语语篇的信息加工及提取时,有偏重内容意义的倾向。各个语义内容成分其复述结果会受语篇中所处位置的影响; 在复述时学习者会采用一些认知处理策略,像内容添加、细节省略、顺序改变、内容改变等等。此外,学习者对语篇信息提取加工、进行重新编码时,与原文相比,对同一语义内容会使用不同的形式,语序会发生变化,字词也有丢失等情况出现。那么,这些发现有何理论价值呢? 以下结合研究的问题作些探讨。

本研究的问题之一是对语义成分的回忆是否受语篇中所在位置的影响? 目前的分析结果应为"是"。复述结果表明: 语篇中部的语义成分最难被回忆出来,换言之,语篇中部的语义成分较难在短期记忆中停留。这一点,与VanPatten (1996, 2004) 在线处理策略中的"易受句中所在位置的影响"有着一致性。比句子长的语言单位,语义成分的处理也受语篇中所在位置的影响,认知心理机制也在起一定作用。

本研究问题之二: 日本汉语学习者在对语义内容复述时使用了什么样的认知处理策略? 具体表现如何? 从分析中可看到学习者的复述有种种变化,比如细节省略、内容添加、顺序改变、内容改变等等。这些策略很可能与学习者的中介语规则、母语或他们的认知心理机制有关,但也应与目的语语言形式的特点特别是其内容意义的强弱有关。内容意义的强弱要在具体语境中看该部分的内容意义对整体内容的影响有多大。文中提到,整体的语义成分复述正确率基本呈V字形,即开头末尾高中间低。复述的质量与语义成分在语段中的位置有关,也与该语义成分是否表示细节等有关。同样,即使不在中部的表示细节的语义成分,其复述的正确率也相应变低。比如,调查中使用的"很"等词语,对一些学习者来说它的有无对整体内容的影响似乎不太大,其内容意义相对要弱一些。学习者的复述中"很"的使用率较低,从侧面说明他们未能很好地处理"很"。这与汉语初学者二语的短期记忆容量非常有限、抓主要内容的认知策略以及"很"的中介语规则有关系。

在学习者的复述中存在原先没有的内容被"添加"、"改变"等现象,这种现象看似随意其实是有规律的,它与理解内容时学习者所作的推理假设有关。比如"在电影院门口拿到了票"等复述内容很可能就是学习者的"看电影"的图示在起作用。前面提到认知心理学的研究表明人们在记忆时采用的并非是照相式的保存方式,而是利用自身经历积累而成的图式作为心理机制,把输入进行加工并完成图式的再构筑。因此,图式对记忆有很强的指导作用。再回到学习者的复述"我坐地铁去大通的电影院,在电影院门口拿到了票",与原文的"朋友"有电影票,"我"和"朋友"在学校门口见面后一起去看电影的顺序有出入。一般在日本常见的情况是到电影院门口以后当场买票。因此看电影的图式很可能是"去看电影→去电影院→在电影院门口买票",难怪有的学习者会"推迟"拿到电影票的时间。同样与朋友见面的地点也有改在"电影院"门口的,这恐怕也是学习者的"预理解结构"—图式在发挥一定作用,受图式的影响学习者会生成自己的理解并反映到记忆的"产品"中去。

本研究问题之三: 日本汉语学习者复述时用汉语目的语重新编码的语言形式有何特点?从对10份用汉语所做的复述的分析结果可以看到: 学习者倾向于抓主要内容意思, 复述中也以表达主要内容为主的倾向。学习者在用目的语汉语重新编码时, 与原文比较, 他们的复述对同一语义内容会使用不同的形式, 语序会发生变化, 字词也有丢失等情况出现, 也表现出多用简单结构少用复杂结构的倾向。学习者在处理输入时, 很自然地知道哪些部分表达的是主要内容; 他们记忆的产品也表现出"重"内容意义 (中心词语), "轻"形式的特点, 这种策略与语言形式的规则特点有关, 也与认知心理机制有关。

了解学习者在复述时使用的认知加工策略, 可以帮助我们结合心理机制的角度探讨为什么有些语义成分没记住, 为什么有些语言形式在复述时发生变形或根本未出现的现象。语序变化、丢词语等现象告诉我们学习者对一些语言形式 (规则) 未能处理或只做了部分处理, 未能在短期记忆中得以储存。像"很"之类的虚词, 其意义内容有"虚"的一面, 而且多与"细节"密切相关, 学习者很可能在抓主要内容、省略细节时也连带把"虚词"一起省略了。这既与学习者的认知心理机制有关也与虚词的语言形式规则特点有关。VanPatten (1996, pp. 23–27) 指出: 每个语言形式 (含语序) 在语境中都有自己的交际价值, 语言形式的交际价值与其所表达的语义对整体内容的贡献度有关。它包含两个方面: 内在含有的语义 (inherent semantic value), 以及该语言形式在句子(或话语)中是否只起语法作用, 在整个话语中是否是多余的语义成分。简单地说, 与该语言形式在语义上含义的多寡强弱有关系。VanPatten补充说: 有些语言形式与其他语言形式相比, 在语义上常常会表现出它的冗余性 (redundancy), 其语言形式的交际价值相对要低一些。对二语学习者来说, 交际价值高的处理起来容易些, 交际价值低的就不太容易。汉语的虚词具有语法功能较强而实际的语义相对较弱的特点。是否可以假设, 这样的虚词其语言形式的交际价值相对较低, 在汉语学习初级阶段常不易被较好地处理 (建立"形式-意义"联系)。

从学习者的复述结果也能看到母语的影响。虽然不能过分强调母语的负迁移作用, 但母语对二语习得的影响还是存在的。本调查中一些日本学习者在复述时将第一人称作主语的修饰性成分"我"省去了, 这个倾向在他们用母语复述的结果中也很突出。同样, 日语汉字的发音和汉语发音的混同导致学习者将"下午"理解成"下雨", 这种处理应该说母语的影响占有一定比重。

分析学习者的复述结果也促使我们考虑, 学习者是否也受到了其他外语学习经验的影响。在介绍中看到, 像学习者12"我经常去大通看电影坐地铁"复述的语序发生了变化。学习者首先处理的是内容意义而不是语序, 复述在语序上的变化很可能源于学习者的中介语规则、对语序处理得不充分, 学习者的中介语规则很可能也受到其他外语学习经验的影响。比如日常教学中常遇到的一些类似的偏误, 学习者常会说"*我吃午饭在食堂"、"*我去学校走路"、"*我来学校明天"。这些句子若按日语的语序来说, 其语序与汉语基本相同。但为什么日本学习者还出现这类处理呢? 汉语对日本学习者来说是外语, 但他们对外语的最初认识一般先来自英语, 很可能有些学习者把英语的一些规则, 特别是语序规则迁移到了汉语上。

考察学习者的复述, 可以帮助我们推测学习者所使用的中介语规则、猜测什么样的语言形式优先被处理、或不易被处理, 因而不易处理的语言形式与偏误间的关系也就能进一步明瞭, 让我们可以从新的角度对待学习者的偏误, 更好地制订教学对策。学习者的偏误可能与母语干扰、其他外语学习经验、学习过程的进展有关, 同时也与其他因素有关, 比如心理机制和语言规则特点等都会影响二语习得的进程。比如在教学中常常会碰到"*我有多中国朋友"之类的偏误, 我们不妨换个角度考虑, 初级阶段学习者倾向于不注意或不使用"很"这样的语言形式, 那我们在教学中是否足够考虑学习者的认知特点、我们的教学是否能促使学习者充分处理这样的语言形式呢?

综上所述, 学习者的复述不是依葫芦画瓢, 是一个先抓大意、理解加工后的过程。如认知心理学所指出的那样, 学习者短期记忆过程中的东西是语义信息的聚合而非语言形式句法结构的汇集。这个复述过程会受到来自短时记忆容量、内容意义优先策略、语言规则特点、母语以及其他外语学习经验、图式等多方面的影响。本调查的初步结果可以提醒我们在设计教学用语料、练习时要考虑学习者的认知特点。语篇阅读、听力练习常见的练习类型多集中在内容大意的理解，一般较少涉及语言规则。作为二语的教学，仅靠理解大意抓主要内容是达不到促进中介语系统的完善的发展 (Doughty & Williams, 1998)，还需要在练习当中重点突出一些容易被学习者忽略的"细节"，把学习者的注意引导至"冗余"的成分，改善他们一些不当的认知策略。从认知角度探讨教与学如何有机地结合将是我们今后的课题。

由于语篇语段记忆过程所涉及的因素繁多，本调查受到词汇、语法项目、样本数量等诸多限制，远未做到全面科学。作为初探，期望能起到抛砖引玉的作用。

References

Abe, J., Momouchi, Y., Kaneko, Y., & Yi, K. (1994). 人間の言語情報処理――言語理解の認知科学 [Cognitive science and information processing]. Tokyo, Japan: Saiensu' sha.

Cravotta, J. S., III. (2001). Second language acquisition, schema, and international tourism. *Memoirs of Osaka Meijo University, 1,* 51–59.

Doughty, C., & Williams, J. (1998). *Focus on form in classroom second language acquisition.* Cambridge, England: Cambridge University Press.

Ellis, R. (1994). *The study of second language acquisition.* Oxford, England: Oxford University Press.

Ellis, R. (1997). *Second language acquisition.* Oxford, England: Oxford University Press.

Ellis, R., & Barkhuizen, G. (2005). *Analysing learner language.* Oxford, England: Oxford University Press.

Gass, S. M. (1997). *Input, interaction, and the second language learner.* Mahwah, NJ: Lawrence Erlbaum.

Gui, S. (2000). 新编心理语言学 [New version of psycholinguistics]. Shanghai, China: Foreign Language Education Publisher.

Li, H., Li, Y., & Liu, J. (2002). 大学生语篇记忆心理认知浅析 [Analysis of paragraph memorization among college students]. 外语与外语教学 [Foreign Languages and Foreign Language Instruction], 2, 25–27.

Liu, G. (2005). 影响语篇记忆诸因素研究之评述 [Overview of factors affecting paragraph memorization]. 长春师范学院学报 (人文社会科学版) [Journal of Changchun Normal College, Social Science Edition], 24, 104–107.

Liu, W. (1996). 在短时记忆中考察外国留学生理解汉语句子的实验报告 [An investigation of sentence comprehension in short-term memory among foreign students]. In 中国对外汉语教学学会第五次学术讨论会论文选 [Proceedings of the Fifth National Teaching Chinese as a Second Language Conference] (pp. 202–215). Beijing, China: Beijing Language and Culture University Press.

Peng, X. (2004). 关于对外汉语语篇教学的新思考 [New thoughts on paragraph instruction in teaching Chinese as a foreign language]. 汉语学习 [Chinese Learning], 2, 50–55.

Shirahada, T., Tomita, Y., Murano, I., & Wakabayashi, S. (1999). *Dictionary of terminology for English education.* Tokyo: Taishukan Publishing Co., Ltd.

VanPatten, B. (1996). *Input processing and grammar instruction in second language acquisition.* Norwood, NJ: Ablex.

VanPatten, B. (2004). *Processing instruction: Theory, research, and commentary.* Mahwah, NJ: Lawrence Erlbaum.

Xu, Z. (2000). 汉语作为外语教学的认知理论研究 [*Studies on cognition of Chinese as a second language*]. Beijing, China: Chinese Education Publisher.

Xu, Z. (2003). 学习主体感知和记忆汉语的特点 [On the characteristics of learners' perception and memorization]. In 对外汉语研究的跨学科探索 [*Cross disciplinary studies on teaching Chinese as a foreign language*] (pp. 299–309). Beijing, China: Beijing Language and Culture University Publisher.

Zhu, Q. (2001). 语篇分析技巧在汉语精读课中的运用 [The paragraph analysis strategies in intensive Chinese language class]. In 中山大学学报论丛 [*Forum of Zhongshan University*], 6, 72–77.

Discourse Features and Development in Chinese L2 Writing

Yun Xiao
Bryant University, Smithfield, Rhode Island

The discourse features and development of Chinese L2 writing was explored by examining 4 CFL learners' (2 heritage and 2 nonheritage) diary entry samples collected over 2 consecutive semesters. The participants' written samples were rewritten by a Chinese native speaker (NS) and commented on by 7 graduate students in their problem-solving papers, which were both consulted in the data analysis. The results showed no significant difference between the participants and the NS in the use of references and conjunctions, but significant or borderline differences were observed in the use of sentence structures, zero pronouns, and topic chains. The participants' discourse features showed no notable changes over the developmental time, although some progress was made by particular individuals and in particular features. The participants, heritage and nonheritage alike, consistently produced structurally simple and discursively loose SVO structures, and the heritage learners did not show meaningful advantages over their nonheritage counterparts in this regard. Pedagogically, the study suggests that both written and oral discourses should be equally represented in L2 teaching practices.

本调查旨在探讨外国学生在中文习作中的语段构筑特点及发展情况,并就此对华裔和非华裔学生进行了比较。在美国,中文是作为外国语或第二语言来学习的,华裔学生也不例外。从第二语言习得的角度来说,它的研究目标是要通过对习得者的语料进行采集分析,从而探讨习得者对目的语语法的掌握情况(Ellis, 1994)。在语料分析中,还要把与第二语言习得有关的一些因素考虑进去。多年来,第二语言习得研究沿袭母语习得理论,认为初学者的语法知识只要通过口语交流便可获得。一个显见的例子就是我们现有的大多数的第二语言或外语教材,特别是低年级教材,简单的日常对话占绝对优势,书面语则寥寥无几。篇章研究表明,口笔语属两种不同的文体,它们之间差距很大。比如说,口语受语境限制,句子零碎,结构松散;而书面语则大量运用语言技巧,句子结构紧密,上下呼应,连成篇章。双语读写(bilingual literacy)研究进一步证实了这一理念,研

究人员发现 (Cummins, 1980, 1984),双语语言能力分两个层次:基本口语交际能力和书面读写能力,这两种能力各自独立,且对后者的掌握难于前者。

此外,对比修辞语言学 (contrastive rhetoric) 认为,语言与文字属文化现象,每种语言都有自己独特的辞语篇章特点 (Connor, 1996)。以中英文两种语言来说,它们在句型结构和语段连接等方面都有很大的区别。英文是主语明显的语言,篇章的通顺主要依靠指代和连接来完成,且每个句子都必须有主语,不允许用零代词来代替。而中文是话题明显的语言,句子主语往往用零代词来代替,与控制话题构成话题链,使句子篇章连贯通顺。对语言加工 (language processing) 的调查发现,第二语言习得者在目的语的习得过程中受母语的各种语言技巧影响 (Tao & Healy, 1998)。中文二外认知调查也发现,以英文为母语的学生往往受英文语法影响,往往过多地使用名代词,回避零代词,他们学习中最大的困难是使用话题链 (Cui, 2003; Jin, 1994)。按照这些理论和研究成果,我们可以预料以母语为英文的学生在用中文写作时,很有可能把英文的语段构筑技巧迁移过来。那么华裔学生的情况又是如何?华裔与非华裔这两组学生在中文写作时,会使用什么样的语段构筑技巧?他们之间有什么样的不同?随着时间的推移,又会有什么样的变化?中文教材对学生们构筑语段篇章能力的发展又有什么样的影响?这些问题就是本调查所要探讨的。

本调查所采用的数据资料为四位大学中文初级 (中高层次) 学生的周记,取自上下两个不同的时段,中间相距一个学期。这四位学生中,有两位华裔,两位非华裔。在资料分析之前,他们的周记分别由中文系的七位研究生进行了分析与评论,其中一位来自中国的研究生将所有周记重写了一遍。他们的评论和重写的周记用在本文中作为比较材料。本文的数据分析侧重于语段构筑的特点和其发展状况。参试者的周记样本及样本重写分两个时段来统计。用作分析的资料先分为三大类:句型,篇章特点,和话题链,然后又进一步分为七小类:简单句,复合句,指代,关连,零代词,话题链,松散句 (该用话题链而未用的句子),按各类的频率进行统计。调查结果表明参试者的周记和研究生的重写之间在指使和关连词的使用方面没有统计意义上的显著性差异,但在句型结构,零代词,和话题链的使用方面有显著性或近乎显著性的差异。此外,在第二时段中,尽管个别参试者或个别语段构筑技巧有了某种进步,但整体上并没有统计意义上的显著差异。所有参试者都一致倾向于使用结构简单篇章松散的主谓 (宾) 齐全的句子,华裔学生在这方面并未显示出什么特别的优势。根据调查结果,本研究对中文教学提出了一些建议,认为初级教材应该增加书面语,均衡口语和书面语学习材料。

The goal of second-language acquisition (SLA) research is to describe learners' underlying grammar knowledge, that is, linguistic competence, by examining samples of their performance. According to Ellis (1994), SLA research comprises four classic questions: What do second language (L2) learners acquire? How do learners acquire an L2? What individual differences are there? What effect does instruction have on SLA? To date, such inquiry has been extensive in English as an L2, but it is relatively uncharted territory for Chinese as a foreign language (CFL), especially when examining learners' written samples as the testing ground. Many issues are involved. In the following section, a few are briefly discussed.

Second-language acquisition and written communication

Inspired by the evidence from first-language acquisition research that children acquire syntactic structures through conversations, SLA researchers have formulated similar theories: Through oral interactions, L2 learners effectively acquire the target grammar and develop the target syntactic structures (Hatch, 1978; Krashen & Terrell, 1988). Mainstream L2 classrooms have since focused on face-to-face interactions (Harklau, 2002) without paying much attention to written communication, and L2 teaching materials are mostly written in the grammar and diction of oral conversations, especially at the beginning level. Ellis (1994, p. 187) noted that, consequently, we know something about how "contextualized" acts such as requests, apologies, and refusals are acquired, but we know little about how learners acquire the ability to perform acts found in decontextualized, written language. Research in bilingual literacy demonstrates that to be literate, learners need to understand the spoken form of the target language and to know how it is represented in its written form (Durgunoglu, Mir, & Arino-Mart, 2002). Based on the context of learning and communication and level of difficulty, Cummins (1980, 1984) classified bilingual proficiency as being composed of two major dimensions: basic interpersonal communication skills (BICS), such as daily social oral skills, and cognitive academic language proficiency (CALP), such as literacy-related reading and writing. He hypothesized that these two types of skills are independent of each other and that the acquisition of BICS is easier and faster than that of CALP.

From the perspective of discourse analysis, Brown and Yule (1983) posited that oral and written languages differ from each other in a number of ways. For one thing, oral language is situationally contextualized and typically much less syntactically structured and thus, is marked by simple sequences of phrases, or fragments. On the other hand, written language is much more syntactically structured and operates with extensive metalingual markers to organize the sentences into large segments of discourse. Likewise, Chinese written text is remarkably different from the spoken form in that text continuity is required more in written discourse than in oral discourse (Chu, 1998).

Oral and written languages are two distinct communicative modularities. In principle, they should be equally represented in teaching practices. However, a disproportionate preference has been observed in L2 teaching materials. For example, the researcher conducted a survey of *Integrated Chinese Level I* (Parts I & II; Yao & Liu, 2005), one of the most popular Chinese textbooks in the US. This series advocates the integration of four Chinese language skills—listening, speaking, reading, and writing—into CFL learning and prepares learners to progress from the novice to low-intermediate level. The results of the survey revealed that in the 23 lessons were 41 conversations (89.14%), two letters (4.34%), and three narratives (6.52%). As evident in these results, spoken language is represented predominantly in these CFL teaching materials, while written language (letters and narratives in this case) is marginalized. Given such a strong preference for spoken discourse, how CFL learners acquire the target written discourse is unclear.

Mixed learner populations in CFL classrooms

As an immigrant country, foreign-language classrooms in the United States accommodate two distinct student populations. One of them is composed of American English speakers who have no prior experience in learning the target language, while the other is composed of heritage language (HL) learners, who are born into families who speak the HL and have the ability to engage in some level of oral communication (National Standards in Foreign Language Education Project, 1999). In her previous studies (Xiao, 2004, 2006), the researcher found that Chinese HL students did significantly better than their nonheritage counterparts in listening, speaking, and grammar/translation tests. The remarkable linguistic disparity between these two populations deserves attention from L2 research and the education system. As the literature indicates, we know that HL learners typically acquire their HL at a young age, lose it after entering mainstream schools (Wong-Fillmore, 1991), and relearn it as a foreign language after entering colleges or universities. Consequently, they arrive in L2 classrooms not entirely as L1 nor as L2 speakers (Lynch, 2003).

Cross-linguistic differences

Contrastive rhetoric maintains that language and writing are cultural phenomena. As a direct consequence, each language has rhetorical conventions unique to it (Connor, 1996, p. 5).

Chinese, like English, has grammatically simple and composite (i.e., complex, compound, and compound-complex) sentence structures (Chao, 1968). Typologically, Chinese and English contrast with each other in such features as the role of the subject and topic, the use of overt noun phrases, and various discourse relations. English is a subject-prominent language, in which the SVO word order is predominant, the subject plays a prominent role, and noun phrase (NP) deletion in subject and object positions is not allowed (C. N. Li & Thompson, 1976). For an English sentence to be considered complete, it must have a subject. At the discourse level, English text connectivity is maintained by cohesive devices, such as reference, substitution, ellipsis, conjunction, and lexicality (Halliday & Hasan, 1976).

Unlike English, Chinese is a topic-prominent language, in which the topic rather than the subject plays a prominent role, and topic-controlled NPs are frequently deleted in subject and object positions (C. N. Li & Thompson, 1981). For Chinese discourse to be coherent, sentences must delete the topic-controlled subject or object NPs. The deleted NPs, defined as zero pronouns, form *topic chains* or antecedent-referent relationships with the controlling topics. In English, references, substitutions, conjunctions, and lexical items are important cohesive devices, whereas, in Chinese, zero pronouns, instead of overt pronouns, and topic chains are the major cohesive devices. At the discourse level, Chinese text continuity is largely maintained by topic chains (Chu, 1998). In a topic chain, the topic extends its semantic domain over several clauses or sentences, *chaining* a segment, sometimes a long segment, of discourse with its controlled zero pronouns (Tsao, 1979), which, in contrast, would be a run-on sentence in English. The following are examples.

1. (这 个 人)$_1$, 我 不 喜欢Ø$_1$, 我妈妈 也 不 喜欢Ø$_1$. (Tsao, 1979, p. 44)
   this MW person I not like my mother also not like
   *"This person, I don't like. My mother does not like, either."

2. (这 棵 树)$_1$ 的 叶子 又 细 又 长,Ø$_1$ 很 难看. (Tsao, 1979, p. 87)
   this MW tree ATR leaves both slim and long, very ugly
   *"The leaves of the tree are small and long, are very ugly."

3. 他$_1$ 肚子 饿,Ø$_1$ 又 找 不 到 东西 吃, 所以Ø$_1$ 躺 在 床上.
   (Tsao, 1990, p. 124)
   he stomach hungry and find not CMP things eat so lie at bed-top
   *"His stomach empty, and couldn't find anything to eat, so lay in bed."

As shown above, each string contains a topic chain, in which the controlling topic chains a number of clauses by means of zero pronouns. Conversely, the translation shows that such discourse relations are not acceptable in English. Moreover, a Chinese topic chain can consist of more than one controlling topic or antecedent-referent relationship. Based on the number of controlling topics or antecedent-referent relationships, topic chains can be classified as single-link, double-link, or three-link chains. For example,

4. 我₁ 一边 吃饭,∅₁ 一边 听 录音,
   I while eat while listen-to recording,
   九 点钟∅₁ 到 教室 去 上课. (Yao & Liu, 1997, p. 148)
   nine o'clock to classroom go attend-class
   "While eating, I listened to a recording; at nine o'clock, I went to the classroom to attend class."

5. 今天早上 他 在 报纸上 看到 (一个 广告)₁,
   this-morning he at newspaper-top saw an advertisement
   ∅₁ 说 学校 附近 有 (一个 公寓)₂ 出租,
   said school near there-was an apartment on-lease.
   ∅₂ 离 学校 只 有 一 公里, ∅₂ 很 方便. (Yao & Liu, 1997, p. 113)
   from school only have one kilometer very convenient
   "He saw an advertisement in the newspaper this morning. It said that there was an apartment for rent near the school. The apartment is only one kilometer away from the school. It is very convenient."

Example 4 can be considered a single-link chain that has only one controlling topic, 我₁, or one antecedent-referent relationship. On the other hand, Example 5 can be considered a double-link chain that has two controlling topics, (一个广告)₁ and (一个公寓)₂, or two antecedent-referent relationships.

L1 transfer

Research in language processing has shown that languages differ in their discourse patterns and that L2 learners tend to transfer their L1 discourse processing strategies into their L2s (Tao & Healy, 1998). Ample evidence has been found in SLA studies that many aspects of learners' L2 use can be traced to their L1s (Kellerman & Sharwood Smith, 1986; Lado, 1957; Odlin, 1989). Properties similar in the L1 and L2 tend to transfer, while those that are different do not (Ard & Homburg, 1992; Kellerman, 1983). Such findings are supported by recent CFL research, which has reported that CFL learners with English as their L1 were largely influenced by English grammar when dealing with Chinese discourse (Cui, 2003; Jin, 1994; W. Li, 2004). Using production data, Jin found that, compared with Chinese native speakers, English-speaking CFL learners tended to overproduce nouns and pronouns and underuse zero pronouns. Cui reported that CFL learners often made errors due to their lack or partial knowledge of Chinese discourse, especially with topic chains, even though topic chains were frequently used in the textbooks. W. Li found that, although CFL learners were exposed to topic chains early and frequently, control of these structures was not acquired until later. The results of these CFL studies all showed that zero pronouns and topic chains are the most difficult aspects of Chinese discourse for learners to acquire and use.

Whether Chinese HL learners were included in these studies is not clear, and if they were, the similarities or differences between HL and non-HL learners are not clear. By examining written CFL samples produced by HL and non-HL learners, the present study explores such differences and similarities and seeks to answer the following research questions:

1. What discourse features and developmental trends are prominent in the L2 writing of Chinese?
2. How does the written discourse of HL and non-HL learners of Chinese differ?
3. What impact do current CFL teaching materials have on learners' acquisition of Chinese written discourse?

Method

Participants

The participants were students enrolled in the beginning intensive Chinese language program (6 hours of class meetings per week) at an American university. The textbooks they used were *Integrated Chinese Level I* (Parts I & II) by Yao and Liu (1997). As one homework assignment, the students were given suggested topics and asked to write weekly diaries. This task was designed for students to use their recently learned vocabulary words and expressions with writing topics that were personal, familiar, and level appropriate so that they could communicate in writing without time or peer pressures. The samples of 4 students (2 HL and 2 non-HL), submitted at each of the data collection periods, were randomly selected, with a total of 8 samples being used for analysis. The 2 non-HL students were American English speakers who had no exposure to Chinese language prior to taking this course. The 2 HL students were born in the US and studied Chinese in community HL schools for a short period of time before they started grade school. The parents of both HL students spoke at least one of the Chinese dialects. Pseudonyms are used for all of the participants' names in the data analysis.

Data collection

Data were collected around the end of fall semester 2004 and spring semester 2005, with one semester in between. In the fall semester of 2005, the selected samples were preliminarily analyzed by seven graduate students as an assignment for a graduate course in CFL pedagogy that they were taking from the researcher. Of the seven graduate students, four were Chinese native speakers and three were American English speakers who had studied Chinese language in China or Taiwan for more than 1 year. In their papers, these students were asked to analyze the participants' written samples, comment on the discourse features, and accordingly make pedagogical suggestions. One of the NS students rewrote all of the 8 samples. Her rewrites were used as models for the analysis, and the comments and suggestions made in the problem-solving papers by the graduate students were also consulted.

Data analysis

The data analysis focused on the discourse features of the participants' written samples. The participants' samples and the NS model were both coded for two time periods: Time 1 for the first data collection and Time 2 for the second data collection. The coding categories included sentence structures, cohesive devices, and the use of topic chains. The three coding categories were further broken down into seven features: simple sentences, composite sentences (compound, complex, or compound complex), references, conjunctions, zero pronouns, topic chains, and loose sentences. Loose sentences were those not topic chained and were either simple or composite constructions. The frequency of the use of each feature was computed for comparison and statistical tests.

Results

Discourse features at Time 1

The following tables show the written samples and statistics of the participants and the NS model for Time 1, in which the topic chains are identified and numbered and zero pronouns are signaled with Ø and co-indexed with their controlling topics. The results showed notable differences overall in the use of sentence structures, zero pronouns, topic chains, and loose sentences between the participants and the NS model but not much difference in the use of references and conjunctions.

Table 1. Comparison of discourse features of Dave and the NS at Time 1

	Dave (nonheritage learner)	NS
	大维的一篇日记.十一月二十八日.星期日,二零零五	大维的一篇日记 二零零五年,十一月二十八日, 星期日
	我今天下午四点半回学校o这个周末是快了o 我现在就得做功课o {我1一边听音乐Ø1一边写字o}C1 因为明天很多早上的课所以后来我得睡觉o	这个周末快结束了o{我1今天下午四点半回学校, Ø1现在就得做功课,因为明天的课在早上,所以Ø1得早点儿睡觉o}C1 {我1一边听音乐, Ø1一边写字o}C2 {明天我1有(一节课)2, Ø2是中文o (这篇课文)2很有意思,可是Ø2很难o 因为(星期一)3 Ø1只有一节课, 所以Ø3比较容易o}C3
	明天我有一节课是中文o {我觉得(这篇课)1很有意思可是Ø1很难o}C2 因为只第一节所以星期一是一个容易天o	
	星期二我一起我的朋友上课o 这是英文课o	星期二我和我的朋友一起去上课o {这是英文课,我1觉得(英文课)2不好,可是Ø1得去, 因为Ø1没有别的课o}C4 {我1无法描述Ø2: Ø1只是觉得Ø2很容易 o}C5
	我觉得英文课不好可是我得去了o 我没别的课只一节o 我不会告诉多:只是容易 o	
	学校生活很好可是我喜欢夏天o 你已经知道了吗?	学校生活很好,可是我喜欢夏天□你已经知道了吗?
simple sentences	15	3
composite sentences	1	10
references	2	2
conjunctions	6	7
zero pronouns	2	12
topic chains	2	5
loose sentences	13	4

The written samples and statistics of Dave and the NS model for Time 1 are shown in Table 1. The differences between the two are notable. Dave wrote 16 sentences, of which 15 (93.75%) were simple SVO constructions, with the subjects all being retained. In some sentences, Dave used conjunctions such as 因为…, 所以…, and 可是…, but he did not use commas to separate the clauses. This indicates that Dave did not have the target grammar knowledge to analyze these sentences with compound/complex relationships but rather treated them as single SVO units. Moreover, Dave used an excessive number of nouns and pronouns, which resulted in the majority of his sentences (86.67%) being loose or unchained. Compared with the NS, he made many fewer topic chains, and his chains were simple and short, with one link per chain and one zero pronoun per link. In contrast, the NS used five topic chains, most of which were more complicated and longer, with two links per chain and two to three zero pronouns per link. A number of Dave's sentences were literal translations from English, for instance, "我觉得英文课不好可是我得去了。我没别的课只一节。我不会告诉多:只是容易。" This is almost a word-for-word translation of the English sentences "I feel English class is not good but I have to go. I do not have other classes but this one. I cannot tell you more: (it) is only easy." In the last sentence, he substituted a blank for "it," which shows that he did not know the Chinese equivalent for "it" and chose to avoid it. Overall, his discourse was described as "choppy," "incoherent," "redundant," "wooden and clunky-sounding," or the "results of transfer from English" by the graduate students in their problem-solving papers.

Table 2. Comparison of discourse features of Amy and the NS at Time 1

	Amy (nonheritage learner)	NS
	爱美十一月二十日, 二零零五年	爱美 二零零五年十一月二十日
	我是大学生。我也很高兴上学。我没有专业,但是我喜欢所有的课。我有中文课,两个跳舞课,哲学课, sociology 。我有很多朋友。周末的时候,我的朋友和我一起 看电影,买东西,和吃饭。因为我的朋友有大家,所以我喜欢去她家玩。上个周末,我回家吃火鸡。我看见我妈妈,爸爸,和我的猫。它的名字是Lucky。我有一个很 快乐的周末。	{我$_1$是大学生, $\emptyset_1$很高兴上学。虽然$\emptyset_1$还没有专业,但是我喜欢 所有的课。}$_{C1}$ 我有中文课,两门跳舞课,哲学课,和社会学课。我有很多 朋友。{周末的时候,(我的朋友)$_1$和我一起看电影,买东西,吃饭。因为我$_1$家很大,所以我喜欢去$\emptyset_1$玩。}$_{C2}$ {上个周末,我回家吃火鸡, $\emptyset_1$看见我妈妈,爸爸,和我的猫。}$_{C3}$它的名字是Lucky。我有一个很 快乐的周末。
simple sentences	9	5
composite sentences	2	4
references	2	2
conjunctions	2	2
zero pronouns	0	4
topic chains	0	3
loose sentences	11	4

The written samples and statistics of Amy and the NS model at Time 1 are shown in Table 2. Amy's discourse has a similar pattern to that of Dave. Amy wrote 11 sentences, of which 9 (81.82%) were simple sentences. She did not use any zero pronouns or topic chains, which resulted in 100% of her sentences being loose. She used the pronoun 我 in each of her sentences, which the graduate students commented made the discourse "sound like talking about several different people instead of herself alone." Like Dave's, her discourse was described as "incoherent" and "redundant" by the graduate students in their problem-solving papers.

Table 3. Comparison of discourse features of Min and the NS at Time 1

	Min (heritage learner)	**NS**
	敏的一篇日记,十一月二十九日,二零零五年	敏的一篇日记,二零零五年十一月二十九日
	{我1今天早上九点起床, $\emptyset_1$洗了澡以后$\emptyset_1$就去上课o $\emptyset_1$十点十分到教室去上课o}$_{C1}$ {第一节课是中文(mythology)1, $\emptyset_1$是容易o}$_{C2}$ 第二节课是中文poetry,这篇课文没有意思o 中午我和朋友们一起去吃午饭o{我们)1一边吃, $\emptyset_1$一边聊天儿o}$_{C3}$ {我下午一点三刻才去(第三节课)1, $\emptyset_1$是中文o}$_{C4}$ 老师教我们发音和生词o {第四节课是(mycology)1, $\emptyset_1$很难o}$_{C5}$ 我四点三刻去工作o 我七点回家o {我1九点吃晚饭o以后$\emptyset_1$一边吃晚饭, $\emptyset_1$一边看电视o}$_{C6}$ {$\emptyset_1$睡觉以前, 我1brush my teeth o}$_{C7}$ 我半夜睡觉,因为我明天早上七点半得起床o	{我1今天早上九点起床, $\emptyset_1$洗了澡以后$\emptyset_1$就去上课o $\emptyset_1$十点十分到教室o}$_{C1}$ {第一节课是(中国神话)1, $\emptyset_1$很容易o}$_{C2}$ {第二节课是(中国诗歌)1, $\emptyset_1$没有意思o}$_{C3}$ 中午我和朋友们一起去吃午饭o {(我们)1一边吃, $\emptyset_1$一边聊天儿o}$_{C4}$ {我1下午一点三刻才去上(第三节课)1, $\emptyset_1$是中文o}$_{C5}$ 老师教我们发音和生词o {第四节课是(真菌课)1, $\emptyset_1$很难o}$_{C6}$ {我1四点三刻去工作, $\emptyset_1$七点回家, $\emptyset_1$九点吃晚饭, $\emptyset_1$一边吃晚饭, $\emptyset_1$一边看电视, $\emptyset_1$睡觉以前$\emptyset_1$刷牙o}$_{C7}$ {我1半夜睡觉,因为$\emptyset_1$明天早上七点半得起床o}$_{C8}$
simple sentences	6	3
composite sentences	9	8
references	2	0
conjunctions	5	5
zero pronouns	10	15
topic chains	7	8
loose sentences	6	2

The written samples and statistics of Min and the NS model at Time 1 are shown in Table 3. Min's discourse was relatively close to that of the NS. Min wrote 15 sentences, of which 6 (40%) were simple sentences, which was fairly close to the NS model. Min formed seven (53.85%) topic chains; however, her topic chains were on average shorter than those of the NS. For instance, in the NS model, Topic Chain 7 consisted of six zero pronouns, which formed a chain of $Pro_1 \rightarrow \emptyset_1 \rightarrow \emptyset_1 \rightarrow \emptyset_1 \rightarrow \emptyset_1 \rightarrow \emptyset_1 \rightarrow \emptyset_1$. For the same length of discourse, Min made two chains. Like her non-HL counterparts, Min repeated the same subject NPs again and again, even though she could have omitted them. Also, the level of coherence was different between the first half and the second half of her story. While the first half was highly coherent through the use of correct zero pronouns and topic chains, the second half was redundant with repetitive overt pronouns. The researcher noticed that the sentences used in the first half were imitations of those sentences she had recently learned in her narrative text. For the second half, the textbook had no model sentences for her to draw upon. To express herself, she had to assemble utterances scattered around the conversations in the textbook. Unable to transform the oral language into written discourse, she reverted to English grammar by retaining the sentence subjects (that should have been deleted) to keep the sentences "complete." Nonetheless, Min's discourse was described as "fairly coherent," and "more advanced than the non-HL learners'" by the graduate students in their problem-solving papers.

Table 4. Comparison of discourse features of Hui and the NS at Time 1

	Hui (heritage learner)	NS
	辉的一篇日记,十一月十九日,二零零五年	辉的一篇日记 二零零五年十一月十九日
	我是二年级的大学生o每天我有好多课o{星期一我1有四节课,星期三Ø1也有四节课o星期二和星期四比较容易,Ø1只有两节课o}C1{Ø1上课以后我1喜欢打球和跳舞可是我没空,Ø1有太多功课o}C2有时候我早上两点钟才睡觉o我平常去图书馆学statistics 和 accounting因为这两节很难o我最近进步一点儿o我希望我可以懂得我的功课所以我能跟我的朋友玩o	{我1是二年级的大学生,每天Ø1有好多课o}C1 {星期一我1有四节课,星期三Ø1也有四节课,星期二和星期四比较容易,Ø1只有两节课o}C2 {Ø1下课以后我1喜欢打球和跳舞,可是Ø1没空,Ø1有太多功课,有时候Ø1早上两点钟才睡觉o}C3 我平常去图书馆学统计学 和会计学,因为这两门课很难o我最近有点儿进步o {我1希望Ø1可以学好自己的功课,然后Ø1能跟Ø1朋友们玩o}C4
simple sentences	6	1
composite sentences	3	5
references	1	1
conjunctions	4	4
zero pronouns	4	10
topic chains	2	4
loose sentences	6	2

The written samples and statistics of Hui and the NS model at Time 1 are shown in Table 4. As indicated, Hui's discourse did not bear much similarity to that of the NS. Hui wrote nine sentences, of which six (66.67%) were simple, which was far more than the NS model (16.67%). Moreover, Hui used many fewer zero pronouns than the NS, which resulted in six of her sentences being loose. She also only used two topic chains, which bound a small portion of the discourse. Some comments on Hui's sample from the graduate students in their problem-solving papers were "largely incoherent and redundant" and "very much like those of the non-HL learners."

Discourse features at Time 2

The following are the written samples and statistics of the participants and the NS model at Time 2. The results again show notable differences in the use of sentence structures, topic chains, zero pronouns, and loose sentences between the participants and the NS, but not much difference in the use of references and conjunctions.

Table 5. Comparison of discourse features of Dave and the NS at Time 2

	Dave (nonheritage learner)	NS
	大维的一篇日记.三月二十日,二零零六年 {(我的朋友)$_1$想买一个家$_2$ o 他$_1$早就看$\emptyset_2$在Amherst o}$_{C1}$ {他喜欢很多家$_1$,可是他的女朋友都不喜欢$\emptyset_1$ o}$_{C2}$ {再说 (那个家)$_1$很贵所以$\emptyset_2$别的城也看$\emptyset_1$ o 他$_2$看$\emptyset_1$多时间, $\emptyset_2$一个家也没喜欢 o}$_{C3}$他的爸爸一个日去看学校 o 他不知道他的儿子看过新家 o {他$_1$有很多(公寓)$_2$, $\emptyset_1$给儿子一个$\emptyset_1$ o}$_{C4}$ {他$_1$高兴得跳了起来 o $\emptyset_1$住在那每天越来越高兴 o}$_{C5}$ 他现在睡得好极了 o	大维的一篇日记二零零六年三月二十日 {(我的朋友)$_1$想买一个(公寓)$_2$ o 他$_1$早就在安城 到处找$\emptyset_2$ o 他喜欢很多处$\emptyset_2$,可是他的女朋友都不喜欢$\emptyset_2$ o}$_{C1}$ {再说(它们)$_1$都很贵, 所以他也在别的城市找$\emptyset_1$ o 他$_2$找$\emptyset_1$了很长时间, 可是$\emptyset_1$一个$\emptyset_1$也不喜欢 o}$_{C2}$ 一天他的爸爸来学校看他 o {他$_1$不知道$\emptyset_1$儿子已经看过很多公寓 o}$_{C3}$ {他$_1$有很多(公寓)$_2$, $\emptyset_1$给了儿子一个$\emptyset_2$ o}$_{C4}$ {(我的朋友)$_1$高兴得跳了起来 o 他$_1$住在那儿越来越高兴, $\emptyset_1$每天睡得好极了 o}$_{C5}$
simple sentences	7	5
composite sentences	4	5
references	3	4
conjunctions	2	3
zero pronouns	9	11
topic chains	5	5
loose sentences	3	1

The written samples and statistics of Dave and the NS model at Time 2 are shown in Table 5. Dave's discourse, unlike that at Time 1, was much closer to that of the NS. Dave wrote 11 sentences, of which 7 (63.64%) were simple sentences, which showed noticeable progress compared with the percentage at Time 1 (93.75%). Also, Dave made a compound sentence with the conjunction 可以, in which he separated the connected clauses with a comma. This indicates that Dave was able to analyze compound sentences as such without treating them as single formulaic chunks as he did at Time 1. Moreover, he formed five topic chains and used nine zero pronouns, with two of his topic chains demonstrating complexity in the antecedent-referent relationships through the use of two links in each chain. However, the researcher noticed that a number of his sentences were imitations of those in a narrative text in his textbook. Overall, Dave was considered by the graduate students in their problem-solving papers to "have made remarkable progress," with his discourse being described as "well-understandable" and "considerably coherent."

Table 6. Comparison of discourse features of Amy and the NS at Time 2

	Amy (nonheritage learner)	**NS**
	爱美. 三月二十日,二零零六年 去年我在学校的宿舍住o 我不喜欢那里o 我觉得房门太小,洗澡间不好o 我常常想搬出去o 今年我想在公寓住o 我和我的朋友想一起住o 我们在报纸上看到广o 有一天我们找到公寓o 这个公寓有两个卧室,一个大的厨房,一个洗澡间,和一个客厅o 我们很高兴!我们跟房东说话o 现在我们住那里o	爱美 二零零六年三月二十日 {去年我$_1$住在(学校的宿舍)$_2$, 可是Ø$_1$不喜欢Ø$_2$, Ø$_1$觉得Ø$_2$ 房间太小, 洗澡间不好, Ø$_1$常常想搬出去o}$_{C1}$ {今年我想住在校外的(公寓)$_1$ o 我和我的朋友想住在一起o 我们在报纸上看到广告o 有一天我们找到了一个Ø$_1$ o}$_{C2}$ 它有两个卧室,一个大的厨房,一个洗澡间,和一个客厅o {(我们)$_1$很高兴, Ø$_1$马上跟房东说定了o}$_{C3}$ 我们现在就住在那里o
simple sentences	11	6
composite sentences	1	2
references	1	2
conjunctions	0	1
zero pronouns	0	6
topic chains	0	3
loose sentences	3	1

The written samples and statistics of Amy and the NS model at Time 2 at shown in Table 6. Amy's discourse was very much like that at Time 1; it did not show any notable change. Amy wrote 12 sentences, of which 11 (91.67%) were simple sentences. Moreover, as at Time 1, she did not use any zero pronouns or topic chains. Her discourse was described as "redundant," "incoherent," and having "no change over time" by the graduate students in their problem-solving papers.

The written samples and statistics of Min and the NS model at Time 2 are shown in Table 7. Min's discourse did not, as at Time 1, bear much similarity to that of the NS. Min wrote 13 sentences, of which 10 (76.92%) were simple sentences. Min used many fewer zero pronouns than the NS and formed only two (15.38%) topic chains, while 11 of her sentences were loose or not topic-chained. Moreover, Min's two topic chains were both simple and short, with one link per chain and one zero pronoun per link. The researcher noted that there was no narrative in the textbook that could provide the model sentences she needed to express her relationship with her boyfriend. Instead, she had to assemble utterances scattered around in the textbook conversations to express herself. Her discourse was described as "redundant," "not (Chinese) native-like," "more like English," or "regressed" by the graduate students in their problem-solving papers.

Discourse Features and Development in Chinese L2 Writing 145

Table 7. Comparison of discourse features of Min and the NS at Time 2

	Min (heritage learner)	NS
	敏的一篇日记,三月九日,二零零六年 我最喜欢的男朋友叫Michael。他很可爱也有一点儿帅。{(我们)1认识已经快十一个月了,Ø1在UMass学校。}C1我们成了好朋友。Michael的腿很长,所以他很高。他的眼睛得很漂亮。他是美国人。他二十三岁了。我跟他同一个organization/club。{他1常常请我去看电影,Ø1也吃晚饭。}C2他费了很多钱□我们常常玩儿得很高兴。明天我们去Cinemark看美国电影<Be Cool>。	敏的一篇日记 二零零六年三月九日 我最喜欢的男朋友叫麦克。他很可爱也有一点儿帅。{(我们)1认识已经快十一个月了,Ø1是在麻大安城分校认识的。Ø1后来成了好朋友。}C1 {(麦克)1的腿很长,所以Ø1很高,Ø1眼睛也很漂亮。}C2{他1是美国人,Ø1二十三岁了。}C3我跟他在同一个俱乐部。{他1常常请我去看电影,Ø1也常常跟我一起吃晚饭,Ø1费了很多钱。}C4 我们玩儿得很高兴。明天我们去电影院看美国电影<帅哥>。
simple sentences	10	6
composite sentences	3	4
references	2	2
conjunctions	2	2
zero pronouns	2	7
topic chains	2	4
loose sentences	11	4

Table 8. Comparison of discourse features of Hui and the NS at Time 2

	Hui (heritage learner)	NS
	辉的一篇日记, 三月十一日,二零零六年 我和我四个最好的朋友去租房子在Amherst。这个学期完了时候 我们要搬出去宿舍。我们的公寓有三个房间,一个大大的厨房,一个干净的洗澡间,和一个客厅已有家俱。{(公寓)1离学校不远,Ø1很方便。}C1{有时候我们会吵别人因为周末我们喜欢请朋友来听音乐,喝啤酒,聊天儿。Ø1每一个月是 房租$250, Ø1还要付水电费和饭。Ø1下个期会很好玩。}C2	辉的一篇日记 二零零六年三月十一日 我和我四个最好的朋友去安城租房子。这个学期结束以后,我们要搬出学校宿舍。{(我们的新公寓)1有三个卧室,一个大大的厨房,一个干净的洗澡间,和一个客厅,Ø1已有家俱。}C1{(公寓)1离学校不远,Ø1很方便。}C2{有时候(我们)1会吵闹别人,因为周末Ø1喜欢请朋友来听音乐,喝啤酒,聊天儿。Ø1每一个月的房租是$250,Ø1还要付水电费和伙食费。Ø1下个学期会 很好玩。}C3

continued...

Table 8. Comparison of discourse features of Hui and the NS at Time 2 *(cont.)*

	Hui (heritage learner)	NS
simple sentences	6	2
composite sentences	1	5
references	1	1
conjunctions	2	2
zero pronouns	4	6
topic chains	2	3
loose sentences	3	2

The written samples and statistics of Hui and the NS model at Time 2 are shown in Table 8. Hui's discourse was, unlike at Time 1, fairly close to that of the NS. Hui wrote seven sentences, of which six (85.71%) were simple, while the NS rewrite had only two simple sentences. Nonetheless, she made two (40%) topic chains, with the second chain covering a relatively long portion of discourse. Comments on her discourse by the graduate students in their problem-solving papers included "a number of the pronouns should be omitted," "although still redundant, she made progress," and "the last part of her diary is native-like."

Discourse features over time

As shown above, the participants' development of discourse features over 1 academic year was individual and feature-specific. Specifically, while one non-HL learner (Dave) and one HL learner (Hui) showed progress, the others did not. While some discourse features showed change, others did not. Using the NS model for comparison, ANOVA tests were conducted. Given the small number of participants, the results were suggestive at best, but they reveal the trend of the L2 Chinese discourse development. Specifically, a one-way ANOVA on the scores at Time 1 showed notable differences between the NS and the participants in the use of simple sentence structures, $F(1, 6)=6.97$, $p<.05$, and loose or unchained sentences, $F(1, 6)=10.29$, $p<.05$. This means that the participants used more simple sentence structures than the NS and that more of their sentences were loose or unchained. Moreover, the results indicated that the participants used fewer zero pronouns than the NS but that the difference between them was not significant, $F(1, 6)=3.88$, $p<.1$.

A one-way ANOVA on the scores at Time 2 revealed a notable difference between the participants and the NS in the use of simple sentence structures, $F(1, 6)=6.08$, $p<.05$, but the use of loose sentences changed from being significant at Time 1 to borderline at Time 2, $F(1, 6)=3.87$, $p<.1$, and the use of zero pronouns was changed from being borderline significant at Time 1 to not being significant at Time 2, $F(1, 6)=2.73$, $p>.14$. This suggests that, over the developmental time, the participants increased their use of zero pronouns and topic chains but did not significantly change in their use of simple sentence structures.

A one-way ANOVA on the accumulated scores at both Times 1 and 2, with the learners as the independent variable, revealed that there was no significant difference between these two learner groups on any of the discourse features, although there was close to a borderline difference between them in their uses of simple sentence structures: $F(1, 6)=3.13$, $p>.13$. This suggests that the non-HL learners wrote more simple sentence structures than their HL counterparts, but the difference between them was not statistically significant.

Summary and discussion

The results showed that there was no significant difference between the participants and the NS model in the use of references and conjunctions, but notable differences between them in the use of sentence structures, zero pronouns, topic chains, and loose or unchained sentences. Compared with the NS model, the participants tended to use repetitive, short, and choppy simple sentences, excessive nouns and pronouns, and insufficient topic chains. Even when they used topic chains, their chains were shorter and had less complexity than those of the NS. This suggests that some discourse features are easier and faster to learn than others. In this case, references and conjunctions, which are cohesive devices similar in the learners' L1 and L2, were easier and faster to learn than zero pronouns and topic chains, which are Chinese-specific and in direct contrast to the learners' L1, that is, primary English-language grammar. Such results seem to support the previous L2 findings that properties similar in a learner's L1 and L2 tended to transfer, while those that were different did not (Ard & Homburg, 1992; Kellerman, 1983).

The data also show that, overall, there was no significant change in the participants' discourse features over time, although some level of progress was made by particular individuals or in particular features. The participants consistently produced structurally simple SVO constructions, and even in the case where conjunctions were used, those sentences were often not analyzed for compound/complex relationships but rather as formulaic simple SVO strings. The participants also constructed a large number of unconnected sentences, resulting in loose or incoherent discourses. This may suggest that, to L2 learners, compound/complex sentences are more difficult than simple ones, and discourse building is more difficult than sentence building.

Moreover, the results reveal that the HL learners did not show any meaningful advantage over their nonheritage counterparts when creating discourse in Chinese. Specifically, both HL and non-HL learners had difficulty using zero pronouns and topic chains and tended to start new sentences with overt nouns or pronouns, which resulted in an overwhelmingly large number of simple SVO structures with retained subjects. Such structures conform to English grammar but not to Chinese grammar. These findings support previous CFL research indicating that learners with English as their L1 were largely influenced by English grammar when dealing with Chinese discourse (Cui, 2003; Jin, 1994; W. Li, 2004). They also suggest that the Chinese HL learners were similar to the L2 speakers when composing written discourse in Chinese, although the HL learners came to their language learning with prior oral skills. The finding that the HL learners' prior oral skills did not meaningfully contribute to their production of Chinese written discourse seems puzzling and is apparently contrary to what L1A and SLA theories predicted. However, this is not surprising to veteran CFL professionals. In reviewing this chapter, Professor Al Cohen, a leading CFL scholar and researcher for 35 years, commented on the oral skills of the Chinese HL learners by noting, "with few exceptions, they have a very shallow level of fluency in Chinese. They know how to talk about household subjects, swear words, 'gossip language' but cannot talk about many serious subjects and Chinese cultural subjects. Their comments about Chinese cultural subjects are very frequently inaccurate and not even very rational" (review comments, July 29, 2006). His insight was supported by a 4-year study of HL literacy learning in Chinese community schools (Wang, 2004) in which the researcher noted that many Chinese HL students were comfortable in using Chinese on simple topics related to daily life, but when dealing with more abstract topics such as expressing their viewpoints or arguing about current events, they often resorted to single words or phrases, or completely switched to English (Wang, 2004, p. 362). Such observations suggest that Chinese HL learners' oral skills are limited and that their oral discourse is, in general, underdeveloped; the use of such skills is unlikely to provide sufficient experience for coherent written discourse. If their spoken language is this underdeveloped, any written stylistics are probably underdeveloped as well. The present data also support Cummins' (1980, 1984) hypothesis about the two types of bilingual proficiencies, BICS and CALP, which he states are independent of each other and have different developmental rates; that is, daily social oral skills are easier and faster to acquire than the proficiency that deals with the type of language used and developed in classroom-based learning.

Furthermore, the results showed that both the HL and non-HL groups did better when they had model sentences to draw on from a written text in their textbooks, but not when such models were unavailable. Such results suggest that CFL pedagogy and teaching materials, especially at the beginning level, need to provide learners with sufficient input to learn Chinese written discourse or the skills needed to transform oral discourse into written form. According to Ellis (1994, p. 187) learners cannot construct native-speaker-like discourse unless they possess the linguistic means to do so. Lack of input will result in persistent errors if writers have little exposure to the look and feel of target-language written texts (Carson, 2001, p. 196). In this regard, research should examine the validity of the mainstream SLA theories, which are biased toward face-to-face oral interactions without giving a role to written communications or a place to HL learners who already have oral skills before arriving in foreign-language classrooms.

A number of other factors may influence the L2 writing of Chinese. First, the more complex a particular feature is, the harder and slower it is likely to be to learn. In Chinese discourse, topic chains are more discursively complex than simple sentences. While the former involves a number of concepts such as controlling topic, NP deletion, and referent-antecedent relationships, the latter merely have grammatical relations of subject + verb + object. The second factor is likely to be the learners' low proficiency at this level. Ample evidence shows that in early L1A and SLA, children and L2 beginners tend to produce simple sentence structures (Givon, 1984; Gruber, 1967; Rutherford, 1983). The third factor is the participants' likely use of avoidance strategies (i.e., avoiding the use of a particular grammar point if it is not understood) when confronted with features that are new and in direct contrast to their L1 or primary language grammar, in this case, the use of zero pronouns and topic chains.

As the research unfolds, the existing SLA pedagogy does not have an appropriate place for HL learners. With a vastly increasing number of students of immigrant descent from kindergarten to college or university in the US, there is an urgent need for detailed description and documentation of these learners' prior knowledge and relevant pedagogy to deal with issues at various developmental stages. Currently, the L2 teaching methodology is for adults who do not have a background in the target language. Which acquisition theories and teaching methodologies are most workable for HL learners is not clear. So far, a number of college and university Chinese programs have adopted a two-track system, which places HL and non-HL learners in separate classrooms. However, they are scrambling for teaching methods and materials for the HL group due to the lack of well-grounded theoretical guidance in this regard. Many of the teaching practitioners have the same dilemma as Lynch (2003): that HL learners arriving in foreign-language classrooms seem not to be entirely L1 or L2 speakers. The present study provides initial data to show that, when composing

Chinese written discourse, Chinese HL learners are more similar to L2 English speakers than to L1 Chinese speakers.

Because both HL and non-HL learners should strive to be bilingual and biliterate, SLA theories and pedagogy should find ways and means for the learners to reach the goal. In CFL pedagogy, while both HL and non-HL learners' needs should be identified and addressed, the teaching materials should, in general, increase learner's exposure to the target written discourse by including proportionate written texts and explicit explanations of the target discourse features. CFL instructors should also incorporate skills related to discourse coherence and emphasize the use of NPs, including overt and covert pronoun forms. In addition, topic chains should be overtly taught and practiced throughout the learning process so that students are not only exposed to these structures but also trained in using them in their own discourse production. Because reading and writing are intertwined skills, CFL reading instructions should raise students' awareness of the omitted subjects and objects in the texts and teach them how to recover their referents from the context.

CFL is a new area of research. We still know little about how classroom-instructed language learning takes place, what shapes learners' underlying grammar knowledge, what impedes learners' writing abilities, and what is the best teaching methodology for HL learners. Due to the small sample in the present study, the findings are suggestive at best. Future CFL research should further describe learner language and individual differences in the hope that learner-directed CFL curriculum and teaching materials can be generated so that the neither-L1-nor-L2-speaker HL dilemma can be resolved.

References

Ard, J., & Homburg, T. (1992). Verification of language transfer. In S. Gass & L. Selinker (Eds.), *Language transfer in language learning* (pp. 47–70). Amsterdam: John Benjamins Publishing Company.

Brown, G., & Yule, G. (1983). *Discourse analysis.* New York: Cambridge University Press.

Carson, J. G. (2001). Second language writing and second language acquisition. In T. Silva & P. K. Matsuda (Eds.), *On second language writing* (pp. 191–199). Mahwah, NJ: Lawrence Erlbaum Associates, Publishers.

Chao, Y. (1968). *A grammar of spoken Chinese.* Berkeley and Los Angeles: University of California Press.

Chu, C. C. (1998). *A discourse grammar of Mandarin Chinese.* New York: Peter Lang.

Connor, U. M. (1996). *Contrastive rhetoric: Cross-cultural aspects of second-language writing.* Cambridge, England: Cambridge University Press.

Cui, S. R. (2003). 淺談篇章語法的定義與教學問題 [On definition and instruction of grammar of sections and chapters]. *Journal of the Chinese Language Teachers Association,* 38(1), 1–24.

Cummins, J. (1980). The construct of language proficiency in bilingual education. In J. E. Alaitis (Ed.), *Georgetown University Round Table on languages and linguistics: Current issues in bilingual education* (pp. 81–103). Washington, DC: Georgetown University Press.

Cummins, J. (1984). Wanted: A theoretical framework for relating language proficiency to academic achievement among bilingual students. In C. Rivera (Ed.), *Language proficiency and academic achievement* (pp. 21–46). *Multilingual Matters, 10.*

Durgunoglu, A. Y., Mir, M., & Arino-Mart, S. (2002). The relationships between bilingual children's reading and writing in their two languages. In S. Ransdell & M. L.

Barbier (Eds.), *New directions for research in L2 writing* (pp. 81–101). Boston: Kluwer Academic Publishers.

Ellis, R. (1994). *The study of second language acquisition.* Oxford, England: Oxford University Press.

Givon, T. (1984). Universals of discourse structures and second language acquisition. In W. Rutherford (Ed.), *Language universals and second language acquisition* (pp. 109–136). Amsterdam: John Benjamins Publishing Company.

Gruber, J. (1967). Topicalization in child language. *Foundations of Language, 3,* 37–65.

Halliday, M. A. K., & Hasan, R. (1976). *Cohesion in English.* London and New York: Longman.

Harklau, L. (2002). The role of writing in classroom second language acquisition. *Journal of Second language Writing, 11,* 329–350.

Hatch, E. (Ed.). (1978). *Second language acquisition.* Rowley, MA: Newbury House.

Jin, H. G. (1994). Topic-prominence and subject-prominence in L2 acquisition: Evidence of English-to-Chinese typological transfer. *Language Learning, 44,* 101–121.

Kellerman, E. (1983). Now you see it, now you don't. In S. Gass & L. Selinker (Eds.), *Language transfer in language learning* (pp. 112–134). Rowley, MA: Newbury House.

Kellerman, E., & Sharwood Smith, M. (1986). *Crosslinguistic influence in second language acquisition.* New York: Pergamon Press.

Krashen, S. D., & Terrell, T. D. (1988). *The natural approach: Language acquisition in the classroom.* London: Prentice Hall.

Lado, R. (1957). *Linguistics across cultures.* Ann Arbor: University of Michigan Press.

Li, C. N., & Thompson, S. A. (1976). Subject and topic: A new typology of language. In C. N. Li (Ed.), *Subject and topic* (pp. 457–490). New York: Academic Press, Inc,

Li, C. N., & Thompson, S. A. (1981). *Mandarin Chinese: A functional reference grammar.* Berkeley: University of California Press.

Li, W. (2004). The discourse perspective in teaching Chinese grammar. *Journal of the Chinese Language Teachers Association, 39*(1), 25–44.

Lynch, A. (2003). *The Heritage Language Journal 1*(1). Retrieved March 21, 2003, from http://www.international.ucla.edu/languages/heritagelanguages/journal

National Standards in Foreign Language Education Project. (1999). *Standards for Foreign Language Learning in the 21st Century.*

Odlin, T. (1989). *Language transfer: Cross-linguistic influence in language learning.* New York: Cambridge University Press.

Rutherford, W. (1983). Language typology and language transfer. In S. Gass & L. Selinker (Eds.), *Language transfer in language learning* (pp. 358–370). Rowley, MA: Newbury House Publishers, Inc.

Tao, L., & Healy, A. F. (1998). Anaphora in language processing: Transfer of cognitive strategies by native Chinese, Dutch, English, and Japanese speakers. In A. F. Healy & L. E. Bourne, Jr. (Eds.), *Foreign language learning: Psycholinguistic studies on training and retention* (pp. 193–212). Mahwah, NJ: Lawrence Erlbaum Associates, Publishers.

Tsao, F. (1979). *A functional study of topic in Chinese: The first step towards discourse analysis.* Taipei, Taiwan: Student Book Co., Ltd.

Tsao, F. (1990). *Sentence and clause structure in Chinese: A functional perspective.* Taipei, Taiwan: Student Book Co., Ltd.

Wang, C. S. (2004). *Biliteracy resource eco-system of intergenerational language and culture transmission: An ethnographic study of a Chinese-American community.* Unpublished doctoral dissertation, University of Pennsylvania, Philadelphia.

Wong Fillmore, L. (1991). When learning a second language means losing the first. *Early Childhood Research Quarterly, 6,* 323–346.

Yao, T., & Liu, Y. (1997). *Integrated Chinese: Level I Part I.* Boston: Cheng & Tsui Company.

Yao, T., & Liu, Y. (2005). *Integrated Chinese: Level I Part I* (Rev. ed.). Boston: Cheng & Tsui Company.

Xiao, Y. (2004). L2 acquisition of Chinese topic-prominent constructions. *Journal of the Chinese Language Teachers Association, 39*(3), 65–84.

Xiao, Y. (2006). Heritage learners in foreign language classroom: Home background knowledge and language development. *Heritage Language Journal, 4*(1), 47–57. Retrieved September 21, 2006, from http://www.heritagelanguages.org

Intermediate Distance Learners of Chinese Look Back: A Survey Study

Isabel Tasker
University of New England, New South Wales, Australia

This chapter reports on a qualitative study of 41 adults who had been studying Mandarin Chinese using distance learning at an Australian university for at least 2 years. Social, affective, and conceptual aspects of their learning experience were investigated. A survey, incorporating a significant proportion of open-ended questions, provides a rich source of data about each learner's background, the chronology of their episodes of Chinese-language learning, their perceptions and beliefs about learning Chinese, and their attitudes and feelings about distance learning as a way of studying Chinese. These data were coded and analysed to look for major themes and connections. What insights can these students give about their strategies and approaches for learning Chinese? What advice would they offer to others just starting out in distance language learning? How is the distance language-learning context situated in relation to other contexts of learning such as informal and independent learning? The conclusions drawn in this chapter are of relevance to the design, teaching, and support of current and future distance-learning programmes in Mandarin.

本文乃对于四十一位通过大学远程教育学习汉语的澳大利亚成人学生的质的研究，重在考察他们学习经验中的社会的、情感的、和观念的方面的问题。一份从这些学生中收上来的主要由开放性问题构成的问卷调查向我们提供了关于每位学生的背景、学习汉语的经过、他们对学习的理解和信仰、以及他们对远程汉语教学的态度和感受的丰富的数据。通过对这些数据的分类和分析，本文试图从中找出一些主题和相互间的联系。这些学生能为他们的汉语学习的策略和方法提供怎样的识见？他们能给其他刚刚开始通过远程教育学习汉语的人提供怎样的建议？远程语言教学于其他的学习方式诸如非正式学习或独立学习存在怎样的关系？本文的研究成果可以为目前以及将来的汉语远程教育的课程设计、教学以及教学管理等方面问题提供参考。

Tasker, I. (2010). Intermediate distance learners of Chinese look back: A survey study. In M. E. Everson & H. H. Shen (Eds.), *Research among learners of Chinese as a foreign language* (Chinese Language Teachers Association Monograph Series: Vol. 4). (pp. 153–177). Honolulu: University of Hawai'i, National Foreign Language Resource Center.

Historically, Western countries have offered few opportunities for studying the Chinese language using distance education. However, the current rapid expansion of interest in learning Chinese as a foreign language, together with increasing acceptance of open and flexible learning methods (often incorporating web-based communication), spells a coming period of growth in the demand for and provision of various forms of distance learning of the Chinese language. For sound institutional and pedagogical choices to be made in the planning, administration, and teaching of such courses, it is useful to consider current practice and knowledge about the teaching and learning of Chinese using the distance mode. This chapter reports on research that focuses on current distance learners of Chinese and aims to illuminate these learners' expressed needs and perceptions. The learners who participated in the research were studying at an Australian university that is an established provider of distance education and has offered Mandarin courses in both on- and off-campus modes for students in Australia and overseas for many years.

The need for inquiry of this kind is becoming increasingly widely voiced in the field of second-language acquisition (SLA). White (2003), for example, put it very clearly:

> An informed understanding of distance learners is a critical issue for distance education since inadequate or incomplete knowledge or awareness in this area severely compromises the quality of the learning experiences that are provided and developed… An important avenue of professional development for distance language teachers is to focus on extending their practical knowledge base of distance learners, in different contexts, and at different stages of a distance course. (p. 123)

If the field of teaching Chinese as a foreign language (TCFL) is viewed through a corresponding lens, research can be claimed to have a comparable role to play in enhancing our practical knowledge base of learners of Chinese in different modes and contexts and at different stages of their Chinese study. The current investigation of distance learners of Chinese is therefore illuminating in two ways: First, it contributes to the "informed understanding" of distance learners called for by White (2003, p. 123), and second, it offers a fresh perspective, from a relatively underreported group of learners, to professional understanding of aspects of the process and experience of Chinese language learning.

Theoretical and methodological context

This study situates itself in the context of an emerging trend in SLA towards qualitative research that can provide a holistically oriented description of the experience of the learner. Qualitative research is based on the key philosophical assumption that reality is constructed by individuals in interaction with their social worlds, and therefore, "there are many 'realities' rather than the one, observable, measurable reality which is key to research based in the positivist paradigm" (Merriam & Simpson, 2000, p. 97). Thus, qualitative research starts from a question to be explored rather than a hypothesis to be tested. Taking an emic, that is, participant-relevant, view of phenomena, it aims to represent diversity rather than to make generalisations. The basic aim of this type of research is "to achieve an understanding of how people make sense out of their lives, to delineate the process (rather than the outcome or the product) of meaning-making, and to describe how people interpret what they experience" (Merriam & Simpson, p. 98). In fields such as adult education and distance education, an understanding of the experiences of participants can contribute to the improvement of practice.

In the field of SLA, such research focuses on social, affective, and conceptual aspects of the learner's experience. Among those who argue for a more socially sensitive approach to research that would enrich our understanding of the language-learning process is

Block (2003). He noted an increase in research that takes as its data learners' accounts of their language-learning experiences and observed that this represents a shift from seeing outcomes of encounters with languages only in linguistic or metacognitive terms to seeing them in sociohistorical terms. Similarly, in a recent overview of developments in the TESOL field over the last 15 years, the necessity was highlighted "to orient ourselves to our learners in more specific ways, taking into account their diverse learning contexts and needs" (Canagarajah, 2006, p. 14). An indicator of the growth of this research orientation is also to be found in a sample of the titles of several important collections of work taking such approaches published between 2001 and 2005: "Learner Contributions to Language Learning" (Breen, 2001); "Portraits of the L2 User" (Cook, 2002); "Beliefs about SLA: New Research Approaches" (Kalaja & Ferreira Barcelos, 2003); "Learner Stories: Difference and Diversity" (Benson & Nunan, 2005).

The research reported here follows this development by investigating Chinese language learning from the learner perspective, rather than from the course perspective or the teacher perspective. In the field of TCFL, the learner perspective is relatively underrepresented. Those studies that have taken this approach to a greater or lesser degree have investigated a variety of issues including the motivations of university students from Asian and Asian-American backgrounds to learn Chinese (Wen, 1997), beliefs of 1st-year Chinese learners and their instructors (Samimy & Lee, 1997), attitudes and beliefs about script and literacy (Bell, 1998), strategies of foreign students learning Chinese in China (Xu, 1999) and in Australia (Postmus, 1999), learner experiences of immersion courses in Chinese (de Courcy, 2002), a sociocultural analysis of a student's failed attempt to learn Chinese as a foreign language at an intensive Chinese summer course (Lantolf & Genung, 2003), and motivations of international learners of Chinese as a foreign language (Z. Wang, Ni, Wang, & Jiang, 2004). The majority of these studies focused on learners in their 1st and 2nd years of tertiary study.

The learners who are the subject of this chapter are more experienced, having each studied Chinese for 2 years or more. The levels of proficiency that they have attained vary widely from one individual to another, but proficiency is not a concern here; what is of interest is that every individual in this group has had at least 2 years' experience of the process of learning Chinese. While they may or may not be advanced Mandarin users, they are all experienced as Mandarin learners. A primary aim of this research is to probe their perceptions and beliefs about Chinese language learning, developed through their experience of the process.[1]

The other important identifying feature of the participants in this research is that they all were studying Chinese by means of distance learning. Distance learning is a type of formal learning in which the student follows a planned and guided learning experience (Holmberg, 1986). It implies a geographical distance separating the learner from the teacher, and usually the learner is also geographically separate from the learning group. In some, but not all distance-learning environments, learners who are geographically distant from each other are linked as a virtual group using the Internet and online tools; however, distance learning of languages is not necessarily synonymous with online learning. Online learning is a tool that can be used in a variety of learning modes and course structures. For example, in a networked classroom with the teacher present, online learning may involve interacting with a class of native speakers of the target language in another country; in other circumstances,

---

[1] The study of the construction of beliefs about second-language acquisition in everyday practice and their development in social contexts of learning is illustrated in the work of Barcelos, Kalaja, and others. (Kalaja & Ferreira Barcelos, 2003; Ferreira Barcelos 2003).

a language course that is mainly taught in the traditional face-to-face classroom at a large university may be supplemented by online activities or quizzes that students must complete in their own time; yet neither of those scenarios is likely to be termed *distance language learning.*

Distance language learning (DLL) is a growing field of research that is now in its fourth decade, marked by significant publications and collections (Holmberg, Shelley, & White, 2005; White, 2003). A recent very comprehensive state-of-the-art article identified a shift in the research literature over that period from a focus on course design and delivery mechanisms to the social process of learning, through communication opportunities facilitated by Internet and communications technology (White, 2006). The principal focus of research has tended until relatively recently to be on such aspects as methodology, course design and delivery, new technologies, and new learning environments; recently, however, a focus has developed that extends Breen's (2001) notion of learner contributions to language learning to the distance language-learning context. Hurd (2000) has identified the need to "find out as much as we can about our learners to be in a position to target their needs and respond appropriately" (p. 78), and White (2005) has asserted that "we know relatively little about the reality of DLL from the point of view of those who are most involved, the learners" (p. 62). The current study situates itself within this emerging trend of explorations of the learners' experiences and shaping of the DLL process.

While DLL must not be equated with online learning, DLL is clearly a learning mode that increasingly makes use of new technology to allow for higher levels of interaction and collaboration, and this in turn requires the learners in this mode to develop new learning skills to add to their existing repertoire. In addition, research has demonstrated that the DLL context typically requires a high degree of self-awareness from learners and skills in self-management. (Hurd, 2005; Murphy, 2005; White, 2003). Cotterall (2003) has identified "the need to study the way in which individual learners gain the confidence, knowledge and skill to begin taking independent decisions in relation to their learning" (p. 6).

To date, research into the learning and teaching of Chinese as a foreign language has tended to focus on the classroom context or the in-country context, and studies of learning Chinese in a distance context are not numerous. The development of a Mandarin distance learning course in South Africa has been reported by Hau-Yoon (1994), and Internet-based videoconferencing as a tool for the distance learning of Chinese has been investigated by Y. Wang (2004a, 2004b). White (1995, 1997) conducted a pair of linked comparative studies of classroom and distance learners of French, German, Japanese, and Chinese in their 1st year of study at a New Zealand university; White's studies throw light on students' experiences of the 1st year of learning a language within a distance environment and report a shift in locus of control from internal to external.

The research reported in this chapter focuses on distance language learners who are at a later stage, at least 2 years into their Chinese learning journey. They have adapted to the demands of the initial phase and chosen to continue studying Chinese beyond the beginner level. In so doing, they have each developed an identity as a distance learner. In this study, they were invited to look back upon the road travelled, evaluate their achievements and the changes in their awareness and perspectives on distance learning as a mode of study, and to share their view of the road ahead. This is the second focus of this research. The method of enquiry was influenced by the narrative or (auto)biographical method used in the social sciences, which "seeks to understand the changing experiences and outlooks of individuals in their daily lives, what they see as important, and how to provide interpretations of the accounts they give of their past, present and future" (Roberts, 2002, p. 1)[2]. The use of narrative or life history research methodology in the fields of SLA and ESL has been discussed in some detail by Kouritzin (2000), who concluded that "it is perhaps a necessary addition to ESL research methodology" (p. 30) and by Benson (2005), who suggested that the introspective diary studies and case studies of the late 1970s, which gave an increasingly important role to the description of language-learning experiences and their nonlinguistic outcomes, can be considered precursors of more recent SLA studies explicitly adopting the narrative methods of the social sciences.

In this regard, a further important orientation of the current study is the recognition that each individual learner creates and follows a unique language-learning trajectory. The trajectory of each learner in this study includes a period of distance language education. However, that is not the full story. As White (2003) observed,

> [P]eople generally learn languages through a mixed means learning route, including teach-yourself courses, interactions with native speakers, some classroom-based learning, and accessing target language sources on the web. In other words, the distance course is likely to be only one learning context among many in the experience (past, current, and future) of learners. (p. 205).

Similarly, Kennett (2003), in her work on biographies of Australians learning Japanese, looked at language learning as an ongoing pursuit in the lives of long-term learners, noting the need for "research that tracks learners to informal learning environments" and "recognition that learners will experience various different formal and informal learning situations over their life trajectories and educational careers" (p. 77).

This research takes up the themes outlined in this section and investigates adults studying Chinese in the distance language-learning mode to gain deeper understandings of (a) their individual learning trajectories, (b) their perceptions and beliefs about learning Chinese, and (c) their perceptions and beliefs about distance learning as a way of learning Chinese.

Local context

The Eastern Australia University (EAU)[3] is one of the few institutions in Australia where all of the studies for a full undergraduate major in Chinese can be done by distance education. EAU is a regional university in the eastern part of Australia, with a tradition as a provider of distance education as well as on-campus education. The distance, or external, mode of study is an option that has equal status with the on-campus or internal mode. The curriculum, materials, assessments, and credits are all the same, and the degree awarded on completion of a course of study does not distinguish between the internal and external modes; indeed, students can combine distance and on-campus attendance modes in a single degree if they wish and are able to. The learners who were the subject of this research had all studied Chinese for at least 2 years, during which at least one semester of study had been by distance mode at EAU (and for many participants, all of their study had been by distance mode).

Students taking Chinese units[4] in the distance mode typically work on a weekly schedule with a textbook, audio recordings, and extensive study-guide materials written by the EAU teaching staff. They can communicate with the staff and fellow students via a threaded

---

[2] This methodology has influenced the approach to responses to open-ended questions in the survey and follow-up research that is not the subject of this chapter.

[3] This is a pseudonym for the university in question.

[4] In EAU terminology, a unit is a semester-long course of study in a particular subject, for example, CHIN 101 and CHIN 312.

discussion forum on a private unit website and by phone or e-mail when necessary. Study notes and practical exercises are also available on the web. They submit regular written and audio-recorded assignments that are returned with detailed individualised written and audio-recorded corrections, and they take an examination every semester. Once or twice a year, they have opportunities to attend intensive residential schools in Chinese and meet their teaching staff.

Data collection and analysis

A survey was completed by intermediate-level learners of Chinese at the end of 2005.[5] The participants were selected by the criterion sampling method, defined as picking all the cases that meet certain criteria (Patton, 2002). In this case, they were current and past students who met two criteria: They had been learning Chinese for 2 years or more, and they had been studying in the distance mode for at least some of that time.

Initially, 61 people who potentially met the criteria were identified and were sent a letter briefly outlining the research project, explaining what was involved in completing the surveys, and asking if they were interested in participating (and if so whether they preferred to complete the survey online or on paper). Positive responses were received from 51 people, and each of those respondents was sent a printed survey or a secure URL at which they could access the online version of the survey. In the end, 41 completed surveys were received. The relatively high rate of return (80.34%) may be due to having established personal contact with potential respondents in advance rather than sending the surveys out cold. A further factor is that the researcher was known, by name at least, to most of the respondents as a staff member in the university department where they had all studied Chinese, resulting in a sense of personal connection. As a nonnative speaker of Mandarin who has studied the language herself through university courses and various other means since the 1970s, the researcher can claim equivalent experience to the participants, qualifying her with the *member's competence* (Woods, 1996) that helps to neutralise potential power imbalances in the research situation. Although she had taught some of the participants in the past, the researcher was no longer in a teacher-student relationship with any of the participants at the time they were surveyed (except for 2, who finished the 2nd-year class taught by the researcher within a month of completing the survey).

The survey[6] consisted of 30 questions, divided into four broad sections corresponding to the four foci, and was a mixture of closed and open-ended items as appropriate. Open-ended questions have the purpose of eliciting a wider range of possible responses from participants, and consequently may provide information that is unanticipated (Merriam & Simpson, 2000). After an introduction requesting demographic information on gender, age group, and residential area, the first section of the survey investigated the learners' study environments and the demands on their time made by their daily occupations and family and social participation. It also gathered information about language background and proficiency in other languages. The second section asked each learner to provide a chronology or timeline of their language learning in terms of different courses or modes of study (both formal and informal) undertaken at different times. Section 3 consisted of 11 open-ended questions probing the development of each learner's perceptions and beliefs about learning the Chinese language. The 10 questions in the final section focused on their feelings about distance learning as a way of learning Chinese.

---

[5] This research forms a part of a larger in-depth longitudinal study which will be concluded in 2010.

[6] The survey instrument is attached in the Appendix. The text format in which it is presented shows the content but does not retain the original presentation and layout.

Apart from the demographic and background information that is presented here in tabular form with commentary, the rest of the data were analysed using comparative strategies of iterative coding and categorisation loosely derived from grounded-theory methodology. Grounded theory is a method that aims to generate theory from data (rather than the reverse), reflecting the lived experiences of the research participants. Coding involves the breaking down, analysis, comparison, and categorisation of data. Comparison involves such processes as "(a) comparing different people, such as their views, situations, actions, accounts and experiences, (b) comparing data from the same individuals with themselves at different points in time, (c) comparing incident with incident, (d) comparing data with category, and (e) comparing a category with other categories." (Charmaz, 2003, p. 259)

The data management and relational database program *NVivo* was used because it is well suited to this type of analysis: It allows the researcher to map relationships within the data, test tentative theorising about such relationships, track data analysis, and log and save search results. It is a tool that enables a researcher to demonstrate the integrity, robustness and therefore, trustworthiness of an investigation (Smyth, 2006). These methods have been used to identify major themes emerging from the data and to search for connections. No attempt is made to correlate the themes with learning outcomes; rather, this type of approach is suited to identifying processes at work and to gaining a deeper understanding of the dimensions of individual learners' experiences in real life contexts from their own words (Glaser & Strauss, 1967; Morse & Richards, 2002; Strauss & Corbin, 1998).

Findings

Who were the participants?

This section reports on the demographic and background details of the participants to try to build up a picture of what kind of people take on and persevere at the study of Chinese by distance learning at the Eastern Australia University.

The survey was completed by 18 male and 23 female participants. Their distribution by age band and gender is shown in Table 1. Clearly, more of this group of university students are in their 30s, 40s, and 50s than are in their 20s. Such an age distribution differs significantly from the age makeup of students enrolled in classroom-based on-campus courses, where the majority are in their late teens or early 20s. (This balance is reflected in the general statistics for internal and external enrolments at EAU.) Therefore, the term *adult learners* is sometimes used in this chapter to refer to the research participants. Female learners significantly outnumbered male in the 30–39 and 40–49 year-old bands, but up to 30 and beyond 50 years of age, that was not the case (Table 1).

Table 1. Distribution of participants by age and gender

	20–29	30–39	40–49	50–59	60–69	70
male	4	3	3	4	3	1
female	3	8	7	4	0	1
total	7	11	10	8	3	2

Place of residence was classified as either metropolitan Australia, regional Australia, China, other Chinese-speaking country or region, or other overseas country, and the gender of the participants residing in each area was noted. A striking finding, shown in Table 2, is that all but 1 of the 14 learners who were located in the major Australian cities were male, and all but 3 of the 17 learners located in regional Australia were female. Place of residence may have an influence on study in a variety of ways. Those students residing in metropolitan areas (mostly male) may have easier access to Chinese-speaking interactions and communities. On the other hand, metropolitan residents are more likely to be time-poor than regional residents due to the extended time needed to commute to work and may not necessarily be able to avail themselves of those study opportunities. Further investigation may be warranted of the effects of place of residence on study opportunities and the implications of any related gender distribution.

Table 2. Place of residence and gender

	male	female	total
metropolitan Australia	13	1	14
regional Australia	3	14	17
China	0	5	5
other Chinese-speaking country or region	1	1	2
other overseas country	1	2	3

The participants were asked to self-classify their current working situation so as to get an idea of the demands on their time. The majority were engaged in either paid or unpaid work, as shown in Table 3. Of the 5 participants not in paid work, 4 were full-time students, and 1 was suffering from ill health.

Table 3. Current working situation

part-time paid	full time paid	home duties only	not in paid work	volunteer work	unknown
10	18	3	5	3	2

To add further depth to the picture of the demands on participants' time, they were asked about their home situation: whether they lived alone, with a partner, with friends and housemates, with dependent children, with grown children, or with aged relatives. A wide variety of combinations of these home situations was reported.

An enquiry into the current study mode of the participants revealed that most were studying part time rather than full time, as displayed in Table 4. This is quite a common feature of distance-education students at EAU. Of the 7 participants studying full time, 2 were men between the ages of 20 and 29, 4 were women in the 30–39 age group, and 1 was a woman in the 40–49 age group. Those that were not enrolled at the time of the survey nonetheless fulfilled the criterion of having studied Chinese for at least 2 years, some or all of which was by distance learning.

Table 4. Study situation

full-time	part-time	not enrolled
7	28	6

The language backgrounds of the participants, based on their own definitions of their first language, are shown in Table 5.[7] They were also asked whether they had family connections either with China (9 positive responses) or Chinese language (10 positive responses). These connections included grandparents or parents, Chinese in-laws, and adopted children, and 3 participants had a non-Mandarin dialect of Chinese as their first language.

Table 5. Language background

English	Chinese dialect	Indonesian	Arabic	German	Czech	Hungarian
32	3	1	1	2	1	1

How did their Chinese learning journeys begin?

One of the purposes of this research is to step back from the view of an individual's learning as commencing and finishing with his or her enrolment at this or another university and to get a broader perspective on her or his story, looking at the ways in which the episodes of external study fit in to the overall trajectory of an individual's Chinese learning. In this respect, it has connections with the work of Kennett (2003), who investigated language learning as an ongoing pursuit and the interplay of formal and informal learning in the lives of six long-term learners and users of Japanese. Kennett has identified "a lack of research that tracks learners to informal learning environments and little recognition that learners will experience various different formal and informal learning situations over their life trajectories and educational careers" (p. 77).

The first experience of learning Chinese language for many of the participants was surprisingly early. The survey was conducted at the end of 2005, and 18 of the participants had begun Chinese in the year 2000 or after. That leaves 23 participants who first 'had a go' at learning some Chinese between 6 and 40 years previously: 16 participants began in the 1990s, 3 in the 80s, and 4 as far back as the 1960s and 1970s. The years of the participants' first experiences of studying Chinese are shown in Table 6.

Table 6. Year of first experience learning Chinese

year	1966	1971	1974	1986	1989	1991	1992	1993	1996	1998	1999	2000	2001	2002	2003	2004
number of studendents commencing	1	2	1	1	2	1	4	1	4	1	5	2	5	7	3	1

These first experiences included such scenarios as informal community-based teaching or evening classes, independent structured learning using 'teach yourself' courses, and local tuition during visits to China. A picture emerges of people having an early encounter with learning Chinese and then much later resuming or restarting their study by a different means and at some point being drawn to university-level study, often attracted by its planned and guided nature. Some learners went through several completely separate episodes of

---

[7] In the survey instrument, this question was carefully worded with a note as follows: "The term 'first language' can refer to either the first language you learnt in your life (the chronological sense) or to the language that is most important in your life (the dominant sense). If this is relevant to you, feel free to nominate a first language in both senses of the word. If you feel you have more than one first language in either sense, please specify."

learning Chinese by different means. In addition, even after beginning distance learning at EAU, some participants had gaps in their enrolment of a semester or more when they did not formally study Chinese for a variety of academic, family, and work-related reasons.

These findings about learning patterns and trajectories are interesting for a variety of reasons. They show us that adult distance learners cannot be assumed to follow a continuous, linear trail in their studies of Chinese and that teaching institutions offering them a degree of flexibility to opt out of and back into a course would serve them well. They also demonstrate that adults enrolled in beginner-level units are actually quite likely to be false beginners, perhaps with some background knowledge or experience of the language, fossilised language skills, and some previous Chinese learning experience on which they are likely to draw. A further implication is that such learners may be pursuing or reviving a long-held goal or interest in learning Chinese, which will strengthen their motivation for study.

An analysis of the reasons given by the participants in retrospect for beginning to learn Chinese reveals a mix of instrumental and integrative motivations and several major recurring themes. Learning Chinese is seen as a challenge, an adventure, and a new world to explore; it is also frequently viewed as a mystery or riddle to be solved. For some, the perceived rarity value of Chinese as a foreign language in Australia appeals; for others, Chinese is a means of communicating with (and impressing) family members. The aesthetic and cultural world that the Chinese language represents is another theme drawing members of this group to begin studying it.

Recent research in motivation in foreign-language study suggests the value of taking a process-oriented approach, to interpret and integrate fluctuations and changes in motivation over time (Dörnyei & Ushioda, 2009; Shedivy, 2004; Shoaib & Dornyei, 2004; Ushioda, 2009). In the current study, after inviting the participants' self-reports of reasons for beginning their study of Chinese at least 2 years previously, the participants were asked what kept them studying it.

The reasons which were impelling learners to continue with their study of Chinese were rather different from those which had initially motivated them to begin studying it. The picture that emerges is one of the rewards and challenges of having made progress on a difficult journey. "It's like getting a pay packet: to get the goodies, there has been a lot of work but I feel satisfaction" (Scott).[8] The challenge of learning Chinese is frequently likened to hard physical effort over an extended period of time in rough terrain, such as climbing a mountain, swimming against the tide, or finding your way through a dense fog or thick forest, but the rewards experienced or glimpsed ahead seem to keep some of the learners going. "It's like bushwalking in remote areas—sometimes challenging, exhausting and frightening, and other times exhilarating" (Michelle). "It's like walking on a LONG, long road where I'm just starting to see the beautiful views ahead" (Stella).

For some, the mysteries and riddles that sparked their curiosity to commence Chinese study are now beginning to be cracked: "It's like finding the key to a difficult riddle" (Sonia). For other learners, however, the puzzles continue to tantalise. "Now, learning Chinese is like trying to solve a puzzle that becomes more difficult, the closer you get to figuring it out" (Lola).

A recurring theme in maintaining the motivation to continue with Chinese learning is the sense of joy that attaches to the development of skills in communication and successful attempts to communicate in Chinese:

---

[8] All participants are referred to by pseudonyms.

"It's the thrill of understanding the structure of the language and being able to use it—even in a most elemental [sic] way." (Harry) "Work hard, take all the opportunities to chat with Chinese. Practice every week, write Chinese character in a flash card. Write diary... then one day, when you can understand what the Chinese person said and you can answer his questions. That happiness might be one of the reward that I think." (Charlotte)

What is striking about these comments is the intensity of emotion associated with the personal choices to learn and continue learning Chinese. As the author has discussed elsewhere (Tasker, 2006),[9] an illuminating way of interpreting the imagery attached to these descriptions of the task of Chinese learning is to use the metaphor of the quest: an arduous journey incorporating challenging tasks and struggles, leading to the attainment of an elusive goal, and in the process, bringing about profound changes or insights. Similar metaphors and emotional intensity are reported in Kramsch's (in press) research with young adults learning another language in a U.S. university campus setting.

Looking back: The lessons of experience in learning Chinese

From their vantage point midway in their journey of Chinese learning, the participants were asked to look back towards their starting point. They were asked what advice they would give someone who was just beginning to learn Chinese and whether there was anything that they knew then that they wished someone had told them when they started learning. The purpose of such questions was to invite reflection about study strategies and approaches and to identify what the participants perceived as being crucial to their learning at the point that they were at, past the beginner stage. Several salient themes emerged from this part of the analysis, which can be seen as reflecting understandings or awarenesses acquired by the learners through their experience of the nature and requirements of the task of learning Chinese. Four broad themes are presented here in terms of what the learners recognised as significant outcomes of their engagement with learning.

Theme 1: Recognition of the complexity of the task and reevaluation of the years it will take; acceptance of a long-term commitment

These learners perceived their current task of learning Chinese to be complex and gradual and accepted the fact that it requires a lengthy commitment of time. They felt that the intrinsic interest of the task made it worthwhile.

> It is a very rewarding language that takes a lot of effort and time to understand. (Russell)

> Naively enough, I certainly didn't think it was going to be this difficult when I started and I didn't realise it was a lifetime commitment, especially if you want to be well versed in the culture and language. (Keith)

> Chinese is a really complex but interesting language. It's not something you can learn immediately and be really good at it. It takes time. (Ruby)

> Recognise that it's not going to be easy, but endure and savour the growth along the way. (Shelley)

This aspect is not something that is stressed to beginning students by teaching staff or course advisors, probably because of a reluctance to frighten them away! Indeed, the responses suggested that perhaps recognition of the scale of the task can only take place in tandem with learners' discoveries of the rewards of continuing study:

---

[9] The paper referred to here is written by the author, Isabel Tasker, and published under her Chinese name, 谭以诗 (**Tán Yǐshī**).

If someone had told me, maybe I would never have started and I have only benefited from learning along the way. (Rachel)

Theme 2: Recognition of the extent of formal linguistic differences between Chinese and English (and other European languages)

Learning Chinese, for speakers of English and European languages, tends to involve a gradual unlearning of Eurocentric understandings of how a language works. Their comments demonstrate the challenges of learning a noncognate language and the value for learners of developing an awareness of formal aspects of language through interlanguage comparison.

> Forget all pre-conceptions about structure and form of language. (Shay)

> Don't be put off by the apparent total different structure of the written characters. (Hugh)

> I wish someone had told me the key characteristics NOT to expect, or TO expect. (e.g., "Please accept that a language without articles 'a' or 'the' can be coherent"—dozens of them.) (Hans)

These distance learners found it helpful that aspects of comparative grammar and semantics were incorporated in their introductory-level learning materials, in terms of activities providing focus on form and encouraging reflective comparison between Chinese and other languages with which they were familiar. Their comments also suggest that a deeper understanding and acceptance of the different way that Chinese encodes and expresses meanings only begins to be realised after a significant period of learning and exposure to Chinese in authentic contexts.

Theme 3: Recognition of the importance of developing competence in all skills at the same time

Just as individuals display different learning styles, they also have different motivations for learning Chinese that will affect their orientation towards listening, speaking, reading, and writing and the various learning tasks involved. As independent learners with some flexibility about how they organise and tackle their study tasks, distance learners sometimes respond to the significant time demands of their Chinese course by prioritising one aspect of the language at a time. However, looking back over their learning experiences so far, a frequently expressed view was that it was counterproductive to focus on particular skills at the expense of others.

> I truly wished I had started learning to read and write at the same time as learning to speak whilst I was in Guangzhou, instead of just trying to survive initially. (Caroline)

> Learn the correct pronunciation of each and every word and character's tones from the BEGINNING… do not tell yourself they don't matter because people will understand you in a contextual sense…it is very difficult to break bad habits. (Pat)

> [T]he importance of listening and trying to learn to speak the language concurrently with other aspects of learning. Each component is only part of the whole, but compliments [sic] the others. To practice them all at the same rate makes learning easier. (Stephanie)

Recognition of the crucial nature of the interrelationship between Chinese characters, meanings, and sounds tends to develop towards the end of the 1st year of study. An understanding of the importance of speaking and listening skills and the role played by tone (which beginning students tend to treat as an optional extra, especially when they are focusing on other aspects of a task) develops in tandem with exposure to situations where authentic spoken interaction in Chinese takes place. Distance learners of Chinese greatly vary in the extent to which they are able to access such interactive situations, apart from those opportunities that are built into their course materials and language tasks. The participants demonstrated awareness of this issue and had developed strategies for addressing it, to be discussed in a following section.

Theme 4: Recognition of the benefits of a relaxed, playful, self-nurturing attitude toward learning

Learner anxiety is relatively common among adult distance learners: partly because they are often either commencing tertiary study for the first time or returning to it after a long break and because their isolation from their classmates exacerbates feelings of uncertainty about whether their progress and performance is acceptable, together with worries that "I'm the only one that can't understand this bit." Learner anxiety is an emotional state that can stifle learning as the learner becomes increasingly worried about performance and study outcomes. The comments elicited in this study demonstrate that the participants recognised such tendencies and have developed strategies and self-talk for dealing with the anxiety. They echo the findings of Hauck and Hurd (2005) on the strategies deployed by distance language learners to reduce anxiety.

> Ask questions, especially the "silly" ones. (Lola)
>
> Don't be shy—go and talk to native speakers and classmates in Chinese! (Donna)
>
> Don't forget to laugh at your mistakes. (Scott)
>
> Don't give yourself a hard time if at times it seems too difficult. Slow steady progress is always best. Try to enjoy the journey and keep in touch with fellow students. (Michelle)
>
> Relax and have fun. Keep listening, speaking and watching Mandarin if they can. (Sharon)
>
> Don't be afraid to push yourself a little and remember that the blunders and mistakes provide the best opportunities for progress. Also remember that progress can be slow, but when it appears, it's great! (Stephanie)

The distance tutor has an important role to play in providing support and encouragement for isolated learners and in encouraging participation in virtual learning communities of whatever type is appropriate to the situation. For those learners who continue beyond the beginner level, the acceptance of a lengthy timescale for achieving goals in Chinese learning contributes to reducing the pressure of time and allows for the cultivation of a lighter attitude where appropriate.

Other themes arising here were the need for conversation partners and the need to persevere with regular study. They will be discussed elsewhere in relation to the particular requirements of distance learning.

Distance language learning: Opinions and choices

Initially, why did the learners choose to study in the distance-learning mode? The reasons cited by the participants fall into and across several categories. Financial concerns were high: either the need to work and earn a living or support a family precluded attendance at on-campus classes, or the travel to and from on-campus classes was too expensive, or the university distance-education classes were more affordable than private tuition. Time concerns were closely linked to financial ones, and for many participants, full-time work and family responsibilities did not allow the time to attend classes at a campus. Factors of location and geography were also high: Many respondents were simply too far away to attend any classes in Chinese. Some lived in remote areas of Australia, some travelled extensively for their work, while others were located overseas (including in China) but wished to study and gain credit towards an Australian degree or diploma.

Whereas some learners saw distance learning as one of the few study options open to them due to the limitations imposed by time, place, and money, others articulated it as a positive choice. Recommendations from friends or previous personal experiences of learning other subjects by distance education with the same institution featured strongly for some. Distance learning was perceived by a number of participants as offering choice and flexibility, offering them the chance to study while living in the place of their choice:

> I was living in a beautiful small community and did not want to live anywhere else to study, yet wanted to complete my degree (B. Arts). (Michelle)

> I wanted to do as much as I could at once while young and single so thought I'd travel and see another country as an exchange student—but needing to continue Chinese as my major, switched to distance education to be able to do both. (Marty)

Some students expressed a preference for studying independently and being able to find their own pace outside of a classroom environment. Others were attracted to the distance learning of Chinese because it offered structure and motivation:

> I also wanted to send in work to see it marked—see feedback and real meaningful signposts indicating actual progress. (Tom)

Asked whether they planned to continue studying Chinese in distance mode, 28 of the participants said that they did, echoing the reasons for which they began it but adding the aspect of being settled in DLL as a familiar mode of study with which they now felt confident. Most learners considered their distance-learning Chinese units to be central to their study of Chinese, providing structure and goals to work towards, though several students expressed the opinion that while central, they needed to be supplemented by face-to-face work with a tutor. For the learners based in Chinese-speaking countries, the distance learning units tended to be seen as something additional, providing a structure and a means of checking progress and working towards a qualification. Among the 8 respondents who did not plan to continue, 5 had completed their degree and either wanted a break from formal study of Chinese for a while or were looking for an appropriate course to move on to, and 3 found that the distance-learning mode did not suit them and planned to search for other modes or opportunities to continue their study.

Distance language learning: Advice for new learners

The participants were asked to identify some of the challenges they had faced in learning Chinese in the distance mode and were asked what advice they would give to someone planning to begin to study Chinese by distance learning. A group of themes emerged very strongly, and comparing the two sets of responses demonstrated that having identified challenges, the learners had also developed individual strategies to meet those challenges. These findings are congruent with recent research into the metacognitive knowledge of distance language learners (White, 1995) and the skills and strategies that successful learners are required to develop (Hurd, 2001).

The first area of challenge was that of isolation from other students and thinking of oneself as the only one facing difficulties. The strategies suggested in response to this were to keep in contact with lecturer and classmates by using of all the means provided: participating in the online discussion forum, calling the lecturer, and attending any residential schools offered. The value of finding a study companion was also important, for instance, as Anya wrote, "Find a study buddy. It's great to have someone to bounce things off if you're not sure."

Another big issue was the difficulty of developing speaking skills when studying in an external mode. A widely advocated solution was to find a conversation partner or native-speaker tutor and organise regular face-to-face meetings. Learners displayed considerable initiative in doing this through work, social, and local networks and reported positively on the experience. For Carl, the requirements of studying Chinese in distance mode impelled him to take this step: "[It's] a reason to engage with Chinese people you don't know! It leaves one with no choice but to get out there and chase the language."

For some located in fairly remote areas of Australia, though, finding suitable local Mandarin speakers was not always possible. The use of Internet technology to facilitate conversation practice was not widely mentioned as a strategy.

Apart from finding a conversation partner, another suggestion that emerged strongly amongst the chorus of learners' voices was that distance learners should create or find and use other resources or opportunities to suit their personal preferences for practising their Chinese, especially their speaking and listening skills. These ranged from watching the Mandarin news on television,[10] listening to Mandarin pop songs, buying children's books, and reading the Bible or the Dao De Jing in Chinese, through to going on a holiday or course in China.

Maintaining discipline and consistency in study was also perceived as a difficulty. Advice offered for beginners was to be rigorous in making a study schedule and keeping to it without falling behind; the use of effective time-management techniques was seen as very important. A further strong theme was the necessity to set time aside every day to work on Chinese.

A degree of self-awareness of one's learning style and individual learning needs was perceived to be helpful: "They have to look at their own personality in terms of whether or not they like to attend class" (Keith); "Distance is good if you have the motivation to push yourself" (Russell).

Many of these learners had also developed a strategy of using self-talk and self-encouragement to help them through the challenges of studying Chinese in distance mode: "Be encouraged by any progress and see it as your personal achievement" (Ann).

Discussion and recommendations

These suggestions and strategies for dealing with the demands of learning Chinese from a distance demonstrate that after 2 or more years of study, these learners had developed considerable levels of awareness of their own agency in the teaching and learning situation. Asked whether her distance learning units were central or peripheral to her study of Chinese, Stephanie, who had been studying externally for over 3 years, replied, "Initially they were central to my study because I had no knowledge of the language and little of the culture. Now I have more of an idea of my direction and how I learn, so the units still enhance my knowledge, but have become an additional source of knowledge."

Increasingly, as they gain experience in distance learning, these students are by no means passive consumers of the educational materials they receive, but are actively creating their Chinese 'course' or programme of learning. They select the aspects of the materials and instruction they receive that meet their needs, and they are able to identify the gaps where their needs are not being met and seek means to fill those gaps. Cohen and White

---

[10] The news in Mandarin is relayed from China daily over the SBS TV network in Australia.

(2008) have observed that such skills are similar to those required for new generations of language learners who "will be faced with an increasing array of choices in terms of learning environments, learning partners, and learning experiences" and who will therefore need to be "equipped to make informed judgements about how they will best invest their time, energy and resources in learning, what constitutes a quality learning experience, and how they may further enhance that experience," (p. 203).

From the perspective of teaching and program design, these findings suggest that investigation and trialling must continue of advances in Internet and communications technology to enable further practical and feasible opportunities for speaking and interactive language practice to be offered to distance learners of Chinese. Methods of voice communication over the Internet are becoming more easily available to students and can be used to incorporate more speaking practice into Chinese units. Not all students, though, are willing or able to take up such methods. Equally important, therefore, is that emphasis be placed on building activities into beginner-level distance and online Chinese courses that aim to do the following: (a) support students in developing independent language-learning skills such as habits of reflection (Murphy, 2005) and awareness of their own learning styles and preferred learning strategies and (b) help and encourage them to identify and take up possibilities for other informal learning activities that their particular local environment and mix of circumstances might offer.

One unexpected outcome of the data collection was the effect on the participants of the individual contact afforded by the research situation, which gave them a stimulus or a chance to reflect upon their Chinese studies. In several cases, the participants found that the reflection involved in completing the survey gave them renewed interest in taking up studies that had lapsed or in resuming study plans. Both the reflection and the personal contact influenced them. The relatively high percentage of positive responses to the initial proposal to participate in the research, discussed above, suggests a willingness to reflect upon their learning and share their experiences with an interested and informed audience. Other studies of distance learners have had similar findings (Sataporn & Lamb, 2005).

This study has shown that the learning pathways of adult learners of Chinese are likely to include stops and starts, periods of formal enrolment in distance learning interspersed with gaps in formal study and periods of learning by other means. At any time, there will be learners who are at a stage in their learning journey when they are not enrolled in a formal course but are perhaps undertaking structured independent study or self-directed informal learning or language maintenance, or using their Chinese in some way, or taking a break from Chinese. Although from the institutional perspective, such learners are not visible and appear to have dropped out, from the learner's perspective, the fact that they are not enrolled in a Chinese unit does not mean that they see themselves as having finished, or finished with their Chinese learning.

Responses and feedback from the learners completing the survey suggest that they find it valuable and stimulating to have a mentor or someone taking an interest in their study journey, which is an individual journey crafted from various episodes and sources. The chance to reflect upon their learning and to articulate their reflections acted variously as a trigger to consider resuming their study or to pick up unfinished business, a reminder of the pleasures of learning Chinese, or a stimulus to revive their interest in it. At a university level, the support networks that are offered in connection with specific formal courses or degree programmes are not normally available to those learners who are considered by the institution to be inactive because they are not currently enrolled. Because, however, the interest of an 'informed other' sometimes seems the only trigger that is required to encourage students to resume their study, conducting regular follow-ups with previous students for this purpose is worth considering.

Conclusion

Overall, this study has pointed to the value of investigating the perspective of experienced learners of Chinese. It can illuminate their current situation and their future needs as they move towards assuming identities as advanced learners of Chinese. It can also help us to understand better the needs and concerns of those engaged in DLL. It is insightful to view distance learners as active agents creating their own learning, discovering what works for them, and choosing their methods of learning to suit their learning styles and their different goals.

In addition, the perspective of the experienced learner of Chinese can cast a new light on the challenges and affordances facing beginners, helping us to understand questions such as the following: What can help them to persevere in their studies? What contributes to transforming a beginner into an experienced, committed learner? What aspects of learning take place in the first years apart from that of curriculum content?

Finding answers to these questions can be of practical use to teachers and course developers for planning curriculum design and delivery of Chinese distance learning. As interest in Chinese increases, some forms of the distance learning mode will likely become more widely used for learning and teaching the language, and empirical research such as that presented here may be of use in drawing attention to the learner perspective and flagging questions to be borne in mind in the development of such courses. Many of the findings can also be extrapolated to the teaching of other languages in distance mode, including less commonly taught languages.

On a different level, the findings from this study can serve an important function of encouraging teacher recognition of the significant affective aspects of the experiences that learners go through in their early years of learning Chinese. A survey participant eloquently captured the intensity and ambiguity of the feelings that her emotional involvement with Chinese learning engendered: "Overwhelming, mind-straining and totally enthralling would be my first words to describe how learning Chinese has affected me" (Helga).

It is hoped that this kind of research can serve to foster among staff involved in (or considering involvement in) distance language education an awareness of the learner's perspective and an empathy for the commitments, challenges, and emotions that are associated for many students with the task of learning Chinese in the distance mode.

References

Bell, J. S. (1998). *Literacy, culture and identity*. New York: Peter Lang.

Benson, P. (2005). The rise of (auto)biographical research? In P. Benson & D. Nunan (Eds.), *Learners' stories: Difference and diversity in language learning* (pp. 4–21). Cambridge, England: Cambridge University Press.

Benson, P., & Nunan, D. (Eds.). (2005). *Learners' stories: Difference and diversity in language learning*. Cambridge, England: Cambridge University Press.

Block, D. (2003). *The social turn in second language acquisition*. Edinburgh, Scotland: Edinburgh University Press

Breen, M. P. (Ed.). (2001). *Learner contributions to language learning: New directions in research*. Harlow, England: Pearson Longman.

Canagarajah, A. S. (2006). TESOL at forty: What are the issues? *TESOL Quarterly, 40*(1), 9–34.

Charmaz, K. (2003). Grounded theory: Objective and constructivist methods. In N. K. Denzin & Y. S. Lincoln (Eds.), *Strategies of qualitative Inquiry* (2nd ed.) (pp. 249–291). Thousand Oaks, CA: Sage.

Cohen, A. D., & White, C. (2008). Language learners as informed consumers of language instruction. In A. Stavans & I. Kupferberg (Eds.), *Studies in language and language education: Essays in honor of Elite Olshtain*. Jerusalem: The Hebrew University Magnes Press.

Cook, V. (Ed.). (2002). *Portraits of the L2 user*. Clevedon, England: Multilingual Matters Ltd.

Cotterall, S. (2003). Learner independence: Reflecting on experience. *Proceedings of The Independent Learning Conference 2003* (pp. 1–6). Retrieved January 20, 2010 from http://independentlearning.org/ILA/ila03/ila03_cotterall.pdf

de Courcy, M. (2002). *Learners' experiences of immersion education: Case studies of French and Chinese*. Clevedon: Multilingual Matters.

Dörnyei, Z., & Ushioda, E. (Eds.). (2009). *Motivation, language identity, and the L2 self*. Clevedon, England: Multilingual Matters.

Ferreira Barcelos, A. M. (2003). Researching beliefs about SLA: A critical review. In P. Kalaja & A. M. Ferreira Barcelos (Eds.), *Beliefs about SLA: New research approaches* (pp. 7–33). Dordrecht: Kluwer Academic.

Glaser, B. G., & Strauss, A. L. (1967). *The discovery of grounded theory: Strategies for qualitative research*. Chicago: Aldine.

Hau-Yoon, L. (1994). The development of a self-study Mandarin Chinese language course for distance learners at the University of South Africa. *Progressio, 16*(1), 70–80.

Hauck, M., & Hurd, S. (2005). Exploring the link between language anxiety and learner self-management in open language learning contexts. *European Journal of Open, Distance and E-learning, 2005*(II). Retrieved January 20, 2010 from http://www.eurodl.org/materials/contrib/2005/Mirjam_Hauck.htm

Holmberg, B. (1986). *Growth and structure of distance education*. London: Croom Helm.

Holmberg, B., Shelley, M., & White, C. (Eds.). (2005). *Distance education and languages: Evolution and change*. Clevedon, England: Multilingual Matters.

Hurd, S. (2000). Distance language learners and learner support: Beliefs, difficulties and use of strategies. *Links and Letters, 7*, 61–80.

Hurd, S. (2001). Managing and supporting language learners in open and distance learning environments. In M. Mozzon-McPherson & R. Vismans (Eds.), *Beyond language teaching towards language advising* (pp. 135–148). London: CILT.

Hurd, S. (2005). Autonomy and the distance language learner. In B. Holmberg, M. Shelley, & C. White (Eds.), *Distance education and languages* (pp. 1–19). Clevedon, England: Multilingual Matters.

Kalaja, P., & Ferreira Barcelos, A. M. (Eds.). (2003). *Beliefs about SLA: New research approaches*. Dordrecht, Netherlands: Kluwer Academic Publishers.

Kennett, B. (2003). *Resourcing identities: Biographies of Australians learning Japanese*. Unpublished doctoral dissertation, University of Queensland, St. Lucia, Australia.

Kouritzin, S. (2000). Bringing life to research: Life history research and ESL. *TESL Canada Journal, 17*(2), 1–35.

Kramsch, C. (in press). *The multilingual subject: What foreign language learners say about their experience and why it matters*. Oxford, England: Oxford University Press.

Lantolf, J. P., & Genung, P. B. (2003). "I'd rather switch than fight": An activity-theoretic study of power, failure and success in a foreign language classroom. In C. Kramsch (Ed.), *Language acquisition and socialisation: Ecological perspectives* (pp. 175–197). New York: Continuum Press.

Merriam, S. B., & Simpson, E. L. (2000). *A guide to research for educators and trainers of adults* (2nd ed.). Malabar, FL: Krieger.

Morse, J. M., & Richards, L. (2002). *Readme first for a user's guide to qualitative methods*. Thousand Oaks, CA: Sage.

Murphy, L. (2005). Critical reflection and autonomy: A study of distance learners of French, German and Spanish. In B. Holmberg, M. Shelley, & C. White (Eds.), *Distance education and languages: Evolution and change* (pp. 20–39). Clevedon, England: Multilingual Matters.

Patton, M. Q. (2002). *Qualitative research and evaluation methods*. Thousand Oaks, CA: Sage.

Postmus, M. A. (1999). *Metalinguistic thinking and learner strategies during the early acquisition of a foreign language: A comparative study of monolingual and multilingual tertiary students learning Mandarin Chinese in an Australian university*. Unpublished master's thesis, University of Western Australia, Perth, Australia.

Roberts, B. (2002). *Biographical research*. Buckingham, England: Open University Press.

Samimy, K. K., & Lee, Y.-A. (1997). Beliefs about language learning: Perspectives of first-year Chinese learners and their instructors. *Journal of the Chinese Language Teachers Association, 32*(1), 40–60.

Sataporn, S., & Lamb, M. (2005). Accommodation zone: Two learners' struggles to cope with a distance learning English course. In P. Benson & D. Nunan (Eds.), *Learners' stories: Difference and diversity in language learning*. Cambridge, England: Cambridge University Press.

Shedivy, S. L. (2004). Factors that lead some students to continue the study of foreign language past the usual 2 years in high school. *System, 32*(1), 103–119.

Shoaib, A., & Dornyei, Z. (2004). Affect in lifelong learning: Exploring L2 motivation as a dynamic process. In P. Benson & D. Nunan (Eds.), *Learners' stories: Difference and diversity in language learning* (pp. 119–134). Cambridge, England: Cambridge University Press.

Smyth, R. (2006). Exploring congruence between Habermasian philosophy, mixed-method research and managing data using *NVivo*. *International Journal of Qualitative Methods, 5*(2). Retrieved January 20, 2010 from http://www.ualberta.ca/~iiqm/backissues/5_2/pdf/smyth.pdf

Strauss, A. L., & Corbin, J. (1998). *Basics of qualitative research: Grounded theory procedures and techniques*. London: Sage.

Tasker, I [谭以诗](2006, August). *Learning Chinese entails a metamorphosis: The personal significance of Chinese language study for adult Australian distance learners and independent learners*. Paper presented at the 5th International Conference on Chinese Language Teaching, Shanghai, China.

Ushioda, E. (2009). A person-in-context relational view of emergent motivation, self and identity. In Z. Dörnyei & E. Ushioda (Eds.), *Motivation, language identity and the L2 self* (pp. 215–228).

Wang, Y. (2004a). Distance language learning: Interactivity and fourth-generation Internet-based videoconferencing. *CALICO Journal, 21*(2), 373–395.

Wang, Y. (2004b). Supporting synchronous distance language learning with desktop videoconferencing. *Language Learning and Technology, 8*(3), 90–121.

Wang, Z., Ni, C., Wang, J., & Jiang, M. (2004). An investigation of the purposes of international learners of Chinese as a foreign language. *Shijie Hanyu Jiaoxue, 2004*(3), 67–78.

Wen, X. (1997). Motivation and language learning with students of Chinese. *Foreign Language Annals, 30*(2), 235–251.

White, C. (1995). Autonomy and strategy use in distance foreign language learning: Research findings. *System, 23*(2), 207–221.

White, C. (1997). Effects of mode of study on foreign language learning. *Distance Education, 18*(1), 178–196.

White, C. (2003). *Language learning in distance education*. Cambridge, England: Cambridge University Press.

White, C. (2005). Towards a learner-based theory of distance language learning: The concept of the learner-context interface. In B. Holmberg, M. Shelley, & C. White (Eds.), *Distance education and languages* (pp. 55–71). Clevedon, England: Multilingual Matters.

White, C. (2006). Distance learning of foreign languages. *Language Teaching, 39*(4), 247–264.

Woods, D. (1996). *Teacher cognition in language teaching*. Cambridge, England: Cambridge University Press.

Xu, Z. (徐子亮) (1999). 外国学生汉语学习策略的认知心理分析 [Cognitive psychological analysis of the Chinese learning strategies of foreign students.]. *世界汉语教学 [Chinese Teaching in the World], 1999*(04), 174–187.

Tasker Appendix: Survey instrument (abbreviated version without the original layout)

Pathways and Perceptions of Distance Learners of Chinese

Section 1. Background information and demographics (all details will be treated as confidential)

Male ☐ Female ☐

Age group (circle one):   <20   20–29   30–39   40–49   50–59   60–69   70 +

What is your current place of residence?

- ☐ Metropolitan Australia
- ☐ Regional Australia
- ☐ China / other Chinese-speaking country or region
- ☐ other overseas country

Questions 1–4 will help me to understand your study environment and the demands on your time.

1. How would you describe your current working situation?

   Tick one or more boxes, and add explanatory comments if you wish.
   - ☐ Part-time paid work
   - ☐ Full time paid work
   - ☐ Home duties only
   - ☐ Not in paid work
   - ☐ Voluntary work
   - ☐ Other: specify

2. How would you describe your current home situation?

   Tick as many boxes as necessary, and add explanatory comments if you wish.
   - ☐ I live alone
   - ☐ I live with a partner
   - ☐ I live with friends / housemates
   - ☐ I live with dependent children
   - ☐ I live with grown children
   - ☐ I live with aged relatives
   - ☐ Other: describe

3. How would you describe your current study situation?
   - ☐ Full time study. (As defined by your institution. At EAU it is 4 units per semester)
   - ☐ Part time study. I am currently taking _____ unit(s) per semester.

4. If you are currently studying Chinese as part of a degree or diploma programme at university, please name the programme (e.g., BA, Dip Mod Language, Grad Dip in Humanities, non-award, etc.) _____

Questions 5–8 will help me to understand your language background.

5. What is your first language?* _____

   If your first language is a dialect of Chinese, please specify which dialect, e.g., Cantonese, Hokkien, etc. _____

   *Note: the term 'first language' can refer to either the first language you learnt in your life (the chronological sense) or to the language which is most important in your life (the dominant sense). If this is relevant to you, feel free to nominate a first language in both senses of the word. If you feel you have more than one first language in either sense, please specify.

6. What other languages do you speak or have you studied apart from English and Mandarin Chinese? _____

   Please indicate the level of your skill in Speaking, Listening, Reading and Writing in each language as None, Basic, Intermediate, or Fluent. _____

   _____

   _____

7. Do you have any family connections with the Chinese language?

   For example, do any of your family members (by birth, adult relationship, or adoption) speak or understand Mandarin or any other Chinese dialect? Yes / No. If Yes, please describe. _____

   _____

   _____

8. Do you have any family connections with China or a Chinese speaking country?

   For instance, have any of your family (by birth, adult relationship, or adoption) lived or worked in China or a Chinese speaking country?   Yes / No. If Yes, please describe. _____

   _____

   _____

Section 2. Chronology / timeline of your Chinese learning:
This section will help me to understand the different phases which you have gone through in learning Chinese.

9. Please use the following table to supply details of the story of your Chinese learning so far.

   'Period 1' is your first experience of learning Chinese; each time you changed course or mode of study marks the beginning of another 'period.' Include periods where there have been no Chinese-related activities. Also, include any overlapping periods of Chinese learning. Continue on the following page if necessary.

[Table omitted; it contained the following questions for each period of study identified by the respondents]

   9.1 Dates (from month/ year to month/ year)

   9.2 Where were you located during this period?

   9.3 Did you take a formal course with a teacher in this period?

      Yes / No. If Yes, specify the level, institution, and whether full-time or part-time study.

      If No, jump to question 9.6.

9.4 What was your mode of study:

Internal (face to face tuition), or External (distance learning)?

9.5 Did your course include any online activities, such as bulletin board, interactive exercises, or email discussion?

Yes / No. If Yes, describe briefly.

9.6 Did you try any independent but structured study, such as a 'teach-yourself' course, in this period?

Yes / No. If Yes, specify the course, and note if it was Attempted or Completed.

9.7 Did you engage in informal Chinese language learning activities in this period, such as regular reading, watching TV or films, conversation exchanges with native speakers, or other activities?

Yes / No. If Yes, describe briefly.

9.8 What opportunities (if any) did you have for using Chinese during this period, for example in your work or daily life, with colleagues, friends, or family? Please describe briefly.

Section 3. Perceptions and beliefs about learning Chinese

Your answers to the next questions will help me to understand how students' ideas and feelings about learning Chinese develop as they learn it.

10. Initially, what were your reasons for beginning to learn Chinese?_____

_____

_____

How would you classify the reasons you have just described? Tick any number of boxes.

☐ personal

☐ family

☐ work-related

☐ study-related

☐ challenge / curiosity

☐ emotional

☐ other (specify)

11. At this point, what are your reasons for continuing to study Chinese?_____

_____

_____

How would you classify the reasons you have just described? Tick any number of boxes.

☐ personal

☐ family

☐ work-related

☐ study-related

☐ challenge / curiosity

☐ emotional

☐ other (specify)

12. How, if at all, do you expect to continue your Chinese learning to improve or maintain your Chinese language skills?

   a) over the next two years?_____
   _____
   _____

   b) in a longer time frame?_____
   _____
   _____

13. What opportunities do you have for using Chinese at the moment?

14. How do you hope to use your Chinese skills in the future?

15. How would you describe your experience of learning Chinese at first? What could you compare it to? Choose one or two metaphors or phrases that capture your experience at that time.

   "When I started it, learning Chinese was like _____,

   or sometimes like _____."

16. Now, how would you describe learning Chinese? What could you compare it to? Choose one or two metaphors or phrases that capture your recent experience.

   "Now, learning Chinese is like _____,

   or sometimes like _____."

17. Please complete the following sentence:

   "So far, the challenges of learning Chinese for me have been_____."

18. Please complete the following sentence:

   "So far, the rewards of learning Chinese for me have been _____."

19. Is there anything that you know now, that you wish someone had told you when you started learning Chinese?

20. Do you think learning Chinese has changed you in any way?

Section 4. Your opinions about distance learning.

Your answers to questions 21–30 will give me a clearer picture of your feelings about distance learning as a way of learning Chinese. By 'distance learning' I'm referring to formal study where the student is remote from the institution offering the course. Some people use terms like 'external study,' 'correspondence course' or 'open learning' to refer to this.

21. Initially, what were your reasons for studying as a distance learner? _____
   _____
   _____

22. Do you plan to continue studying as a distance learner? Please give reasons. _____
_____
_____

23. Do you consider distance learning courses / units as central to your study of Chinese or as something extra, additional or peripheral? Please explain. _____
_____
_____

24. How would you describe your experiences of distance learning? What could you compare it to? _____
_____
_____

Choose one or two metaphors or phrases that capture your experience.

"Studying a language in distance mode is like _____,

or sometimes like _____."

25. Please complete the following sentence:

"So far, the challenges of learning Chinese in distance mode have been _____
_____."

26. Please complete the following sentence:

"In my experience, the rewards of learning Chinese in distance mode are _____
_____."

27. What advice would you give to someone who was just beginning to learn Chinese? _
_____

28. What further advice would you give that person if they planned to study by distance learning? _____
_____

29. Apart from Chinese, have you any experience of studying other subjects by distance learning? _____
_____

Please give brief details of the year, subject, and institution. _____
_____

30. Do you have any further comments on any of the issues touched upon in the survey? _____
_____

About the Contributors

Editors

Michael E. Everson (PhD, The Ohio State University) is an associate professor of foreign language education at The University of Iowa. He has published and presented widely on topics such as reading in Chinese as a foreign language, Chinese language-teacher development, and less commonly taught language (LCTL) education. He has served on a variety of advisory boards for associations supporting Chinese and other LCTLs and is one of the principle designers of the *Read Chinese!* online lessons sponsored by the National Foreign Language Center. He is involved in a number of national strategic initiatives supporting K–12 Chinese language education.

Helen H. Shen (http://myweb.uiowa.edu/heshen/ is associate professor of Chinese, Department of Asian and Slavic Languages and Literature, The University of Iowa. Her primary research area is second-language acquisition in Chinese reading. She has conducted a series of empirical studies and published extensively in this area. She also published two textbooks for adult Chinese learners and developed the *Chinese Reading World*, a comprehensive web-based Chinese reading program for Chinese learners from beginning to advanced levels. This project is supported by an International Research and Studies grant from the U.S. Department of Education. She received her PhD from the University of Nevada.

Authors

Cecilia Chang is associate professor of Chinese and chair of the Asian Studies Department at Williams College. In addition to teaching modern Chinese at Williams, she offers courses in applied linguistics. Since 2006, she has been involved in teacher training at Middlebury College's Summer Chinese School and in 2008, served as a faculty member at the Middlebury Summer School MA Program in Chinese. She received her EdD from the University of Massachusetts at Amherst. Her current research interests focus on methodologies of reading and teacher development.

Hang Du is an assistant professor in the Chinese Department at Middlebury College. The courses that she has taught include Chinese language courses at various levels and introductory courses on linguistics, language acquisition, Chinese sociolinguistics, and writing systems of the world. She has conducted research and published on child bilingualism and the acquisition of Chinese as a second language. She received her PhD from the Interdisciplinary Ph.D. Program in Second Language Acquisition and Teaching at the University of Arizona. Her current research interest is American college students studying Chinese in China.

Aiqun Liu obtained her BA from Beijing Language Institute in Chinese as a foreign language and her PhD from Hokkaido University in Japan. She is currently teaching Chinese as a foreign language in the Language Education Center at Ritsumeikan University in Japan. She has published textbooks for basic Chinese and articles on Chinese language teaching and topics in applied linguistics such as the acquisition of selected Chinese function words by Japanese-speaking learners. Her current research interest is in the field of second-language acquisition, especially the cognitive approaches involved in teaching Chinese as a foreign language to Japanese-speaking learners.

Chan Lü is currently an assistant professor of applied linguistics at Loyola Marymount University, where she teaches courses on Chinese language and applied linguistics. She received her PhD in second-language acquisition from Carnegie Mellon University and prior to that, an MEd in teaching Chinese as a second language from Beijing Language and Culture University. She was the recipient of the 2006 Jiede Empirical Research Grant for Chinese Pedagogy/Chinese Applied Linguistics from Chinese Language Teachers Association and the *Language Learning* Dissertation Grant in 2009. Her research interests are in second-language reading and biliteracy acquisition.

Isabel Tasker is a lecturer in Chinese at the University of New England, Australia. She has 3 decades of experience teaching Mandarin in Europe and Australia in a variety of modes and contexts: full- and part-time, adult and community education, university campus based, by distance education and online. She has worked in a range of curriculum development, assessment, and teacher-training initiatives, and her research and publications reflect her interests in Chinese pedagogy and learner perspectives. She earned her MA at the School of Oriental and African Studies in London, and her doctoral research is on the experiences of long-term learners of Chinese.

Miao-fen Tseng received her PhD in second-language acquisition and teacher education from the University of Illinois, Urbana-Champaign, and is currently teaching at the University of Virginia. She was the recipient of the first Ron Walton Presentation Prize and the Jiede Empirical Research Grant in 2005. Her current interests include teacher training and Chinese language pedagogy. She has published articles in refereed journals and two books on AP Chinese. As the founder and president of the Chinese Language Teachers' Association of Virginia (CLTA-VA), she has continued to present workshops and coordinate K–16 professional development activities. She also serves as the director and key trainer for the Virginia STARTALK Chinese Teacher Program.

Yun Xiao teaches Chinese language courses and conducts Chinese teacher training at Bryant University, where she is associate professor and chair of the Modern Languages Department. Her research interests are second-language acquisition and pedagogy, heritage-language learning, and Chinese teacher education. She has published more than 20 journal articles and book chapters. She also co-authored a readings series in Chinese literature and co-edited and authored a research monograph on Chinese as a heritage language and one on teaching Chinese as a foreign language.

NATIONAL FOREIGN LANGUAGE RESOURCE CENTER
University of Hawai'i at Mānoa

ordering information at nflrc.hawaii.edu

Pragmatics & Interaction
Gabriele Kasper, series editor

Pragmatics & Interaction ("P&I"), a refereed series sponsored by the University of Hawai'i National Foreign Language Resource Center, publishes research on topics in pragmatics and discourse as social interaction from a wide variety of theoretical and methodological perspectives. P&I welcomes particularly studies on languages spoken in the Asian-Pacific region.

TALK-IN-INTERACTION: MULTILINGUAL PERSPECTIVES
KATHLEEN BARDOVI-HARLIG, CÉSAR FÉLIX-BRASDEFER, & ALWIYA S. OMAR (EDITORS), 2006

This volume offers original studies of interaction in a range of languages and language varieties, including Chinese, English, Japanese, Korean, Spanish, Swahili, Thai, and Vietnamese; monolingual and bilingual interactions, and activities designed for second or foreign language learning. Conducted from the perspectives of conversation analysis and membership categorization analysis, the chapters examine ordinary conversation and institutional activities in face-to-face, telephone, and computer-mediated environments..
430 pp., ISBN(10): 0–8248–3137–3, ISBN(13): 978–0–8248–3137–0 $30.

Pragmatics & Language Learning
Gabriele Kasper, series editor

Pragmatics & Language Learning ("PLL"), a refereed series sponsored by the National Foreign Language Resource Center, publishes selected papers from the biannual International Pragmatics & Language Learning conference under the editorship of the conference hosts and the series editor. Check the NFLRC website for upcoming PLL conferences and PLL volumes.

PRAGMATICS AND LANGUAGE LEARNING VOLUME 11
KATHLEEN BARDOVI-HARLIG, CÉSAR FÉLIX-BRASDEFER, & ALWIYA S. OMAR (EDITORS), 2006

This volume features cutting-edge theoretical and empirical research on pragmatics and language learning among a wide-variety of learners in diverse learning contexts from a variety of language backgrounds (English, German, Japanese, Persian, and Spanish) and target languages (English, German, Japanese, Kiswahili, and Spanish). This collection of papers from researchers around the world includes critical appraisals on the role of formulas in interlanguage pragmatics and speech-act research from a conversation-analytic perspective. Empirical studies examine learner data using innovative methods of analysis and investigate issues in pragmatic development and the instruction of pragmatics.

430 pp., ISBN(10): 0–8248–3137–3, ISBN(13): 978–0–8248–3137–0 $30.

NFLRC Monographs
Richard Schmidt, series editor

Monographs of the National Foreign Language Resource Center present the findings of recent work in applied linguistics that is of relevance to language teaching and learning (with a focus on the less commonly-taught languages of Asia and the Pacific) and are of particular interest to foreign language educators, applied linguists, and researchers. Prior to 2006, these monographs were published as "SLTCC Technical Reports."

TOWARD USEFUL PROGRAM EVALUATION IN COLLEGE FOREIGN LANGUAGE EDUCATION
JOHN M. NORRIS, JOHN McE. DAVIS, CASTLE SINICROPE, & YUKIKO WATANABE (EDITORS), 2009

This volume reports on innovative, useful evaluation work conducted within U.S. college foreign language programs. An introductory chapter scopes out the territory, reporting key findings from research into the concerns, impetuses, and uses for evaluation that FL educators identify. Seven chapters then highlight examples of evaluations conducted in diverse language programs and institutional contexts. Each case is reported by program-internal educators, who walk readers through critical steps, from identifying evaluation uses, users, and questions, to designing methods, interpreting findings, and taking actions. A concluding chapter reflects on the emerging roles for FL program evaluation and articulates an agenda for integrating evaluation into language education practice.

240pp., ISBN 978–0–9800459–3–2 $30.

SECOND LANGUAGE TEACHING AND LEARNING IN THE NET GENERATION
RAQUEL OXFORD & JEFFREY OXFORD (EDITORS), 2009

Today's young people—the Net Generation—have grown up with technology all around them. However, teachers cannot assume that students' familiarity with technology in general transfers successfully to pedagogical settings. This volume examines various technologies and offers concrete advice on how each can be successfully implemented in the second language curriculum.

240pp., ISBN 978–0–9800459–2–5 $30.

CASE STUDIES IN FOREIGN LANGUAGE PLACEMENT: PRACTICES AND POSSIBILITIES
THOM HUDSON & MARTYN CLARK (EDITORS), 2008

Although most language programs make placement decisions on the basis of placement tests, there is surprisingly little published about different contexts and systems of placement testing. The present volume contains case studies of placement programs in foreign language programs at the tertiary level across the United States. The different programs span the spectrum from large programs servicing hundreds of students annually to small language programs with very few students. The contributions to this volume address such issues as how the size of the program, presence or absence of heritage learners, and population changes affect language placement decisions.

201pp., ISBN 978–0–9800459–0–1 $40.

CHINESE AS A HERITAGE LANGUAGE: FOSTERING ROOTED WORLD CITIZENRY
Agnes Weiyun He & Yun Xiao (Editors), 2008

Thirty-two scholars examine the socio-cultural, cognitive-linguistic, and educational-institutional trajectories along which Chinese as a Heritage Language may be acquired, maintained and developed. They draw upon developmental psychology, functional linguistics, linguistic and cultural anthropology, discourse analysis, orthography analysis, reading research, second language acquisition, and bilingualism. This volume aims to lay a foundation for theories, models, and master scripts to be discussed, debated, and developed, and to stimulate research and enhance teaching both within and beyond Chinese language education.

280pp., ISBN 978–08248–3286–5 $40.

PERSPECTIVES ON TEACHING CONNECTED SPEECH TO SECOND LANGUAGE SPEAKERS
James Dean Brown & Kimi Kondo-Brown (Editors), 2006

This book is a collection of fourteen articles on connected speech of interest to teachers, researchers, and materials developers in both ESL/EFL (ten chapters focus on connected speech in English) and Japanese (four chapters focus on Japanese connected speech). The fourteen chapters are divided up into five sections:

- What do we know so far about teaching connected speech?
- Does connected speech instruction work?
- How should connected speech be taught in English?
- How should connected speech be taught in Japanese?
- How should connected speech be tested?

290 pp., ISBN(10) 0–8248–3136–5, ISBN(13) 978–0–8248–3136–3 $38.

CORPUS LINGUISTICS FOR KOREAN LANGUAGE LEARNING AND TEACHING
Robert Bley-Vroman & Hyunsook Ko (Editors), 2006

Dramatic advances in personal-computer technology have given language teachers access to vast quantities of machine-readable text, which can be analyzed with a view toward improving the basis of language instruction. Corpus linguistics provides analytic techniques and practical tools for studying language in use. This volume provides both an introductory framework for the use of corpus linguistics for language teaching and examples of its application for Korean teaching and learning. The collected papers cover topics in Korean syntax, lexicon, and discourse, and second language acquisition research, always with a focus on application in the classroom. An overview of Korean corpus linguistics tools and available Korean corpora are also included.

265 pp., ISBN 0–8248–3062–8 $25.

NEW TECHNOLOGIES AND LANGUAGE LEARNING: CASES IN THE LESS COMMONLY TAUGHT LANGUAGES
Carol Anne Spreen (Editor), 2002

In recent years, the National Security Education Program (NSEP) has supported an increasing number of programs for teaching languages using different technological media. This compilation of case study initiatives funded through the NSEP Institutional Grants Program presents a range of technology-based options for language programming that will help universities make more informed decisions about teaching less commonly taught languages. The eight chapters describe how different types of technologies are used to support language programs (i.e., Web, ITV, and audio- or video-based materials), discuss identifiable trends in elanguage learning, and explore how technology addresses issues of equity, diversity, and opportunity. This book offers many lessons learned and decisions made as technology changes and learning needs become more complex.

188 pp., ISBN 0–8248–2634–5 $25.

AN INVESTIGATION OF SECOND LANGUAGE TASK-BASED PERFORMANCE ASSESSMENTS
James Dean Brown, Thom Hudson, John M. Norris, & William Bonk, 2002

This volume describes the creation of performance assessment instruments and their validation (based on work started in a previous monograph). It begins by explaining the test and rating scale development processes and the administration of the resulting three seven-task tests to 90 university level EFL and ESL students. The results are examined in terms of (a) the effects of test revision; (b) comparisons among the task-dependent, task-independent, and self-rating scales; and (c) reliability and validity issues.

240 pp., ISBN 0–8248–2633–7 $25.

MOTIVATION AND SECOND LANGUAGE ACQUISITION
Zoltán Dörnyei & Richard Schmidt (Editors), 2001

This volume—the second in this series concerned with motivation and foreign language learning—includes papers presented in a state-of-the-art colloquium on L2 motivation at the American Association for Applied Linguistics (Vancouver, 2000) and a number of specially commissioned studies. The 20 chapters, written by some of the best known researchers in the field, cover a wide range of theoretical and research methodological issues, and also offer empirical results (both qualitative and quantitative) concerning the learning of many different languages (Arabic, Chinese, English, Filipino, French, German, Hindi, Italian, Japanese, Russian, and Spanish) in a broad range of learning contexts (Bahrain, Brazil, Canada, Egypt, Finland, Hungary, Ireland, Israel, Japan, Spain, and the US).

520 pp., ISBN 0–8248–2458–X $25.

A FOCUS ON LANGUAGE TEST DEVELOPMENT: EXPANDING THE LANGUAGE PROFICIENCY CONSTRUCT ACROSS A VARIETY OF TESTS
Thom Hudson & James Dean Brown (Editors), 2001

This volume presents eight research studies that introduce a variety of novel, non-traditional forms of second and foreign language assessment. To the extent possible, the studies also show the entire test development process, warts and all. These language testing projects not only demonstrate many of the types of problems that test developers run into in the real world but also afford the reader unique insights into the language test development process.

230 pp., ISBN 0–8248–2351–6 $20.

STUDIES ON KOREAN IN COMMUNITY SCHOOLS
Dong-Jae Lee, Sookeun Cho, Miseon Lee, Minsun Song, & William O'Grady (Editors), 2000

The papers in this volume focus on language teaching and learning in Korean community schools. Drawing on innovative experimental work and research in linguistics, education, and psychology, the contributors address issues of importance to teachers, administrators, and parents. Topics covered include childhood bilingualism, Korean grammar, language acquisition, children's literature, and language teaching methodology. [in Korean]

256 pp., ISBN 0–8248–2352–4 $20.

A COMMUNICATIVE FRAMEWORK FOR INTRODUCTORY JAPANESE LANGUAGE CURRICULA
Washington State Japanese Language Curriculum Guidelines Committee, 2000

In recent years the number of schools offering Japanese nationwide has increased dramatically. Because of the tremendous popularity of the Japanese language and the shortage of teachers, quite a few untrained, non-native and native teachers are in the classrooms and are expected to teach several levels of Japanese. These guidelines are intended to assist individual teachers and professional associations throughout the United States in designing Japanese language curricula. They are meant to serve as a framework from which language teaching can be expanded and are intended to allow teachers to enhance and strengthen the quality of Japanese language instruction.

168 pp., ISBN 0–8248–2350–8 $20.

FOREIGN LANGUAGE TEACHING AND MINORITY LANGUAGE EDUCATION
Kathryn A. Davis (Editor), 1999

This volume seeks to examine the potential for building relationships among foreign language, bilingual, and ESL programs towards fostering bilingualism. Part I of the volume examines the sociopolitical contexts for language partnerships, including:

- obstacles to developing bilingualism
- implications of acculturation, identity, and language issues for linguistic minorities.
- the potential for developing partnerships across primary, secondary, and tertiary institutions

Part II of the volume provides research findings on the Foreign language partnership project designed to capitalize on the resources of immigrant students to enhance foreign language learning.

152 pp., ISBN 0–8248–2067–3 $20.

DESIGNING SECOND LANGUAGE PERFORMANCE ASSESSMENTS
John M. Norris, James Dean Brown, Thom Hudson, & Jim Yoshioka, 1998, 2000

This technical report focuses on the decision-making potential provided by second language performance assessments. The authors first situate performance assessment within a broader discussion of alternatives in language assessment and in educational assessment in general. They then discuss issues in performance assessment design, implementation, reliability, and validity. Finally, they present a prototype framework for second language performance assessment based on the integration of theoretical underpinnings and research findings from the task-based language teaching literature, the language testing literature, and the educational measurement literature. The authors outline test and item specifications, and they present numerous examples of prototypical language tasks. They also propose a research agenda focusing on the operationalization of second language performance assessments.

248 pp., ISBN 0–8248–2109–2 $20.

SECOND LANGUAGE DEVELOPMENT IN WRITING: MEASURES OF FLUENCY, ACCURACY, AND COMPLEXITY
Kate Wolfe-Quintero, Shunji Inagaki, & Hae-Young Kim, 1998, 2002

In this book, the authors analyze and compare the ways that fluency, accuracy, grammatical complexity, and lexical complexity have been measured in studies of language development in second language writing. More than 100 developmental measures are examined, with detailed comparisons of the results across the studies that have used each measure. The authors discuss the theoretical foundations for each type of developmental measure, and they consider the relationship between developmental measures and various types of proficiency measures. They also examine criteria for determining which developmental measures are the most successful and suggest which measures are the most promising for continuing work on language development.

208 pp., ISBN 0–8248–2069–X $20.

THE DEVELOPMENT OF A LEXICAL TONE PHONOLOGY IN AMERICAN ADULT LEARNERS OF STANDARD MANDARIN CHINESE
SYLVIA HENEL SUN, 1998

The study reported is based on an assessment of three decades of research on the SLA of Mandarin tone. It investigates whether differences in learners' tone perception and production are related to differences in the effects of certain linguistic, task, and learner factors. The learners of focus are American students of Mandarin in Beijing, China. Their performances on two perception and three production tasks are analyzed through a host of variables and methods of quantification.

328 pp., ISBN 0–8248–2068–1 $20.

NEW TRENDS AND ISSUES IN TEACHING JAPANESE LANGUAGE AND CULTURE
HARUKO M. COOK, KYOKO HIJIRIDA, & MILDRED TAHARA (EDITORS), 1997

In recent years, Japanese has become the fourth most commonly taught foreign language at the college level in the United States. As the number of students who study Japanese has increased, the teaching of Japanese as a foreign language has been established as an important academic field of study. This technical report includes nine contributions to the advancement of this field, encompassing the following five important issues:

- Literature and literature teaching
- Technology in the language classroom
- Orthography
- Testing
- Grammatical versus pragmatic approaches to language teaching

164 pp., ISBN 0–8248–2067–3 $20.

SIX MEASURES OF JSL PRAGMATICS
SAYOKO OKADA YAMASHITA, 1996

This book investigates differences among tests that can be used to measure the cross-cultural pragmatic ability of English-speaking learners of Japanese. Building on the work of Hudson, Detmer, and Brown (Technical Reports #2 and #7 in this series), the author modified six test types that she used to gather data from North American learners of Japanese. She found numerous problems with the multiple-choice discourse completion test but reported that the other five tests all proved highly reliable and reasonably valid. Practical issues involved in creating and using such language tests are discussed from a variety of perspectives.

213 pp., ISBN 0–8248–1914–4 $15.

LANGUAGE LEARNING STRATEGIES AROUND THE WORLD: CROSS-CULTURAL PERSPECTIVES
REBECCA L. OXFORD (EDITOR), 1996, 1997, 2002

Language learning strategies are the specific steps students take to improve their progress in learning a second or foreign language. Optimizing learning strategies improves language performance. This groundbreaking book presents new information about cultural influences on the use of language learning strategies. It also shows innovative ways to assess students' strategy use and remarkable techniques for helping students improve their choice of strategies, with the goal of peak language learning.

166 pp., ISBN 0-8248-1910-1 $20.

TELECOLLABORATION IN FOREIGN LANGUAGE LEARNING: PROCEEDINGS OF THE HAWAI'I SYMPOSIUM
Mark Warschauer (Editor), 1996

The Symposium on Local & Global Electronic Networking in Foreign Language Learning & Research, part of the National Foreign Language Resource Center's 1995 Summer Institute on Technology & the Human Factor in Foreign Language Education, included presentations of papers and hands-on workshops conducted by Symposium participants to facilitate the sharing of resources, ideas, and information about all aspects of electronic networking for foreign language teaching and research, including electronic discussion and conferencing, international cultural exchanges, real-time communication and simulations, research and resource retrieval via the Internet, and research using networks. This collection presents a sampling of those presentations.

252 pp., ISBN 0-8248-1867-9 $20.

LANGUAGE LEARNING MOTIVATION: PATHWAYS TO THE NEW CENTURY
Rebecca L. Oxford (Editor), 1996

This volume chronicles a revolution in our thinking about what makes students want to learn languages and what causes them to persist in that difficult and rewarding adventure. Topics in this book include the internal structures of and external connections with foreign language motivation; exploring adult language learning motivation, self-efficacy, and anxiety; comparing the motivations and learning strategies of students of Japanese and Spanish; and enhancing the theory of language learning motivation from many psychological and social perspectives.

218 pp., ISBN 0-8248-1849-0 $20.

LINGUISTICS & LANGUAGE TEACHING: PROCEEDINGS OF THE SIXTH JOINT LSH-HATESL CONFERENCE
Cynthia Reves, Caroline Steele, & Cathy S. P. Wong (Editors), 1996

Technical Report #10 contains 18 articles revolving around the following three topics:
- Linguistic issues—These six papers discuss various linguistic issues: ideophones, syllabic nasals, linguistic areas, computation, tonal melody classification, and wh-words.
- Sociolinguistics—Sociolinguistic phenomena in Swahili, signing, Hawaiian, and Japanese are discussed in four of the papers.
- Language teaching and learning—These eight papers cover prosodic modification, note taking, planning in oral production, oral testing, language policy, L2 essay organization, access to dative alternation rules, and child noun phrase structure development.

364 pp., ISBN 0-8248-1851-2 $20.

ATTENTION & AWARENESS IN FOREIGN LANGUAGE LEARNING
Richard Schmidt (Editor), 1996

Issues related to the role of attention and awareness in learning lie at the heart of many theoretical and practical controversies in the foreign language field. This collection of papers presents research into the learning of Spanish, Japanese, Finnish, Hawaiian, and English as a second language (with additional comments and examples from French, German, and miniature artificial languages) that bear on these crucial questions for foreign language pedagogy.

394 pp., ISBN 0-8248-1794-X $20.

VIRTUAL CONNECTIONS: ONLINE ACTIVITIES AND PROJECTS FOR NETWORKING LANGUAGE LEARNERS
MARK WARSCHAUER (EDITOR), 1995, 1996

Computer networking has created dramatic new possibilities for connecting language learners in a single classroom or across the globe. This collection of activities and projects makes use of email, the internet, computer conferencing, and other forms of computer-mediated communication for the foreign and second language classroom at any level of instruction. Teachers from around the world submitted the activities compiled in this volume—activities that they have used successfully in their own classrooms.

417 pp., ISBN 0-8248-1793-1 $30.

DEVELOPING PROTOTYPIC MEASURES OF CROSS-CULTURAL PRAGMATICS
THOM HUDSON, EMILY DETMER, & J. D. BROWN, 1995

Although the study of cross-cultural pragmatics has gained importance in applied linguistics, there are no standard forms of assessment that might make research comparable across studies and languages. The present volume describes the process through which six forms of cross-cultural assessment were developed for second language learners of English. The models may be used for second language learners of other languages. The six forms of assessment involve two forms each of indirect discourse completion tests, oral language production, and self-assessment. The procedures involve the assessment of requests, apologies, and refusals.

198 pp., ISBN 0-8248-1763-X $15.

THE ROLE OF PHONOLOGICAL CODING IN READING KANJI
SACHIKO MATSUNAGA, 1995

In this technical report, the author reports the results of a study that she conducted on phonological coding in reading kanji using an eye-movement monitor and draws some pedagogical implications. In addition, she reviews current literature on the different schools of thought regarding instruction in reading kanji and its role in the teaching of non-alphabetic written languages like Japanese.

64 pp., ISBN 0-8248-1734-6 $10.

PRAGMATICS OF CHINESE AS NATIVE AND TARGET LANGUAGE
GABRIELE KASPER (EDITOR), 1995

This technical report includes six contributions to the study of the pragmatics of Mandarin Chinese:
- A report of an interview study conducted with nonnative speakers of Chinese; and
- Five data-based studies on the performance of different speech acts by native speakers of Mandarin—requesting, refusing, complaining, giving bad news, disagreeing, and complimenting.

312 pp., ISBN 0-8248-1733-8 $15.

A BIBLIOGRAPHY OF PEDAGOGY AND RESEARCH IN INTERPRETATION AND TRANSLATION
ETILVIA ARJONA, 1993

This technical report includes four types of bibliographic information on translation and interpretation studies:

- Research efforts across disciplinary boundaries—cognitive psychology, neurolinguistics, psycholinguistics, sociolinguistics, computational linguistics, measurement, aptitude testing, language policy, decision-making, theses, dissertations;
- Training information covering program design, curriculum studies, instruction, school administration;
- Instruction information detailing course syllabi, methodology, models, available textbooks; and
- Testing information about aptitude, selection, diagnostic tests.

115 pp., ISBN 0–8248–1572–6 $10.

PRAGMATICS OF JAPANESE AS NATIVE AND TARGET LANGUAGE
Gabriele Kasper (Editor), 1992, 1996

This technical report includes three contributions to the study of the pragmatics of Japanese:
- A bibliography on speech act performance, discourse management, and other pragmatic and sociolinguistic features of Japanese;
- A study on introspective methods in examining Japanese learners' performance of refusals; and
- A longitudinal investigation of the acquisition of the particle ne by nonnative speakers of Japanese.

125 pp., ISBN 0–8248–1462–2 $10.

A FRAMEWORK FOR TESTING CROSS-CULTURAL PRAGMATICS
Thom Hudson, Emily Detmer, & J. D. Brown, 1992

This technical report presents a framework for developing methods that assess cross-cultural pragmatic ability. Although the framework has been designed for Japanese and American cross-cultural contrasts, it can serve as a generic approach that can be applied to other language contrasts. The focus is on the variables of social distance, relative power, and the degree of imposition within the speech acts of requests, refusals, and apologies. Evaluation of performance is based on recognition of the speech act, amount of speech, forms or formulæ used, directness, formality, and politeness.

51 pp., ISBN 0–8248–1463–0 $10.

RESEARCH METHODS IN INTERLANGUAGE PRAGMATICS
Gabriele Kasper & Merete Dahl, 1991

This technical report reviews the methods of data collection employed in 39 studies of interlanguage pragmatics, defined narrowly as the investigation of nonnative speakers' comprehension and production of speech acts, and the acquisition of L2-related speech act knowledge. Data collection instruments are distinguished according to the degree to which they constrain informants' responses, and whether they tap speech act perception/comprehension or production. A main focus of discussion is the validity of different types of data, in particular their adequacy to approximate authentic performance of linguistic action.

51 pp., ISBN 0–8248–1419–3 $10.

www.ingramcontent.com/pod-product-compliance
Lightning Source LLC
Chambersburg PA
CBHW080338170426
43194CB00014B/2610